MORE PRAISE . . .

"A LAUGH-OUT-LOUD ROASTING OF CONSERVATIVES . . . Franken is a top-notch political satirist." —*The Denver Post*

"Franken trains a wily, satirical eye on all manner of Washington hypocrisy, taking careful aim at everyone from Arianna Huffington to Newt Gingrich to Bob Dole, then pulling the trigger." —*Elle*

"IRREVERENT . . . with cunning use of research, [Franken] repeatedly skewers the Rushster for his factual failings." —*St. Petersburg Times*

"THE BEST PART OF THE BOOK IS THE INCISIVE, STINGING, HILARIOUS AND INTELLIGENT INDIGNATION FRANKEN UNLEASHES." —*Press Republican* (Plattsburg, N.Y.)

"[A] HILARIOUSLY SCATHING COLLECTION OF HUMOROUS POLITICAL ESSAYS . . . [Franken] takes Limbaugh's tactics and aims them squarely back at him." —*Shreveport Times* (La.)

"SHARP AND RELENTLESS . . . Franken's satire ranges from amusing to laugh-out-loud."
—*The Tampa Tribune*

MORE PRAISE . . .

"HILARIOUS . . . skewers Rush & Friends as no liberal has done in years." —*Publishers Weekly*

"HE'S BACK, AND HIS WIT IS SHARPER THAN EVER . . . [the book] blends wicked satire with sound political thinking." —*The Boston Phoenix*

"FUNNY WOULD PROBABLY BE ENOUGH HERE, BUT FRANKEN'S BOOK IS MORE. He also offers plenty of solid information—from the maligned liberal position, for a change—about GOPAC, the economy, health care, and other issues of the day . . . watch out, Republicans—Franken proves humor is the best revenge." —*Booklist*

"FRANKEN WRITES WHAT MANY PEOPLE HAVE BEEN THINKING BUT WERE TOO SCARED TO SAY." —*Indianapolis News*

"AN UNCOMPROMISING LOOK AT MODERN AMERICAN POLITICS . . . thoroughly skewers Limbaugh with meticulous research." — Cox News Service

"HILARIOUS . . . part satire, part memoir, part liberal diatribe." —*Dallas Morning News*

. . . AND CONDEMNATION!

"A MONUMENTALLY UNFUNNY BOOK . . .
Angry, simple-minded, egotistical abuse, page after
page . . . Rush, Newt Gingrich, Bob Dole and the
gang are subjected to heavy-handed abuse, often in the
coarsest terms . . .
IN THE WORDS OF AYN RAND,
THE BOOK IS A BUCKET OF SLIME EMPTIED
OVER ITS TARGETS."
—*The Detroit News*

RUSH LIMBAUGH IS A BIG FAT IDIOT

and Other Observations

Al Franken

Island BOOKS

ISLAND BOOKS
Published by
Dell Publishing
a division of
Bantam Doubleday Dell Publishing Group, Inc.
1540 Broadway
New York, New York 10036

ISBN: 0-440-22330-X

Printed in the United States of America

Published simultaneously in Canada

November 1996

10 9 8 7 6 5 4 3 2 1

OPM

To my dad

CONTENTS

Preface to Paperback Edition   xv

1. Book Review   1

2. Rush Limbaugh Is a Big Fat Idiot   7

3. One Giant Leap Toward Solving the
Budget Crisis   37

4. Adventures in Politics 1951–1975
My American Journey   41

5. The Newt Cancer Surgery Story
What the Liberal Media Might Not Be
Telling You   54

6. Gingrich: Sex, Giraffes, and
Weightlessness   56

7. Rush Limbaugh's Fact Checker   61

8. Operation Chickenhawk   66

9. Bob Dole's Nightmare of Depravity   85

10. The Invisible Hand of Adam Smith   89

11. Adventures in Politics November 8, 1988
Boston, Mass., Comedian's Nightmare: I
Emcee the Dukakis Victory Celebration   92

12. Phil Gramm, Gun Lover   99

13. Affirmative Action: The Case for the
Mushball Middle   103

14. Something We Can All Get Behind   111

15. Apocryphal Anecdotes: The Republican
Contribution to Public Debate   113

16. This Book Is Not Part of a Conspiracy   121

17. I Get Letters   125

18. Adventures in Politics December 31,
1993
Renaissance Weekend. Hilton Head.
I Meet Wolf Blitzer and Play Touch Football
with the President   126

19. The Secrets of Renaissance Weekend   134

20. Stop This Man Before He Kills Again   136

21. Monetary Policy: A Ticking Time Bomb   140

22. The Reagan Years: Rush Limbaugh Is a
Big Fat Liar   143

23. Newt's Loot   154

24. Lexis-Nexis
The Powerful, Revolutionary Database
Technology   156

25. Back to Newt's Loot   158

26. Adventures in Politics April 23, 1994
I Am Brilliant at the White House
Correspondents Association Dinner   165

27. Phil Gramm: Everybody's Favorite
Bastard   173

28. Fun with Nexis   182

29. Arlen! Arlen! Arlen! And Other
Thoughts on the '96 Election   187

30. Pat Buchanan: Nazi Lover   195

31. The Middle-Class Squeeze   204

32. Rubbernecking on the Infotainment
Superhighway   206

33. Another Fearless Policy Initiative from
Me   210

34. Adventures in Politics April 29, 1995
White House Correspondents Association
Dinner. I Charm the Socks Off Arianna
Huffington, Meet Newt Gingrich, and Offend
Al D'Amato   213

35. More Fun with Rush Limbaugh's Fact
Checker   223

36. Republicans and Environmental
Regulation: Like Mixing Oil and Water.
Literally.   228

37. The Law and Order Party: Us!   235

38. Fair Mean vs. Unfair Mean   241

39. Adventures in Politics August 12–14,
1995
I Attend the Perot Conference in Dallas, and
Personally Get John Kasich to Admit to an
Act of Intellectual Dishonesty   245

40. The Urgent Need for Health Care
Reform   262

41. The Critical Need for Legal Reform   266

42. The Desperate Need for Entitlement
Reform   270

43. Bill Clinton: Greatest President of the
Twentieth Century   275

44. Adventures in Politics September 9, 1995
I Attend the Christian Coalition "Road to
Victory" Conference and Become Ill   280

45. Epilogue: A Time for Healing   294

Special for the Paperback Edition: New Dirt on the Nutcase Right 297

46. Adventures in Marketing January–April 1996
I Go on a Book Tour, Bask in Glory, Taunt My Enemies, and Learn Terrible Things About Deepak Chopra 299

47. Adventures in Politics The 1996 Primary Season
I Cover the Primaries for *Newsweek* and Do a Very Bad Job 312

48. Adventures in Politics May 4, 1996
The Washington Hilton. I Deliver a Speech at the White House Correspondents Dinner and Rankle Newt Gingrich, Who Threatens to Slug Me. 324

49. My Research Assistant Is Not Dead 338

INDEX 342

PREFACE TO
PAPERBACK EDITION

A lot has happened since I started work on the hardcover version of *Rush Limbaugh Is a Big Fat Idiot and Other Observations*. Back then, in the dark days of May 1995, conservative Republicans appeared to be taking over the country. Newt Gingrich's claims that he was leading a "revolution" were interpreted not as the rantings of a delusional megalomaniac but as a reasonable blueprint for the nation's future. Congressional Republicans were targeting federal agencies for elimination at the rate of about one a day. Media pundits were cooing over such rising Republican stars as freshman Representative Enid Waldholtz of Utah, the "Mormon Maggie Thatcher."

In the midst of all this, Bill Clinton held a press conference to declare himself "relevant." No one believed him.

By the time I finished the book in September 1995, all talk in Washington was of the impending showdown over the budget. What would happen? Nobody knew. Would the President cave? Would the Republicans strong-arm him into accepting their budget, thereby ratifying their revolution?

Or would the President stand his ground? And would the public blame the subsequent government shutdown on the Republicans? Would Newt throw a

hugely embarrassing hissy fit over the seating ar-
rangement on *Air Force One*? Would Enid Waldholtz's husband disappear from Washington National
Airport, leaving a trail of bad checks in his wake?
Would the Republican party split open like a rotten
watermelon during the primaries, with Pat Buchanan
urging his followers to take up pitchforks against the
"boys down at the yacht basin"? Would the Republicans end up nominating a 73-year-old Washington
insider with less flair for spoken English than George
Bush?

Finally, would my book sell like hotcakes?

Boy, what a great year!

Of course, in politics, a month is a lifetime. By the
time you read this, the Democrats could be right back
in the toilet. But for now, allow me to gloat. Ha, ha,
ho, ho, wheeeeeee!!!!

Al Franken
New York
July 1996

Book Review

January 7, 1996

RUSH LIMBAUGH IS A BIG FAT IDIOT AND OTHER OBSERVATIONS

By Al Franken
288 pp. Delacorte Press:
$21.95

by Jeane Kirkpatrick

I T REMAINS a mystery why the *New York Times* would ask me to review this dreadfully foul little book. I am an expert on geopolitical strategic paradigms, not on the sort of cheap, mindless mockery that seems to be Mr. Franken's forte. It is almost as if this were the result of some awful mistake by the *Times*. Why, for example, would humorist P. J. O'Rourke be assigned this very same week to review Nigel Hodgeson's wonderful tome *The Falkland Islands War—Six Hundred Years in the Making*? Is it possible that because O'Rourke and I have the same agent, some simple mix-up occurred? Perhaps P.J., our agent, or I should have tried to sort this out. But I have simply been too busy trying to slog through this repugnant collection of vile, unfunny essays.

Rush Limbaugh Is a Big Fat Idiot and Other Observations is not just unfunny. It is confused. While Mr. Franken decries "the loss of civility in public discourse," he himself is a most egregious offender, not just calling Rush Limbaugh "a big fat idiot," but Newt Gingrich "a big fat jerk," and House majority leader Richard Armey "a big dick."

Mr. Franken seems to want to have it both ways,

criticizing Limbaugh for "demonizing" those who disagree with him, but all the while attacking *his* enemies with invective and scurrilous assertions that remain totally unproven. For example, nowhere in the 288-page screed does Franken actually show any real evidence that Limbaugh is indeed fat. There is not one footnoted reference concerning Limbaugh's body weight, and Mr. Franken seems to be relying on sheer guesswork. Indeed, on page 45, he refers to Limbaugh as "a three-hundred pound blimp," while on page 117, he refers to a "size-78 suit squeezing Rush's some six-hundred pound frame like so much sausage casing." Which is it? Three hundred or six hundred?

One begins to wonder if Franken isn't just inventing things out of whole cloth. After a careful reread of *The Bell Curve*, nowhere in its 800-plus pages did I find Murray and Herrnstein refer to jazz as "the music created by morons." And similarly, Newt Gingrich's Contract with America did not "promise to make it easier to sue for divorce a spouse with cancer."

Occasionally Mr. Franken does succeed to amuse. When discussing the Senate Banking Committee's Whitewater investigation, he writes, "Having Al D'Amato lead an ethics investigation is like asking Bob Dornan to head up a mental health task force." I must admit that one made me chortle; Bob Dornan *is* dangerously unstable. Yet only thirty-seven pages later Mr. Franken, for all intents and purposes, *repeats* the joke. "Having Al D'Amato lead an ethics investigation is like asking *Ross Perot* [my emphasis] to head up a mental health task force." Again, funny. But which is it? Bob Dornan or Ross Perot?

As one labors through *Rush Limbaugh Is a Big Fat Idiot and Other Observations* one quickly concludes that Mr. Franken chose the title simply as a craven device to attract readers. Yes, the book's opening essay *is* "Rush Limbaugh Is a Big Fat Idiot." But in it Mr. Franken negates the whole premise of his book, when in referring to Limbaugh's enormous success, he writes: "All right. I guess Limbaugh is not an idiot. But you have to admit, he's big and fat."

In fact, one of the author's goals seems to be to draw Limbaugh into some kind of public feud, as if that would enhance the sales of his book. Calling Limbaugh "a fat bully" who is "too scared to engage in open debate with anyone other than pre-screened callers," Franken gratuitously taunts the talk radio host: "Limbaugh is able to attack women and keep the audience's sympathy for one reason and one reason only. He is clearly a sad, fat loser wounded by a pathetic history with the opposite sex." Again, Franken offers no proof, other than to cite that Limbaugh met his third, and current, wife on CompuServe.

Will Limbaugh rise to the bait? Franken seems to hope so, writing on page 187, "I hope he rises to the bait." Even so, Franken admits that Limbaugh would probably prevail in a one-on-one encounter. Franken, who insists that Bill Clinton is "by far" our best post-war President, admits to being a part of "the fuzzy-headed liberal-middle" and that mano-a-mano he would be no match for Limbaugh's clearheaded, "well thought out," right-wing doctrine. "Besides, I'm a comedian," is his weak defense. Franken's plan, as revealed in his chapter "I Have Smart Friends," is to lure Limbaugh into a live debate on ABC's *Nightline*, then act sick, getting Michael Kinsley to fill in for him at the last second.

As reprehensible as I found this strategem [my word], I was even more appalled by the flippant, smart-alecky tone of the non-Limbaugh chapters, including one entitled "If Abortions Are Outlawed, Only Outlaws Will Have Abortions." My goodness. If this is the kind of mindless tripe that passes for political satire these days, I fear for this nation!

Letters

He Said, She Said

To the Editor:

It was with great horror that I picked up Sunday's *Times* to see that you had assigned Jeane Kirkpatrick to review my book, "Rush Limbaugh Is a Big Fat Idiot and Other Observations" (January 7). It had been my understanding that in the interest of objectivity your paper has had a long-standing policy of not assigning an author's former lover to review his book. As anyone who was familiar with the Manhattan eighties' club scene knows, Ms. Kirkpatrick and I endured a somewhat stormy and all too public affair during her tenure as our country's U.N. Ambassador. Even then Ms. Kirkpatrick, though my lover, had no discernible sense of humor. In fact, a primary cause of our breakup was her almost obdurate unwillingness to understand irony, an unwillingness which is woefully apparent in her uncomprehending review of my very funny book. Come on! Be fair. Next time get someone who isn't my former lover to review my book!

AL FRANKEN
New York

Ambassador Kirkpatrick replies:

I don't know what this horrible, horrible man is talking about. During the time that I served as ambassador to the United Nations I was far too busy defending the people of America, including (unfortunately) Mr. Franken, against the dark forces of Soviet Communism to cheat on my husband, let alone "go clubbing" (my phrase) as Mr. Franken suggests. After careful examination of my appointment calendars from that period, I admit that I did on one occasion step foot inside Studio 54, but I can assure you that once I saw what was going on in that place, I quickly turned on my heel and left. I can assure you as well that Mr. Franken will be hearing from my attorney, as will the *New York Times*. How on earth the *Times* could print his letter and take part in this abhorrent calumny is beyond me.

The editors reply:

It is our policy to allow authors to respond to reviews in the manner they see fit. Since Mr. Franken's claim of an affair between Ms. Kirkpatrick and himself comes down to a matter of "he-said, she-said," we felt the Ambassador's denial was insufficient to prevent us from printing his response. We did, however, edit Mr. Franken's letter, omitting a number of gratuitously lurid descriptions which were entirely irrelevant to his complaint. And, yes, it *is* our policy not to allow a former lover to review an author's book. Our apologies to Mr. Franken.

2
RUSH LIMBAUGH IS
A BIG FAT IDIOT

After Delacorte asked me to write a book on politics, my very first creative act was coming up with the title, *Rush Limbaugh Is a Big Fat Idiot and Other Observations.* I thought the title, aside from the obvious advantage of being personally offensive to Limbaugh, would sell books. Let me explain why: It makes fun of Rush Limbaugh by pointing out that he is a big lardbutt.

Confident that I was now on my way to a bestseller, I took some time off and went to Florida with my wife and kids. But when I returned and sat down to work, it became immediately apparent that the "title tail" was going to wag the "content dog." That is to say, I'd actually have to write about Rush Limbaugh.

Which, of course, meant I'd have to listen to him on radio, read his books, and watch his TV show. "How much am I getting paid for this?" I asked myself.

I was not, after all, totally unfamiliar with

Limbaugh. He is the king of talk radio, with an esti-
mated twenty million listeners in a given week. I had
been one of those twenty million a while back, listening to him spew about "feminazis" and their
"women-as-victim" ideas. Limbaugh was railing
about how feminists believe that all heterosexual sex is
rape, which, I admit, is a belief that's very hard to
defend. The thing is, though, I know a lot of women,
almost all of whom consider themselves feminists,
and I know only one who actually holds this belief.
And we've been married nearly twenty years.

Limbaugh expanded . . . to TV a few years back,
and I had seen his show a number of times. It's been a
considerable success, though I think it was ultimately
a terrible mistake for Limbaugh because we finally
got to see his audience. During the shows I watched,
Limbaugh presented, in a deliberately misleading
way, disinformation that was devoured whole by a
studio audience of rabid—but extraordinarily
straightlaced—right-wing yahoos. These are the fans
who voluntarily—hell, gleefully—call themselves
"dittoheads" in honor of their ability to blindly and
uncritically agree with everything that comes out of
Limbaugh's mouth.

The first time I watched the show was in October,
1992, about a month before the election. President
Bush had been on *Larry King Live* the night before,
and during the interview Bush had said that he was
bothered by Clinton's actions during the Vietnam
War: "Maybe I'm old-fashioned, Larry," he said.
"But to go to a foreign country and demonstrate
against your own country, when your sons and daugh-

ters are dying halfway around the world? I'm sorry, I —I just don't like it. I think it is wrong." To anybody watching *Larry King*, as I happened to be, it was an attack on Clinton's patriotism, and the next day several newspapers ran headlines saying as much.

So Rush shows this headline from the *New York Times* that reads: BUSH ASSAILS CLINTON'S PATRIOTISM DURING VIETNAM WAR PROTEST ERA. Then he starts whining about the liberal media. "He didn't assail Clinton's patriotism. . . . Now let's roll Bush on *Larry King Live* last night, and you be the judge. Did he attack Governor Clinton's patriotism here?"

Then he runs a twenty-second clip from *a totally different part of the interview*. Limbaugh comes back: "I didn't hear one assault on patriotism. I didn't hear one word or syllable questioning Bill Clinton's patriotism. . . . We'll be back in just a moment." Cut to: a hundred and twenty idiots in bad suits applauding wildly.

Subsequent viewings pretty much confirmed that the point of Rush's show is to punish you for actually knowing anything.

Back to my still-unwritten book. Catchy title in hand, I braced myself for an entire season of such punishment. I would spend the summer absorbing Limbaugh—three hours a day, five days a week, listening to conservatism's most powerful (not to mention obnoxious) voice. I am, after all, a professional.

Rush Limbaugh, Radio Icon and Staunch Defender of Constitutional Rights for Neckwear

Spring 1995. I go to the Wiz and buy a boom box for my office at home. I pour a fresh glass of iced tea, settle into a comfortable chair, flip on WABC, and tune in to the first installment of what will be approximately one hundred and eighty hours of listening pleasure. And at 12:15, Rush is peeved:

Let me give you another example here of the press. This may be as good as an example as I could cite to show you how it is that the left has stereotypes. Now you people all know that I have introduced a new line of neckwear, commonly known as ties. And that I have, right now, we've got four styles, four designs that are out there, and we are always working on more. . . .

I was about to learn that the liberal media had deliberately misrepresented his mail-order tie collection:

. . . So I'm at the United Press International wire and I'm reading the People section and there's a story there about the new Rush Limbaugh No Boundaries tie collection, and would you like to hear it described? "Limbaugh's ties are as conservative as he is. Blue, white, red, and gray stripes." My friends. The *last* thing my ties are is conservative. That's why we're calling it No Boundaries! These are . . .

the last thing in the world these ties would be described as would be conservative. There's not one stripe! On any of the ties! . . .

And he won't stop. He's just going on and on about these ties. So I flip around the dial, catch an inning of the Mets game, and then come back to Rush. And his brutally defamed ties:

. . . I mean, that is another example of the stereotypes that the left, and I am including the press in this, have about conservatives. . . . It was my wife Marta who came up with the whole concept, to tell you the truth, of No Boundaries. And she said no themes on these ties, no ties to issues, no ties to politics . . . These are going to be gorgeous, beautiful ties that *anybody* would want to wear to make themselves look better. And they are. And there's not one stripe! Not one stripe! On any tie! . . .

Time for another iced tea. I head to the kitchen, wander around the apartment a bit. Back to my office and . . . the vicious media smear campaign directed against Rush's ties:

. . . They could have called me first to ask me about it. They could have called and said, "Hey, we hear you got some new ties out; we'd like to see them; we're going to write a story." . . .

Back to the fridge. I root around for some leftovers. Make a sandwich. Read the sports page. The Twins are having a pretty tough year. Back to the ties, which —near as I can tell—have now had their civil rights violated by the hounds of attack journalism:

> . . . In this battle for the soul of democracy, it is more and more clear that the press, which has a designed Constitutional role, can't be trusted, cannot be counted on. My gosh, if the press, which Constitutionally is protected so as to get the truth, is this far off as often as they are, then is it any wonder that there is a new media led by me, America's truth detector? No, there's not. Quick break. Back to the phones in just a moment . . .

Only a hundred and seventy-nine hours to go. Hmmm. Maybe it would be okay if I just . . . sampled . . . the show. Every now and then.

KIERKEGAARD, NIETZSCHE—AND LIMBAUGH

After the tie episode, I sent my research assistant Geoff to Barnes and Noble, where he found a paperback of Limbaugh's bestseller *See, I Told You So*.

Picking up a new book is always exciting to a curious person like myself, but I became especially jazzed by Rush's introduction: "Prepare your mind to be challenged as it has never been challenged before." Kierkegaard, Nietzsche, now Limbaugh.

By Chapter Two, I had learned the key to Limbaugh's success. "My show works because people are tired of being insulted elsewhere on the radio or TV dial. They enjoy listening to someone who respects their intelligence."

Fortunately, I was soon treated to an example of just how much respect Rush has for his readers' intelligence:

> With the exception of the military, I defy you to name one government program that has worked and alleviated the problem it was created to solve. Hhhmmmmmmm? I'm waiting. . . . Time's up.

This got me thinking. Now, I'm no expert on government. And besides, I'm a liberal. So my naming ten or twenty of the hundreds of successful government programs isn't going to impress anyone. Hell, I think Rural Electrification worked! That's how big a dumbass liberal I am! So instead, I called a few bona fide conservatives and asked them to name a few:*

---

* I spoke personally with each of these very nice conservatives. As you might guess, I didn't tell them that they were contributing to a book entitled *Rush Limbaugh Is a Big Fat Idiot and Other Observations*. Instead, I told them that I was writing "a satire on the breakdown of civility in public discourse," which in a way is true. I also told them I was calling Democrats and asking them to name government programs that *don't* work. Which, I admit, was a naked lie.

1. George F. Will (grim-faced conservative columnist)—*Rural Electrification*, the Interstate Highway System ("the most successful public works program in the history of the world"). "The federal government has been tremendously successful in disseminating health and safety information, for example, about smoking and seat belts."

2. Rep. John Kasich (R–Ohio; boyishly rugged, straight-talking chairman of the House Budget Committee)—National Institutes of Health, Youth Summer Jobs Program.

3. Rep. Bob Dornan (R–Calif.; Republican candidate for president; crazy homophobe)— The F.A.A., lighthouses, federal penitentiaries ("We gotta keep those guys locked up").

4. Arianna Huffington (enigmatic, Greek-born, Cambridge-educated socialite; conservative commentator; fund-raiser for Newt Gingrich; wife of unsuccessful California Senate candidate Michael Huffington)—The National Park System, guaranteed student loans, aid to Greece.

5. Ben Stein (conservative columnist for the *American Spectator*; former Nixon speechwriter; noted character actor, famous for role as the "Bueller, Bueller, Bueller" teacher in *Ferris Bueller's Day Off*)—Social Security. Medicare. Head Start. Food Stamps. "The Federal Deposit Insurance Corporation is the most wildly successful government program in the history of man."

6. Richard Viguerie (former publisher the *Conservative Digest*, archconservative direct-mail pioneer)—Public libraries, the F.B.I., the G.I. Bill.

So, is Limbaugh that out of touch with conservatives like Will, Kasich, and Dornan? Or does he just take his readers to be complete morons? Hhhmmmmmmm? I'm waiting. . . . Time's up!

DIDIOTS—LIMBAUGH'S LEGION OF FANS

Now, am I saying that dittoheads are ignoramuses? No. I don't need to. Listen to Kathleen Hall Jamieson of the Annenberg School for Communications at the University of Pennsylvania:

We just concluded a study of 360 people, whom we watched watch the health care reform debate for nine months. And at the end of that period, we took the people who said they relied on talk radio, and by this, we mean primarily Rush Limbaugh. . . . And we asked them how well informed they felt. . . . Of all the people we watched, they said they were the best informed. And of all the people we watched, they were the least informed.

What a surprise, huh? Limbaugh listeners *thought* they were the best informed, and yet were the *least informed.*

How is such a thing even measured? Well, like all the other people studied, talk radio listeners were asked questions of "objective fact" such as: "Which groups (the elderly, poor, middle class, etc.) are most likely to be uninsured?" The Limbaugh listeners were "highly likely" to give an incorrect answer such as "the elderly" who, of course, are all covered by Medicare.

But why would people so woefully lacking in the basic facts of an issue think they were the best informed? Social scientists call the phenomenon "pseudo-certainty." I call it "being a fucking moron."*

LIMBAUGH AND WOMEN—A PATHETIC STORY

It's safe to say that most of Limbaugh's fact-challenged dittoheads are men. Limbaugh has tapped into the resentments of "the angry white male," which are quite legitimate. I mean, if you think about it, what chance for advancement have white men really had in this country?

Limbaugh, himself, seems to have a problem with women. He has been married three times. Personally, I am not one for psychoanalyzing public figures. I

---

* Death threats should be sent to Delacorte Press, attn. Salman Rushdie.

wouldn't, for example, attempt to create a psychological construct to explain why a desperately insecure man would weigh three hundred pounds and have difficulty sustaining intimate relationships. Psychobabble mumbo jumbo doesn't interest me, and I would never suggest that a difficult separation from the primary love object at an early age might cause a man to hate women and look to food as a substitute for the mother's teat.

Instead I thought it might be fun (after all, that's what this is about), to juxtapose some of Rush's own words with those of people who know him. (I saw some of this stuff on *Frontline*.)

Rush: Feminism was established so that unattractive, ugly women could have easy access to the mainstream of society.

Millie Limbaugh, Mother: No. He did not date in high school.

Rush: If you want a successful marriage, let your husband do what he wants to do.

David Limbaugh, Brother: I don't think he would have chosen to break up either marriage. I think it was the choice of both of his ex-wives. . . . Women, especially young women, don't want guys to be sedentary.

Rush (Writing to a woman on E-mail): I remain

in an interminable funk, no end in sight—listless, uninspired, and self-flagellating.

Hazel Staloff (The woman): I thought, "What a sad thing to write, and to write to somebody you didn't even know." Later I came to realize that it was probably his way of trying to attract a woman. You know, for a woman to read, "Rush has no friends" and for her to respond, "Let me make it better for you."

Limbaugh later met his third wife, Marta, via E-mail.

LIMBAUGH ON LIBERALS—WE'RE "DIABOLICAL"

Now don't get me wrong. I *like* Limbaugh. I mean we're sort of in the same business. And I'd love to meet him. It's just that I don't think *he'd* like *me*. See, I'm a liberal, and evidently, we are pretty awful people:

"Liberals love misery. It makes them feel necessary."

"Liberals don't want the homeless to hold a job that has any real promise."

"Businesses, according to liberals, are the root of all evil."

"You are morally *superior* to those liberal compassion fascists. . . . You have a real job; they just beg for a living."

"Some of them—many of them, perhaps—are just plain diabolical and dishonest to the core."

I wouldn't want to meet me either. But at least I'm better than a poor person:

> The poor in this country are the biggest piglets at the mother pig and her nipples. The poor feed off the largesse of this government and give nothing back. . . . We need to stop giving them coupons where they can go buy all kinds of junk. We just don't have the money. They're taking out, they put nothing in. And I'm sick and tired of playing the one phony game I've had to play and that is this so-called compassion for the poor. I don't have compassion for the poor.

I guess it's easy to be overcome with compassion fatigue when you're carrying an extra hundred and forty pounds.

Rush Limbaugh—Big Fat Hypocrite

Given his feelings about the poor, you might find it surprising that Limbaugh has himself fed off the largesse of the government. In the form of unemployment insurance. Was Rush temporarily disabled? No.

As you'll read in more detail in the Limbaugh Letter section, this self-described "rugged individual" and scourge of government handouts had the gall to file for unemployment at a time when he was able-bodied and spending his days sitting around the house eating junk food, too lazy to even mow his own lawn.*

Does this make Rush a big fat hypocrite? Yes, it does. And so do a few other interesting facts about his life. For example, did you know *Limbaugh never voted for Ronald Reagan*? That's right. The man who says Ronald Reagan belongs on Mount Rushmore never voted for him. In fact, Rush didn't register to vote until he was 35 years old, after a Sacramento journalist shamed him into it. Phil Gramm, who championed Reagan's economic policies as a member of Congress,

---

* For some reason, Rush made this admission, which I'm sure he regrets, on his radio program on May 10, 1995. I called Limbaugh's producer, Kit Carson, and asked him if Rush would supply the dates that he was on the dole. Kit was very nice and said he'd talk to Rush. The next day, Rush was on the radio:

> Didn't you say Franken called us the other day and wants me to be in a book he's writing? He's got a couple questions for a book he's writing. My instincts then were to say no. If somebody is gonna cream us you don't help him. We know we're gonna get creamed in Al Franken's book. We know that it's gonna be a distorted view. We know it is gonna be based on seven-year-old or four- or five-year-old things he misunderstands.

Kit called me back the next day and said, "As you probably expected, we really don't want to respond to this."

has called himself "a foot soldier in the Reagan Revolution." I guess that makes Rush a draft dodger in the Reagan Revolution.

While we're on the subject, Limbaugh has said several times, "Never ever trust a draft dodger." Meaning never trust a Baby Boomer who actively avoided serving in Vietnam. Guess what? We'll get to that later in the book.

RUSH LIMBAUGH—THIN-SKINNED BULLY

I tried to meet Rush back in 1992. I was the anchor for Comedy Central's convention coverage, "Indecision '92." We thought it would be interesting to have Rush on our program, joining other conservatives like Paul Gigot of the *Wall Street Journal* and regular *American Spectator* contributors Joe Queenan and Ben Stein. Even Roger Ailes, executive producer of Limbaugh's TV show and media adviser to Ronald Reagan and George Bush, appeared with us and was terrific. (Roger, by the way, is also very fat.)

Limbaugh, though, had demands. No one could be on camera with him. No one could comment on anything he said. "Screw that," I said. And no Limbaugh.

Limbaugh knows what's good for him. Whenever he's ventured outside the secure bubble of his studio, the results have been disastrous. In 1990, Limbaugh got what he thought was his chance at the big time, substitute hosting on Pat Sajak's ailing CBS late night show. But the studio wasn't packed with pre-screened dittoheads. When audience members started attacking him for having made fun of AIDS victims, he panicked, and they had to clear the studio. A CBS executive said, "He came out full of bluster and left a very shaken man. I had never seen a man sweat as much in my life."

Limbaugh later apologized for joking about AIDS and promised to "not make fun of the dying." But by early '94, he had forgotten the other lesson: he needs a stacked deck. This time disaster struck on the *Letterman* show. The studio audience turned hostile almost immediately after Rush compared Hillary Clinton's face to "a Pontiac hood ornament." Evidently, that's the kind of thing that kills with the dittoheads, but Letterman's audience wasn't buying. When Letterman ended the interview with: "Do you ever wake up in the middle of the night and just think to yourself, 'I am just full of hot gas'?" the studio erupted in laughter and applause.

Maybe I'm being a little unfair. So what if Rush is a bully who can dish it out to the poor, the homeless,

How Fat Is He?

In 1990, Rush spent a lot of time traveling around the country on his "Rush to Excellence" public speaking tour. This was before he got filthy rich, so he flew coach. But he didn't save all that much money. Why? Because *Rush is so fat he had to buy two seats.*

and "stupid, unskilled Mexicans," but who can't take it when he's the target himself? That's old news. And maybe I'm going too far with the fat jokes. Sure, he's obese. But it's too easy. It's way too easy to quote him: "It's time to start championing old-fashioned virtues like . . . self-restraint, self-discipline" and then write STOP EATING!!!

So I guess maybe I am being a little unfair. At least, that's what I thought until I started subscribing to the Limbaugh Letter.

THE LIMBAUGH LETTER

It was bad enough that I'd been forcing myself to listen to Limbaugh every day. Well, that's a lie. I'd listen every once in a while. Okay, I might as well come clean. At a certain point I started doing everything I could to avoid the man.

I told my research assistant Geoff to listen for an hour a day, but after a couple of weeks, he threatened to quit if I made him continue. Finally, I had to start paying a guy in California to listen for me.

Unfortunately, I made the mistake of subscribing to the monthly Limbaugh Letter. That makes me one of over 475,000, which is about five times the number of subscribers to the *New Republic*.

It also means that once a month my wife says to me, "C'mon, you paid for it. Open it." (It comes in an envelope, and she won't open it either.) Early in July, I got the June issue. The cover had a big picture of

Rush and carried the banner: The Best and the Brightest.

The title was inspired by a stupid controversy from last April involving Clinton's Health and Human Services Secretary Donna Shalala. Shalala had been on CNN's *Capital Gang* and said: "We sent not the best and the brightest's sons to Vietnam. We sent men from small towns and rural areas, we sent kids from the neighborhoods I grew up in, and we exempted the children of the wealthy and of the privileged and it tore this country apart and we must never do that again."

Eleanor Clift, a panelist on the show, jumped in: "Actually, the people who went were the best and the brightest," to which Shalala responded: "Absolutely."

In her first statement, Shalala had been referring to the sons of "the best and the brightest," an ironic, pejorative term coined by David Halberstam for the men in the Kennedy and Johnson administrations who got us into the war.

But her comment was picked up and reported by talk radio as: "The best and the brightest sons didn't go to Vietnam." In other words, Shalala was saying the men who fought in Vietnam were stupid. Limbaugh, Oliver North, and G. Gordon Liddy all started calling for Shalala's resignation.

Now my friend Josette Shiner, the managing editor of the conservative *Washington Times*, was on *Capital Gang* that day with Shalala and Clift. So Josette calls Liddy's show, and they put her on the air with him. She explains what Shalala said, Liddy agrees that

Shalala has been misinterpreted, and explains to his audience that he was wrong.

Meanwhile, Clift goes on North's show. And North, like Liddy, admits that he was wrong.

Then Josette calls one of Limbaugh's top people. She explains that Shalala was completely misunderstood, and Limbaugh's guy responds: "That's her problem."

So, when I got the June Limbaugh Letter, I opened it up to find that he was *still* flogging the Shalala thing:

> "We sent not the best and the brightest sons to Vietnam." This was the declaration on CNN's *Capital Gang* by Health and Human Services Secretary Donna Shalala. . . . My friends, there is no better demonstration of the liberal view of the country than this. Ordinary American kids who fought and bled and died in Southeast Asia—or their parents—were too stupid to know any better. These were not the talented ones, the ones with great promise, the future national leaders, the coming movers and shakers. These were mere working class, the patsies, the chumps, the losers.

So you can imagine my excitement when the new Limbaugh Letter arrived. I didn't open it right away. I thought of a few things I had to do first. The cat box. That always needs cleaning. My wife usually does it, but, hey, I've got to start pulling my weight around here. Also, no one had checked our ATM receipts against our bank statements. I'd been saving those since they invented the ATM, so that took a couple days.

Come to think of it, getting the Limbaugh Letter has had its upside. If an unopened copy of the Limbaugh Letter hadn't been sitting in my office, I probably never would have regrouted the bathroom tiles.

Well, finally I opened it. Greeting me on the cover, once again, was a large picture of a smirking Rush and, this time, a smaller inset of the First Lady, teasing this month's feature: "My 'Conversation' with Hillary Clinton."

Inside I found the three-page "conversation," at the end of which, in very small type, is this disclaimer:

> All the First Lady's words are taken verbatim from transcripts of her speeches, press conferences and comments on the public record. Rush's comments have been added to create this simulated "interview."

This clever literary conceit allows Limbaugh to construct such witty exchanges as the following:

First Lady: There is this undercurrent of discontent.

Rush: Wait a minute. Define "discontent."

First Lady: This sense that somehow economic

growth and prosperity, political democracy and freedom are not enough.

Rush: Oh, I know what you're talking about—the
conclusion most of us arrive at when we are 16 or 17
years old that there's more to life than money and
politics.

First Lady: That we lack at some core level meaning
in our individual lives and meaning collectively. . . .

Rush: Would you like a tissue?

This gave me an idea. Why not *steal* Rush's idea
and use it against him? And so, here goes:

My "Conversation" with Rush Limbaugh

Al: First of all, I'd like to thank you for agreeing to
talk with me. I understand you don't often give interviews.

Rush: I've had 4,635 stories in which I was mentioned in the past year without giving any interviews.
(*Time* magazine, 1/23/95)

Al: By the way, megadittoes on developing this interview technique.

Rush: Thank you so much. (*See, I Told You So*, Ac-
knowledgments)

Al: It reminds me of those old disc jockey routines where they'd intercut song lyrics with goofy questions. Like "What was Queen Elizabeth wearing?" And they cut in: "She wore an itsy-bitsy teeny-weeny yellow polka-dot bikini."

Rush: *Laughs.* (*Playboy* interview, 12/93)

Al: My goodness, you're fat.

Rush: [Y]es. (*The Way Things Ought to Be*, p. 315)

Al: I see you're wearing one of your Rush Limbaugh Collection ties. It's very conservative.

Rush: The *last* thing in the world these ties would be described as would be conservative! (Radio show, 6/12/95)

Al: But those stripes seem pretty conservative.

Rush: There's not one stripe! Not one stripe! (Radio show, 6/12/95)

Al: All right, let's drop that and get back to the issues. Sweet Jesus, you're enormous! You must weigh close to eight hundred pounds!

Rush: Not yet true, but inevitable. (Heritage Foundation, *Policy Review*, Fall 1994, p. 7)

Al: Well, how much do you weigh then?

Rush: More than six hundred. (*See, I Told You So*, p. 2)

Al: Okay, let's move off of how fat you are. Because there's something pretty serious I want to ask you about. Recently on one of your radio—

Rush: Have you ever noticed how all newspaper composite pictures of wanted criminals resemble Jesse Jackson? (*Newsday*, 10/8/90)

Al: My Lord, that is racist. And please don't interrupt me.

Rush: Let's go to the issue of condoms. (Heritage Foundation, *Policy Review*, Fall 1994, p. 8)

Al: No, this is my interview. I want to get into something serious here, which is a startling revelation you made on the radio recently. You broke down and admitted to your listeners that you actually collected unemployment insurance, am I right?

Rush: Well, I was without income once when I was married and my wife made me go and file for unemployment, and it was the most gut-wrenching thing I've ever done. (Radio show, 5/10/95)

Al: Wow! That is astounding! So Rush Limbaugh was actually on the dole? How could you of all people accept money from the government?

Rush: I had a bunch of expenses I couldn't meet. I had one credit card—I couldn't pay my MasterCard bill because it came at a time of the month when the rent came. (Radio, 5/10/95)

Al: My God! You are perhaps the world's biggest hypocrite. I mean in *The Way Things Ought to Be* you say, "The poor in this country are the biggest piglets at the mother pig and her nipples." And yet it turns out that you, yourself, suckled at the federal teat, and are, in fact, a loathsome piglet. I mean pig, because you're so fat.

Rush: I had a cash flow problem . . . grocery stores then didn't take credit cards—I literally, for a couple of years, was going to snack-food kinds of places, that did take credit cards, and buying junk, potato chips and so forth. (Radio show, 5/10/95)

Al: Hence your enormous weight. Lord in heaven, you are a sad person. Can you give us more of your pathetic sob story?

Rush: I was able to afford shelter, but that was it. I wasn't able to afford the upkeep on the shelter. If it weren't for the fact that I had a friend whose boys would mow my yard, then I would have had weeds instead of a yard. (Radio show, 5/10/95)

Al: I think I get the picture. You were unemployed, eating potato chips, and too lazy to mow your own lawn. Could this story get any more pitiful?

Rush: The air conditioner broke down—couldn't get it fixed. Roof, paint, all that. And I eventually had to sell it and lost money in the process, because, of course, the place had turned into a ramshackle old shack. (Radio show, 5/10/95)

Al: Of course. You know, Rush, I still don't understand why you collected unemployment instead of working. There *must* have been some work available in Kansas City for an able-bodied man with three hundred pounds on the hoof. Perhaps as ballast on a barge traveling down the Missouri.

Rush: My wife made me go and file for unemployment. (Radio show, 5/10/95)

Al: That's right, you already said that. I swear, you must be the biggest pussy on God's green Earth.

Rush: [Y]es. (*The Way Things Ought To Be*, p. 315)

Al: My God, you are a sad, sad creature, aren't you? Sort of a she-male?

Rush: [Y]es. (*The Way Things Ought to Be*, p. 315)

Al: Well, that's about it. Before we go, is there anything you'd like to say to my readers about the state of America?

Rush: We're in bad shape in this country when you can't look at a couple of huge knockers and notice it. (TV show, 2/2/94)

RUSH LIMBAUGH—SUCCESS STORY

That was fun, wasn't it? But it's occurred to me that maybe I'm being so rough on Rush because I'm a little jealous. After all, Rush is more successful than I am, at least if you leave out the failed marriages and sad physical condition. He is, after all, the undisputed master of the format radio consultants have dubbed "non-guested confrontation." He does make $25 million a year, maybe more now with the No Boundaries tie collection.

And he's used his platform to become national pre-cinct chairman for the Republican party. As much as anyone, including Newt Gingrich, he is responsible for the current Republican majority in Congress. Just ask the seventy-three freshman Republicans who made Rush an honorary member of the Class of '94. So, yes, Rush deserves more respect. And that's why I've prepared this time line to give you some idea of how and where American conservatism found its voice.

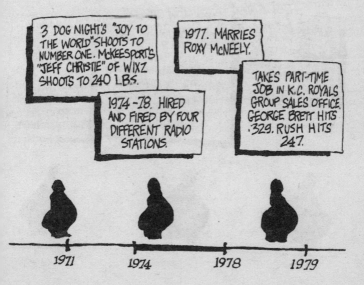

DIVORCED BY
ROXY M. BALLOONS
TO 260 LBS.

HIRED BY KMBZ
IN K.C., WHERE "I
FOUND OUT I WAS
REALLY GOOD AT
INSULTING PEOPLE."

FALL '84. HIRED BY
KFPK, SACRAMENTO.

"UNGUESTED CONFRONTATION"
FORMAT CATCHING ON. LOSES
60 LBS AS SACRAMENTO
SPOKESMAN FOR NUTRI/
SYSTEM. WEIGHS LESS
THAN OPRAH.

MARRIES MICHELLE
SIXTA. LOSES SIX
TO EIGHT LBS.

FIRED BY KMBZ.
PUTS BACK WEIGHT
AND THEN SOME.

1980   1983   1984   1986

NUMBER OF SYN-
DICATED STATIONS
EXCEEDS RUSH'S
WEIGHT IN POUNDS
FOR FIRST TIME—
REACHING 350.

TV SHOW BEGINS.
THE WAY THINGS OUGHT
TO BE TOPS BESTSELLER
LIST. IN IT, RUSH RAILS
AGAINST UGLO-AMERICANS,
ANTI-MALES, SUBSIDY
HOGS, ENVIRO-RELIGIOUS
FANATICS, ANTICAPITALISTS,
AND LIBERALS.

SEE, I TOLD
YOU SO HITS
BESTSELLER
LIST. IN IT RUSH
ANNOUNCES THAT
"I, FOR ONE, AM
TIRED OF ALL
THE NEGATIVITY."

1991   1992   1993

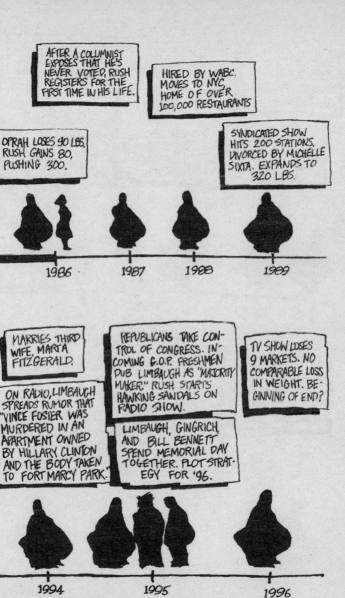

Delacorte Press

FOR IMMEDIATE RELEASE

AL FRANKEN TAKES CREDIT FOR CANCELLATION OF LIMBAUGH TV SHOW

(New York, NY—July 16, 1996) Delacorte Press best-selling author Al Franken claimed today that he is "directly and personally responsible" for the cancellation of Rush Limbaugh's syndicated television show.

Mr. Franken's book *Rush Limbaugh Is a Big Fat Idiot and Other Observations* recently spent twenty-three weeks on the *New York Times* bestseller list, including five weeks in the number-one position.

"Clearly, I have crippled the man," said a jubilant Franken in response to Limbaugh's announcement last Friday that he was abandoning his regular television show. Mr. Limbaugh's statement that "I need to take a step back and look at things again" is, according to Mr. Franken, "a rhetorical fig leaf masking his stunning professional failure."

Mr. Franken also predicted that this autumn's publication of the paperback version of his book will deal "a fatal blow" to Mr. Limbaugh's flagship radio show. "I've got him on the ropes," declared Mr. Franken. "My only regret is that, since he's abandoned all visual media, it will now be impossible to monitor his cyclical weight fluctuations."

Delacorte Press

3
ONE GIANT LEAP TOWARD SOLVING THE BUDGET CRISIS

The big movie last summer was the inspiring rescue story of *Apollo 13*. Yet despite the boost to NASA's public image, the agency is still under the budget knife. That's because the big political story these days is balancing the budget.

How can we cut all these programs, retain civilization as we know it, and become a better and more compassionate country, as the Republicans are suggesting? I've looked at the budget and it can be done, but we need creative thinking to make it work. In the spirit of Gingrich and Kasich, I have an idea.

The new budget includes big cuts for both Medicare and NASA. Now here are two seemingly unrelated facts.

Fact one: 30 percent of Medicare expenditures are incurred by people in the last year of their lives.

Fact two: NASA spends billions per year on as-
          tronaut safety.

Maybe you see where I'm going. Recent poll data
show that our senior citizens are willing to make sacrifices, if they will help lower the staggering debt on
future generations. Most think these sacrifices would
take the form of lower social security benefits. My
idea is more radical.

Why not shoot the elderly into space? Stay with
me. Because I'm not just thinking about the budget
here. I'm talking about science. Just think how many
more manned space operations NASA could under-
take if they didn't have to worry about getting the
astronauts back.

Now, I'm not saying we don't try to get them back.
We just don't make such a big deal about it. That way
we don't have to use the shuttle every time, which is
very expensive. Put an old Mercury capsule on top of
a Saturn rocket, fire it up, and see what happens. And
if the "Houston, we've got a problem" call comes,
Mission Control can simply reply, "Best of luck.
We're rooting for you."

We could learn so much. What is the effect of
weightlessness on arthritis? Let's make it our goal to
perform the first hip replacement in space before the
millennium!

Would aluminum foil make a good space suit for a
space walk? Or would you bake like a potato? That
would be fun to know. Would a '72 Buick Le Sabre
make a good space capsule? This whole thing could
be a tremendous boon to what is called "raw science."

That is, knowledge for which there is no real immediate use, but which could have great long-term benefits. For example, how close to the sun can a person get before he bursts into flame? Would it make any difference if he's fat?

If my idea works, we could expand the program to include the terminally ill. Who doesn't want to go out making a contribution?

Here's a related idea. Stunts. How much did Evel Knievel get for jumping the Snake River Canyon? Millions, right? OK. Every Sunday we put an elderly (or terminally ill) person in a rocket, fire it over the Snake River, and put it on pay-per-view. The revenues go straight to reducing the debt.

Here's another idea. I am not a military expert, so I'm not sure that this is feasible. But here it is. From what I've read I understand there is nothing more terrifying in battle than seeing enemy hordes charging at you with no regard for their own lives. Why have we always insisted on asking our young men, and now young women, in the flower of their lives, to risk themselves in combat? Why not, in the right situation, use a human wave of our elderly to scare the enemy?

Think about it. You're an Iraqi or a North Korean or Serbian soldier. Suddenly, over the horizon, you see a battalion of Americans. They won't attack, you think. America wouldn't risk the blood of its precious youth when it could simply employ their sophisticated, expensive weapons. Then you look through your binoculars, and a chill goes down your spine. Retirees! Thousands and thousands of them! Each one older than the next. Each with a life expectancy of three or four years at most. You think to yourself, "What do these people really have to lose? The four worst years of their lives?" You're terrified. Then they charge. A slow charge, yes, but that makes it even more frightening.

Admittedly, there're some kinks to work out. Mobilization would be tough. Have you ever organized a group of seniors for a theater trip? I don't think training would be that much of a problem. It'd be kind of like, "Go out there and run." And this would give our World War II–era Americans a chance to contribute yet again to our country. Just when they thought they were forgotten.

I guess what I'm saying is let's not just talk about our problems. Let's talk about *solutions*.

4
ADVENTURES IN POLITICS
1951-1975

I've always been fascinated with politics. When I was growing up in Minnesota, my family would discuss current events at the dinner table. My father was a lifelong Republican even though he never made more than eight thousand dollars in a year. I like to say we were lower middle class but didn't know it. Dad was born in New York in 1908, and we didn't move to Minnesota until 1955, when I was four. For those of you in the Michigan Militia, that means I was born in 1951.

We moved to this small town in southern Minnesota, where Dad opened a factory that manufactured quilting. Quilting is the, well, quilted fabric that lines winter coats. My mother's dad, Simon, a Russian immigrant who arrived in this country when he was sixteen speaking no English, built a fabric business and passed up a golden opportunity to become rich during World War II, when he refused to cheat on wartime regulations, which a lot of manufacturers did. At least, this was family lore, but the point is my mom was proud of it, and it was an ethics lesson in our house. So in 1955 Grandpa opened this factory in Albert Lea, Minnesota, and sent my dad, who at 47 had never been west of the Alleghenies, to manage it. I asked Dad a few years ago, why Albert Lea? and Dad said it was because the railroad ran through Albert Lea, but when we got there we found out the railroad wouldn't *stop* in Albert Lea. At least not to pick up our goods. Dad was not a good businessman. Even though he worked fourteen-hour days, the factory failed.

So when I was six, we moved up to Minneapolis. Actually a suburb, St. Louis Park, called "St. Jewish Park" by most of the Twin Cities, because it was the Jewish suburb of Minneapolis, that is to say it was about 20 percent Jewish. Not exactly a *shtetl* (for those of you in the Christian Coalition, a small city of Jews), but by Minnesota standards, a *lot* of Jews. Minneapolis had something of a reputation for anti-Semitism, fueled in part by the pernicious presence of a Jewish organized crime syndicate that Hubert Humphrey chased out in the late 40s when he was mayor.

Dad got work as a printing salesman, and since my brother and I were both in school, Mom got her real estate license. At the dinner table my parents would talk about their day. Dad's highlight was always lunch and one of his buddies' bad jokes. Mom would tell us stories about the practice that didn't have a name at the time but would later become known as redlining. Basically, developers, bankers, and real estate agents had a spoken or unspoken agreement to restrict blacks or Jews from buying homes in certain areas. I assume the term "redline" came from a line, I guess a red one, drawn down streets like Texas Avenue in St. Louis Park. So on one side of Texas you'd have a development with tiny houses owned by people with names like Anderson, Carlson, Lundahl, and Anderson again, and right across the street, living in the exact same houses with the exact same floor plan, families named Goldberg, Shapiro, and Grossman.

Mom wouldn't tell her clients she was Jewish. So every once in a while she'd be driving a couple around, and the woman would say something like, "I don't want to buy a house from a Jew. I hear Jewish women are terrible housekeepers." And my mom would smile and kind of bat her eyes involuntarily, which she'd do when she hated someone, and say something like, "In my experience there are good Jewish housekeepers and a few who aren't so good, just like Christian housekeepers." And leave it at that.

Mom was a Democrat, and I remember the 1960 presidential election as a source of some friction in our home. I was for Nixon, because I liked my dad better than my mom. My older brother, Owen, was for Kennedy. I think it had something to do with a visceral aversion to Nixon. Anyway, in 1964 Dad switched parties. A card-carrying member of the NAACP, he was disgusted with Goldwater's opposition to the 1964 Civil Rights Act. We'd sit in front of the TV and watch them turn police dogs and fire hoses on Negro demonstrators, and Mom and Dad would compare it to the Holocaust and tell us it was our duty as Jews to support civil rights. Dad just couldn't understand how Goldwater or anyone could oppose equal access to public accommodations. But the Republican party, people like Strom Thurmond, and George Bush, and Robert Bork, did reject a law that made it a crime to refuse to serve a person because of the color of his skin.

So Dad left the Republican party and never went back. A man who had voted for Herbert Hoover, Alf Landon, Wendell Willkie, and Thomas Dewey (twice!) turned around and voted for Lyndon Johnson, Hubert Humphrey, George McGovern, Jimmy Carter, Walter Mondale, Michael Dukakis, and finally, at age 84, for Bill Clinton. During Vietnam, Dad didn't want his sons to go to war. Just like Dan Quayle's father. The only difference was Dad didn't want anyone else's son to go to Vietnam. So he demonstrated against it.

So I've always been interested in politics. And I thank my parents for that. As you can see, there was a strong element of moral indignation behind this interest, and indignation is well and good in doses, but I noticed fairly early in life that some people *live* to find stuff to be indignant about. And it's pretty unattractive. That's why I decided to become a wiseass.

1971–1975. I GET MY BROTHER OUT OF THE DRAFT AND GIVE MO UDALL A CRUEL MEASURE OF FALSE HOPE

Late fall 1975. For those of you in the Montana Militia, I was now twenty-four years old. I had my first steady job, writing for a new show on NBC called

Saturday Night Live. It was an exciting time, and my only regret was that my dad wasn't alive to see it. No, wait. What am I saying? He didn't die until 1993.

After our first few shows in October, we had a one-week break. My brother Owen, who also had become a wiseass, though not professionally, was now a photographer, and he suggested I ride the press bus with him in New Hampshire and follow Ronald Reagan around. Reagan was one of those guys who in 1964 opposed the Civil Rights Act. Can't legislate morality was the rationale.

Our first stop was Cambridge, Massachusetts. Mo Udall was speaking at M.I.T., Owen's alma mater. My brother, the first member of our family to go to college (Dad never graduated high school), holds a degree in physics from M.I.T. But he was there during the height of the war and saw that most of the applications of physics at the time involved finding better ways to kill people. So after graduating, he became a photojournalist.

We arrived late at Kresge Auditorium, which was packed with bespectacled young Jewish and Asian American men with slide rules stuffed in the breast pockets of their white shirts. I tried to keep up with Owen as he snaked his way through the crowd to the front, a talent he had developed in his years covering these kinds of events. Also he was very skinny, which was an advantage. In 1971 Owen got out of the draft by being underweight. He's five-ten, and at his draft physical he weighed in at 109. Pounds.

In fact, I was his trainer. I wrestled in high school and knew how to lose weight. (Attention, Rush: It involves diet and exercise.) Owen had graduated and gotten his draft notice. I was a sophomore at Harvard (I tested well in high school), so Owen moved into my dorm room, and I supervised his weight-loss program. We didn't have that far to go; he weighed 125 and we had to get him down below 115–110 to be safe. On the other hand, try getting fifteen pounds off a guy who's built like a whippet.

Basically, I fed him two things. Steamed spinach and raw oysters. The latter on the hope that he'd get some nasty gastrointestinal disorder. And I'd play squash with him for hours at a time. My dorm had squash courts in the basement and you could play twenty-four hours a day. The week of the physical I had Owen down there in the middle of the night in his sweats and he'd literally collapse during volleys. And I'd yell at him, "Get up! Charlie's coming! Charlie's gonna get ya!" Meaning, of course, the Vietcong. Owen would jump right up and play till he collapsed again, and we got him down to 109. He thinks less, because he swears they added some weight to the scale when they saw him coming.

But in Kresge Auditorium Owen was at his fighting weight, now probably 127 pounds, working his way through this mass of wonks, geeks, and techies while hauling three Nikons and a camera bag with all kinds of shit in it. Fortunately, we hadn't missed anything, because Udall was late too.

Very late, it would turn out, and as the crowd grew restless, a young man from the M.I.T. forum committee got up and praised the turnout and went on for about fifteen minutes about participatory democracy and started pissing everybody off. Only he didn't announce that he was from M.I.T. and the crowd thought he was from the Udall campaign. By now, Owen and I were actually on the stage, and I turned to a Udall staffer and said, "Somebody from your campaign really should say something." But the staffer just stared at me.

This guy has no sense of show business, I thought. I who had been in show business for about a month. As the guy from the forum committee wrapped up, there was a smattering of boos, and I looked around for someone with a Udall button to address the situation. The jeers started to build and I just couldn't help myself.

By the time I got to the podium, the boos were pretty deafening. But when I tapped the microphone, they started quieting down. Owen looked at me kinda puzzled, but then started snapping pictures. His little brother was speaking. "The Udall campaign would just like to announce that the tedious gentleman who just spoke was from your institution and not, I repeat, *not* a member of the Udall campaign!"

First came a really big laugh. Then cheers. More than anything it was about the hour and fifteen minutes of mind-numbing boredom that preceded my announcement. And just as the cheer was coming to a crescendo, my gaze went to the back, where Morris Udall was just entering the hall, looking tired and a little distracted. Even his non-glass eye was a little glassy. He was, after all, an hour behind. That's when I got really close to the mike, so everyone could hear my voice booming over the cheers, "Ladies and gentlemen, the next president of the United States, Mo Udall!" A tumultuous roar! The place went nuts! As Udall worked his way through the frenzied crowd, I could see that for probably the first time, and maybe the last, Mo Udall was convinced he could win this thing.

Owen told me not to do that again.

NEW HAMPSHIRE, 1975. I SOW THE SEEDS OF GERALD FORD'S DEMISE

The day after Udall's M.I.T. speech we headed up to New Hampshire. First we went to a Ford event. It was *really* boring. I don't think I even saw him. The press corps and I sat in a high school gymnasium where they piped in a speech Ford was giving to the students in a nearby auditorium. So I just wandered around, talking with press people who were even more bored than me.

I was excited to see Ron Nessen. Now, there's a sentence you don't read every day. Ron Nessen was press secretary to the president, so I was excited to see him, and I struck up a conversation. It came out that I worked for *Saturday Night Live*, which I was surprised to learn he had seen and enjoyed. He even said he liked Chevy Chase's Ford sketches, which depicted the president as a fatuous stumblebum. I said, "You should be on the show." And he said, "I'd love to."

When I went back to work the next week, Lorne Michaels made it clear that, since he, not I, was the producer of *Saturday Night Live*, it was inappropriate for me, an apprentice writer, to invite people to appear on the show. Nevertheless, Nessen did host a few months later, and it was pretty much a total disaster for the president. It was never our intention to "take the President and shove his press secretary up his ass," as Lorne would later put it. It just kind of worked out that way.

Nessen appeared in an Oval Office sketch I helped write in which Chevy as Ford kicked a wastebasket around the room, stapled his ear, and shouted, "Heel, Liberty!" to a stuffed dog. Worse for the White House were sketches Nessen didn't appear in: A couple (Chevy and Jane Curtin) writhing under sheets in their bedroom as robed Supreme Court Justices make sure they don't do anything too kinky; an Emily Litella (Gilda Radner) "Weekend Update" editorial on "presidential erections"; and a hilarious parody of the "with a name like Smuckers, it has to be good" commercial written by Michael O'Donoghue featuring names for jams such as Nose Hair, Death Camp, Mangled Baby Ducks, Dog Vomit, Monkey Pus, and Painful Rectal Itch.

Oh yeah. And Nessen had talked the president into pre-recording an opening for our show. A very, very stilted Gerald Ford saying, "Live from New York, it's *Saturday Night*!" You know, kind of a presidential endorsement. And I forgot the Autumn Fizz parody. Gilda pitching a carbonated douche.

According to wire service reports, White House staffers said the president was "not pleased." When Nessen returned to Washington, he received a handwritten note from the president's son, Jack. "I thought as Press Sec. you're supposed to make professional decisions that get the Pres. good press! If you get a min. I'd be happy to explain to you that your job is to further the Pres. interest, not yours or your family's!" Evidently he agreed with White House aides who found the show "vulgar" and thought it made the president "look stupid."

Fortunately, the White House had a plan to restore the President's stature. The WIN! buttons. Whip Inflation Now!

Same Trip. Lyn Nofziger Throws Me Off the Press Bus for Asking Ronald Reagan a Snide Question

I seemed to be cutting quite a swath through New England. Now Owen and I found ourselves in Hanover, New Hampshire, following Ronald Reagan. We stayed overnight with the rest of the press corps at a quaint hotel on the campus of Dartmouth College, and the bus left very early in the morning for Reagan's first campaign event of the day, an appearance at the most adorable little country store you've ever fucking seen.

I was kind of sleepy, but this was fun! I, like the rest of the press corps (well, I wasn't really part of the press corps, but I was getting confused), was standing about fifteen feet from Reagan inside this set for a Pepperidge Farm commercial as he answered questions from guys named Caleb and Ichabod.

It would be pretty much impossible to overestimate the extent to which I underestimated Ronald Reagan at this point in time. Yes, he was a former two-term governor of California, but I thought of him mainly as the host of *Death Valley Days* and spokesman for Boraxo.

This is probably something you should know about me as you read this book. I do not have the best track record as a prognosticator. Remember back to about 1984 when both Madonna and Cyndi Lauper were emerging? I would have put all my money on Cyndi Lauper. Great voice, really cute and fresh-faced in a saucy kind of way, with a Gracie Allen comic thing happening. Yeah, Cyndi Lauper over Madonna. Of course, in fairness to me, I had no way of knowing at that time the extent to which Madonna would be willing to degrade herself to win such a huge following.

So some guy asks Reagan about mandatory motorcycle helmets, which was a big issue in California. A couple years before, a few thousand Hell's Angels had bombed into Sacramento to protest a proposed law which would have made it mandatory to wear a brain bucket when riding a motorcycle. Now I guess it had become an issue in New Hampshire, and Reagan was on the side of the Angels. "It's a limit to personal freedom," he told the man.

On to the next event, and the next. On and off the bus, then back on. And it's kinda cool; I'm one of the boys on the bus. Back off and we're at a junior high assembly where a kid asks if Reagan favors decriminalizing marijuana. Reagan says no, "because medical evidence shows that marijuana causes brain damage."

The last event is back at the Dartmouth hockey

arena. It's evening, and there are several thousand people, all Reagan supporters, except for those of us in the press who are neutral, sitting in a neutral roped-off area. Reagan gives his speech and then it's time for questions. It's a big arena, so there are microphones in the aisles. So I climb over the rope and get in line to ask my question.

"Yeah. I've been following you on the press bus all day, and this morning in Derby Falls you said you were against mandatory motorcycle helmets because it's a limit to personal freedom. . . ."

People had already started booing.

". . . And then later this afternoon in Cornish Flat you said you were against decriminalizing marijuana because it causes brain damage. . . ."

BOOO!!

"What's your question?" says the candidate.

"Well . . . can't not wearing a motorcycle helmet cause brain damage a lot quicker than marijuana by, for example, the head splitting open so that actual material from the road enters the brain?"

BOOOOOO!!!!!!!

Reagan let the crowd go on for quite some time while he seemed to grope for an answer to my question. Finally, they quieted and he bobbed his head the way he would and said, "Well. If I was on an airplane, and the pilot was drunk, I'd be able to tell. But if he was high on marijuana, I wouldn't. Be able to tell."

Lots of applause.

When I got back to the press bus, Lyn Nofziger was waiting for me. Nofziger was a bulldog of a guy with the kind of a goatee that if he was Jewish and in a little worse shape, you might think he was a pornographer. I think he was Reagan's press secretary at the time. Anyway, he ran the bus. He actually let me on so everyone could hear him say, "Either you're a member of the press or a member of the public!" And, of course, he was right. Then he kicked me off, and I had to walk back to the hotel, which was about three blocks away, and since there was so much traffic from the event, I easily beat the bus back to the hotel and made sure to greet it with a big grin on my face.

When Owen got off the bus, he acted like he didn't know me. Later he suggested that we kind of put a moratorium on these little fraternal campaign junkets.

5
THE NEWT CANCER
SURGERY STORY

WHAT THE LIBERAL MEDIA MIGHT NOT
BE TELLING YOU

You've probably heard the famous story about Newt Gingrich and his first wife, Jackie. The one in which he visited her in the hospital when she was recovering from cancer surgery. As the story goes, Gingrich brought along their two daughters *and* a yellow legal pad with his terms for a divorce, which he read to her while she was still groggy.

One thing you should know about the story is this: It's true. Gingrich has acknowledged all but the groggy part, telling *Time* magazine that the story was "a caricature." And to be fair, there is no way to know what goes on between two people. Anyone who's been married knows that.

In fact, I think the liberal media's portrayal of this whole ugly episode has been a little unfair to Newt. Maybe if we knew the real story, Newt wouldn't come out looking like such a pig.

Maybe it went like this:

Jackie calls Newt at home just before she goes into surgery. "Newt, I'm more certain than ever that I want a divorce."

"But, honey, you're about to undergo cancer surgery! You don't know what you're saying!"

"Newt, please. When you bring the girls today, I also want you to bring a legal pad with terms for a divorce."

"For godsakes! You're having cancer surgery!"

"Would you stop it?! This is what I want. What I *don't* want is for you to blame yourself. You're too good a person for that."

It could have been like that. And to assume otherwise would be unfair.

Of course, what we do know is that after the divorce, he was late with his alimony payments, and she had to take him to court twice to provide adequate support for her and the girls and that her church took up a collection to help them get by. That we do know.

6
GINGRICH: SEX, GIRAFFES, AND WEIGHTLESSNESS

So Newt Gingrich is a deadbeat dad who presented his first wife with terms for divorce while she was in the hospital recovering from cancer surgery. That's not the point of this piece. But it's fun to repeat.

Newt is nothing if not a man of ideas: We should give poor kids laptops. We should put poor kids in orphanages. We should appoint militia-loving Idaho representative Helen Chenoweth to a gun control task force.

Some of Newt's ideas have not been popular among feminazis. Last January, while teaching his "Renewing American Civilization" course, Newt discussed some of the innate differences between the male of the species and the female:

> If combat means living in a ditch, females have biological problems staying in a ditch for 30 days because they get infections. . . . On the

other hand, if combat means being on an aegis class cruiser managing the computer controls for twelve ships, a female may be again dramatically better than a male, who gets very, very frustrated sitting in a chair all the time because males are biologically driven to go out and hunt giraffes.

Two images come to mind. The first is of the grasslands of Africa. During the Neolithic Period. Rush, Newt, and Bill Bennett, all 825 pounds of them, are trying to run down a giraffe. The giraffe is thinking, "No problem here."

The second image is of Newt, about fifteen years ago, explaining to his thirteen-year-old daughter that she just got her first "infection."

The question is: Where does Newt get all of his ideas? Well, I turned to his bestseller *To Renew America* for clues.

If you want a sense of the personal values we should be communicating to children, get the Boy Scout or Girl Scout handbook. Or go and look at *Reader's Digest* and *The Saturday Evening Post* from around 1955.

So I sent my assistant, Geoff, to the New York public library (government program) to do a little research. And wouldn't you know it? He found what appears to be the primary source of Newt's gender theories. From the November 1955 *Reader's Digest* comes "Why Women Act That Way."

The article answers such thorny, politically charged questions as: "Why are women so clumsy at pitching a ball and running?" (bone structure); "Why do women go on periodic frenzies of housecleaning and furniture moving?" (thyroid gland); "Why are women forever smelling something burning or hearing burglars?" (keener senses); and "Why are women such glib fibbers?" (to compensate for lesser strength).

But the core of Newt's beliefs seems to be derived from the section entitled, "Why do women go in for concerts and 'culture' so much more than men?"

> There's a biological basis. Such things call for sitting still, and it's hard for a man to sit still. Woman's greatest avoirdupois is around her hips. This anchors her down in chairs and makes her more comfortable. A man is top-heavy, with his maximum weight around his chest and shoulders. He's built for action, not sitting.

See? Just add the words "aegis class cruiser" and "giraffe."

There is one area of male-female relations, however, in which the Speaker's views seem to diverge sharply from those of our nation's literary condenser of record. To wit: the honeymoon.

For more than a decade, Newt has contended that in the not-so-distant future, couples will be celebrating their nuptials in space. He first suggested this in his 1984 book *Window of Opportunity*, and it's back again in *To Renew America*.

I believe space tourism will be a common fact of life during the adulthood of children born this year, that honeymoons in space will be the vogue by 2020. Imagine weightlessness and its effects and you will understand some of the attractions.

You don't have to be Hugh Hefner to know that Newt is talking about sex. Well, from what I know about sex, Newt couldn't be more wrong. Gravity is an important, maybe even necessary, element in the physics of marital union. This is especially true for the uninitiated, for whom the wedding night is a source of extreme anxiety and apprehension. I refer you to the September 1955 edition of *Reader's Digest** and the article "Before Young People Marry."

People harbor many needless anxieties about sex. Men may be afraid they may be anatomically inadequate; girls may be apprehensive about the first sex experiences. Most of these fears are baseless. Anatomical disproportion is very rare, and the dilation of the hymen is seldom accompanied by much discomfort. . . . Honeymoon experiences are no criterion by which to judge sexual compatibility. Tired from weeks of wedding preparations, both bride and groom may be too exhausted, by the time they

---

* The same issue also features an article entitled "The Negroes Among Us."

are alone, to function normally or to react adequately.

My God! The *last* thing these kids need is to be weightless! What is Gingrich thinking?

Imagine for a moment that you are a bashful young groom, exhausted not just from weeks of preparation and the wedding itself, but from the stress of the massive G-forces exerted on your body during liftoff. It's been a long day.

Now, finally alone in the honeymoon suite of the space station, you and your bride prepare to consummate your marriage. As you offer her a tube of complimentary space champagne, she floats away. As you try to unzip her space suit, she floats away. As you attempt to find the switch for the artificial fireplace, once again, she floats away. What is already a very awkward situation for the both of you becomes a horrifying, potentially scarring, test of acrobatic agility.

If this is any indication of how impractical Gingrich's ideas are, imagine what a mess welfare reform is going to be.

7
RUSH LIMBAUGH'S
FACT CHECKER

What's the easiest job in America? Washington, D.C., Shadow Senator? That's pretty easy. How about "undeclared candidate for president"? That's easy *and* lucrative. Ask Colin Powell's publisher. But if you ask me, the man who has the easiest job in America is Rush Limbaugh's fact checker. I asked my own fact checker, Geoff, to track him down. He called us back and we got it all on tape.

Telephone ring

Geoff: Hello! Rush Limbaugh Is a Big Fat Idiot. How may I direct your call?

Waylon: Excuse me. I thought I was calling Empower USA.

Geoff: Oh. Um . . . I'm sorry, you must have the wrong number.

Waylon: Is this 212-555-0238?

Geoff: Ooooh, no. I guess you misdialed.

Waylon: Sorry.

Geoff: S'okay.

Moments later . . .

Geoff: Hello! Empower USA. How may I direct your call?

Waylon: Oh good. Is this Geoff?

Geoff: Hi, Waylon! Let me put my boss on.

Al: Hi, Waylon! Megadittoes!

Waylon: What?

Al: Megadittoes. You know . . . megadittoes.

Waylon: Oh!! Yeah, right. Megadittoes.

Al: Waylon, thanks for calling. As I think Geoff told you, we here at Empower USA are a brand-new right-wing think tank, and we're just gearing up. Now, I understand you've been Rush Limbaugh's fact checker from the get-go.

Waylon: Yeah, I've been with him for eight, ten years. Something like that.

Al: I guess he must be very happy with you.

Waylon: Well, if it ain't broke.

Al: Waylon, we're trying to get our fact-checking unit up and running, and we thought we'd come to the best. So I wanted to ask you about a few of these . . . facts. First of all, in April of 1994, Rush said on the radio that "there is no conclusive proof that nicotine's addictive. . . . And the same thing with cigarettes causing emphysema, lung cancer, heart disease."

Waylon: Yes. That's a bona fide, one hundred percent correct.

Al: I see. And where did you get that information?

Waylon: Ummm . . . jeez, you know, I got that around here somewhere. The place is kind of a mess. I never throw anything out. 'Cause, you know, fact checker.

Al: Right. Well, here's another one. It seems that on June 9th, 1994, Rush claimed on his TV show that there's a federal regulation which says if you have a Bible at your desk at work, then you're guilty of religious harassment.

Waylon: Okay. Turns out that's wrong. But it wasn't my fault. See, I took June off that year. And July.

Al: You get a lot of vacation?

Waylon: Yeah. Rush is great that way. Makes up for the very low salary.

Al: All right. How 'bout this one? In his second book, *See, I Told You So*, Rush writes, "There are more American Indians alive today than there were when Columbus arrived."

Waylon: There are? That doesn't sound right.

Al: Well, actually, it's not. According to the Bureau of Indian Affairs, in 1492 there were between five and fifteen million Native Americans in what later became the United States. Today, there are fewer than two million Americans who claim Indian ancestry.

Waylon: Wow! How would you find out something like that?

Al: We did a Nexis search. It's a computer database.

Waylon: Hmmm. Is that anything like that E-mail stuff I've been hearing about?

Al: Yeah. Sort of. Well, Waylon, I want to thank you. You've been very—

Waylon: Hey! Guess what! I found that source for that nicotine, lung cancer thingy.

Al: Let me guess. Tobacco Institute.

Waylon: Bingo!

Al: Well, this has been very helpful, Waylon. Thanks.

Waylon: My pleasure. Listen, any time you guys need any information . . . I got great stuff on the poor.

Al: Can't wait.

Waylon: Megadittoes!

Al: Megadittoes!

8
OPERATION CHICKENHAWK

If you've spent any time listening to Limbaugh, you've probably heard him call Bill Clinton a draft dodger. But what about Rush's military service record? Surely a man of his age and political conviction would have volunteered for duty in Vietnam. After all, he supported the war.

So you might wonder where exactly in 'Nam Limbaugh served. The steaming rice paddies of the Delta? Or was he a Marine, dug in at Khe Sanh? Special Forces, perhaps, crossing the DMZ on a Search and Destroy with "Born to Kill" tattooed on his biceps? Or maybe he stayed in Saigon and used that talent on loan from God to entertain the boys in the field. That's it! Of course! Robin Williams's *Good Morning, Vietnam* character must have been based on Rush!

Not quite. When questioned about his draft history in 1992, Limbaugh responded, "I had student deferments in college, and upon taking a physical, was discovered to have a physical—uh, by virtue of what the military says, I didn't even know it existed—a physical deferment and then the lottery system, when they chose your lot by your birth date and mine was high."

Sounds like they discovered some debilitating injury at the draft physical, doesn't it? Nope. Limbaugh, who has said about the draft, "I made no effort to evade or avoid it," never took a draft physical. Instead, records show that Limbaugh pre-empted a physical by providing his draft board with information of some disqualifying condition. Limbaugh's story has changed several times. According to Limbaugh, the physical deferment was for either a "football knee from high school" or a "pilonidal cyst." A pilonidal cyst is a congenital incomplete closure of the neural groove at the base of the spinal cord in which excess tissue and hair may collect, causing discomfort and discharge. As disgusting as this sounds, there is no evidence that Limbaugh's cyst contributed to the breakup of his two marriages. There is, however, also no evidence of a football injury.

It's funny how many hawkish Republicans didn't go. Phil Gramm had student and teaching deferments; George Will had student deferments; Clarence Thomas was 4-F.

So was Pat Buchanan, who had a bad knee. He spent the war writing speeches for Nixon. Interestingly, he is now an avid jogger. Jogs regularly, I understand.

After his *Murphy Brown* speech, Dan Quayle took a

lot of unfair hits, especially from Hollywood. Quayle wasn't attacking single parents; he was talking about the importance of fathers. For example, Quayle's father found his son a slot in the Indiana National Guard, and the boy didn't have to go to 'Nam.

Newt Gingrich didn't go. But sometimes he regrets it. He's said that by avoiding Vietnam, he "missed something . . . a large part of me thinks I should have gone over." I wonder if Bob Kerrey ever thinks: "I'm missing something . . . a large part of me." Just wondering.

Central Highlands, South Vietnam
August 1969

"Shit," murmured Gingrich, wiping the sweat from his brow.

"Are we in trouble?" Quayle whispered. Quayle was "new meat." This was his first night ambush and he was shaking.

"You wanted to know what that smell was," Gingrich said with disgust, as they trudged down the jungle trail. "It's shit. Limbaugh shits his pants whenever he's scared. That's why no one wants to be in a hole with Limbaugh."

"It's my pilonidal cyst!" came the voice from the rear. "It's a congenital incomplete closure of the neural groove at the base of my spinal cord in which excess tissue and hair may collect, causing discomfort and discharge. I shouldn't be here."

"Bullshit!" shouted Buchanan. "You've dropped a load in your shorts, and it stinks!"

"It's my pilonidal cyst!" huffed Limbaugh as he struggled to keep up.

"Fuck your pilonidal cyst! Ah'm sick of hearing about it!" came the thick southern drawl.

"Fuck you, Gramm," the corpulent radio operator shot back.

"Eat me, fatso!"

Now they were all yelling at Limbaugh. Gingrich, Gramm, Thomas, Buchanan. All but Quayle, who was too new and too scared to take sides, and Will, who was too high on acid. That's why Will was the one they called "Stoner."

"Shut up, you meatheads!" Lieutenant North was pissed. "You're gonna get us killed!" North couldn't believe he was out with this bunch of sorry-ass losers. He was platoon leader, and normally a buck sergeant would be taking a squad out on ambush. But this squad was giving his whole platoon a bad rep. Word had spread up and down III Corps: North had a squad of chickenshits who wouldn't fight. Well, tonight, that would change.

North knew that sound carries at night. Fortunately, they were only a few hundred meters from base camp. A reconaissance team had reported "beaucoup NVA movement" a few klicks north, and the chickenshit squad was headed out to surprise a few dinks.

North was still sizing them up. Knowing who you could rely on could save your life. Not knowing could get you killed. "Will, you take point."

"Go ask Alice." The private grinned.

"What?!" North hoped he had heard the man wrong.

"When she's ten feet tall."

He hadn't. "What are you talking about, soldier?!"

"One pill makes you larger, and one pill makes you small," Will explained.

"Gingrich, what's wrong with Will?"

"First day in 'Nam, Stoner saw a buddy get greased. Guy named Bill Bennett. Got it right in the eye. Stoner tried to plug the hole, came up holding a handful of goop that used to be Bennett's brain. It was pretty grotesque. Bizarre and grotesque, to be honest. Stoner hasn't been the same since."

"And the ones that Mother gives you don't do anything at all." Will giggled.

North just shook his head. Too late to send Will back. "Limbaugh, take Will. From now on you two are buddies." Limbaugh nodded. He didn't mind. Will was the only one who didn't complain when he dropped a load. North turned to Thomas. "Clarence, you take point."

"Why?" Thomas shot back indignantly. " 'Cause I'm black?!"

North knew he couldn't tolerate insubordination.

But racial tensions had been high within the platoon. "Okay, Buchanan, you got point."

"But my knee." Buchanan winced to make his point. "Sometimes it goes out, and I scream. You don't want the point man giving away our position." Gramm rolled his eyes. How many times had they heard about Buchanan's knee?

"Buchanan. My momma told me there's two kinds of people." Gramm scrunched his face like a bulldog. "The kind that pulls the wagon, and the kind that rides in the wagon. It's time you got out of the wagon."

"Then *you* take point," the Irishman shot back.

"Ah took it last tahm," drawled the Texan.

"Bullshit!" "*I* took it last time!" "No, *Ah* did!" Gingrich, Limbaugh, and Gramm were at each other now.

North just wanted it to stop. "All right! *I'll* take point. Now, let's move." North started forward, taking the point position about twenty meters in front of his men. As he worked his way down the moonlit trail, North began to get a bad feeling. He had led a lot of men into battle. He had seen fear before. But not like this. And North knew one thing. Fear at night is a killer.

The trail led to a steep embankment. North clutched the M16 close to his chest and slid down feet first on his butt. It was a bumpy ride, but North didn't mind. In fact, he kind of liked it. He just wondered if his men could navigate it. Especially Limbaugh. He's so fat and smelly, thought North. He turned and waited. And waited. Where are they?

By the time North caught up with the squad, they were just fifty meters from the base camp perimeter. "We got lost," shrugged Limbaugh.

"The only rational thing to do was turn back," Gingrich explained.

Gramm nodded. "Gettin' late, sir. Maybe we should pack it in, chalk this one up to bad luck." The others agreed. Will was the last to speak:

"Excuse me, while I kiss the sky."

North planted a pair of claymores in the high grass. That made ten in the kill zone. He ran back to the trees where his men were waiting—cowering, really. They had put in their ambush along a stream about three klicks west of the base. North gave two clackers to Quayle, and pointing to the arm on the firing device, whispered, "You push this down, it sends a current to the blasting cap and detonates the mine."

"Huh?" North couldn't tell if the boy was stupid or just scared stupid. He did know this. Quayle had the look of a deer caught in the headlights.

"Never mind." North gave the clackers to Gingrich and hoped for the best. "It's going to be a long night, men. You wanna catch some z's, work it out with your buddy."

Limbaugh smiled through his fear. He knew Will was too wired to sleep. The rotund radio operator had just polished off both their C rations and was getting drowsy, so he leaned against the radio set and drifted off.

In the dark and silence now, each man sat alone with his thoughts. And his dread. "My God," thought Quayle, "I'm so scared! I should have listened to Dad and taken that place in the National Guard. But no, I was too worried about my political future. I didn't want to look like some rich coward in the year 2004, when I'd be mature enough to run for national political office. God, I'm a fool!"

Thomas used the moonlight to write his girl: "Dear Honeybunch, Sometimes this war frightens

THE NEXT FORTY MINUTES WERE THE LONGEST OF HIS ADULT LIFE...

me to depth of my very soul. But I promise you I'll make it out of here alive, sugar, so I can come home into your embrace and gaze into your loving eyes. Love, Clarence. P.S. Send more pornography."

Ten meters away, Gramm gazed up at the stars. He'd never believed he could kill a man. And so far he hadn't. But women and children were another story. He thought back to the village and how he'd lost control. Funny what fear will do.

Gingrich cursed North under his breath. Four more days and his tour would be over. Then he'd be out of this nightmare. Three hundred and sixty-one days he'd lived with this unbearable, unrelenting, gut-wrenching fear. Fear that had lifted only once. He thought back to the Saigon bar.

"You number one G.I. I fuck you till tomorrow. I suck you all night long," sighed the pouty sex kitten.

"Could you sit athwart my chest," Gingrich asked excitedly, "and make me do terrible things?"

"You number ten G.I. You disgust me." She spit in his face and walked away.

Gingrich smiled at the memory. He hadn't found the release he had sought, but at least the humiliation had taken his mind off the fear.

For the moment anyway, sleep had erased the fear from PFC Quayle's young mind. His dream took him back to the sun-dappled hills of Indiana and a raven-haired beauty named Marilyn. His head cradled in her tender arms, they watched the wind ripple through the rows of Hoosier corn. Caressing him lovingly, she nibbled at his ear, then whispered softly . . .

"We're never going to get out of this jungle." Quayle woke with a start. Someone was still nibbling at his ear.

"I'm so frightened, Quayle. Hold me. Hold me tight." Buchanan's strong arms clutched the new man firmly. Quayle froze in terror. The next forty minutes were the longest of his adult life.

North's catlike eyes pierced the dark. He lifted his

STONER HAD TOKED HIS LAST DOOBIE...

nose to the air. On a good night he could smell Charlie from half a klick away. Not tonight. Not with
Limbaugh fouling the air.

Then he heard it. A twig snapping in the distance.
North ID'd it immediately. Bamboo, seventy-five
yards. They were going to have company.

North saw the scout first. NVA regulars, heading
right for the kill zone. North's mouth split into a grin.
He signaled silently to Gingrich, whose hand tight-
ened on the clacker. In a moment, these dinks would
be in for the surprise of their lives.

Suddenly, the still night silence was shattered.
THE MAGICAL MYSTERY TOUR IS COMING
TO TAKE YOU AWAY! Fucking Will! North yelled
at Stoner to turn off the boom box, but a burst of AK-
47 fire did it for him. The boom box had played its
last tune. And Stoner had toked his last doobie.

The jungle erupted in a maelstrom of hot, flying
lead. North squeezed his M16, cutting down the
scout with a bullet through the head as red tracers
from a spewing NVA M-60 lit up the night.

North turned to see Quayle catch one in the throat,
leaving a gaping wound that spurted blood onto the
terrified Buchanan. Buchanan had just one thought.
Play dead.

When North stopped to reload, he noticed that all
the fire was coming from one direction. His squad
had not shot one round! The lieutenant caught a
glimpse of a panicked Thomas, trying to squeeze the
trigger. "Click off the safety!" North cried as he
slapped in a magazine while dodging a hail of AK-47

bullets. Too late. Thomas jerked backward, the bullet that took his life ripping through his chest.

As North watched thirty NVA regulars charge toward them, he called to Gingrich. "The clacker! Now!" But Gingrich's eyes were wide and his hands frozen with terror. "Now, dammit! They're in the kill zone!" Again nothing. North made a mad dash toward Gingrich, AK rounds whizzing by his head and thudding at his feet. A final dive and roll, his hand pushed the handle down. BLAM!!! The ground shook from the explosion, and thirty dinks went to their gory deaths.

Still they kept coming. My God, North thought, it's a whole company! "Limbaugh! Call in the artillery!!" No response. When North turned to find his radio operator, he couldn't believe his eyes. Limbaugh had pulled Will's corpse over himself, and Stoner's lifeless body heaved in rhythm to the fat man's terror-stricken sobs.

For the first time in my life, thought North, I feel ashamed to be an American.

At first, Gramm had panicked too. But now he knew what to do. "Ah'm not going home in no body bag," he thought. "Phil Gramm's momma didn't raise no fool." He clicked off the safety on his M16, lined up his target, and squeezed the trigger. BLAM! He stared at the smoking hole in his boot, then passed out.

North looked around at his unit. He realized it was just him and the enemy. Thirty yards ahead two NVA's had set up a machine gun and were spitting

WITH QUAYLE'S VIRGIN M-16 IN ONE HAND, AND THOMAS'S IN THE OTHER, HE LEAPT UP AND CHARGED.

out .50 caliber rounds at will. North took one in the leg. His face hardened. He plucked a grenade from his vest, pulled the pin with his teeth, and sent it hurtling through the night air. When the smoke cleared, all that was left was a grisly tangle of flesh and metal.

North emptied the clip in his machine gun, mowing down a couple dozen dinks in the process. Tossing the spent weapon aside, he decided to take the fight to the enemy. He pulled a knife from his belt, placing it between his teeth. Then with Quayle's virgin M16 in one hand and Thomas's in the other, he leapt up and charged. Running, dodging, jumping, shooting, knifing, clubbing, and strangling where necessary, he cut a swath of destruction through the astonished ranks of the enemy.

Meanwhile, Gingrich had snapped out of his stupor. He grabbed the radio. "Limbaugh, tell me how to work this thing!" No answer. Just the feeble whimper of a man sitting in his own excrement.

Gingrich slapped him across the face. "Snap out of

"LIMBAUGH! TELL ME HOW TO WORK THIS THING!"

"SONOFABITCH! AH AM CAPABLE OF KILLING A MAN!"

it!" But Limbaugh couldn't stop crying. "Fuck it, I'll do it myself! Where do you keep the manual?"

Limbaugh had the hiccups. "In, in, in, in . . . in my back pocket."

"Oh, Christ!" This was going to be unpleasant.

First light was appearing on the horizon as North slit the throat of an NVA corporal and tossed his body on the pile. Suddenly, his ears pricked up. The sound was unmistakable. The distant thwop-thwop-thwop of a Huey slick. North turned to see the remains of his unit hobbling toward a clearing in the distance.

The chopper was almost overhead when North caught up with them. "Why the hell you calling in a medevac?! This fire zone is still hot!!"

"But, sir, we've got wounded," shouted Gingrich over the roar of the helicopter. Gramm shook his foot demonstratively, unable to hide his smile.

"There's still a third of a company of NVA back there, dammit! Now you turn and fight or I'll court-martial every damn one of you!!" North spun around on his good leg and started back to engage the enemy.

Gramm turned to Gingrich. "You thinking what I'm thinking?" Gingrich nodded grimly. Limbaugh choked out a feeble, "Uh-huh." Buchanan gave a hearty thumbs up.

Crack! North fell to the earth, facedown. Blood gushed from the hole that had just opened in his back. He rose to his knees, only to fall again as another slug caught him between the shoulder blades.

"Sonofabitch," thought Gramm. "Ah *am* capable of killing a man."

He turned to the others. "Nobody saw nothing, right?"

"Nope."

"Not me."

"Unh, unh, unh . . . unh-unh."

The sun was rising over the battlefield as the Huey lifted the four grunts to safety. Gramm surveyed his wounded foot with a smile. "Purple Heart's gonna look mighty fahn some first Tuesday after the first Monday in November." Gingrich and Buchanan exchanged a look. Solemnly, each man drew his knife and plunged it into the other's thigh.

The pilot turned back to look at them, his nose wrinkling in disgust. Uh-oh, thought Gingrich, he's onto us.

"Hey! Did one of you grunts shit your pants?!"

(Mr. Franken is a regular contributor to Soldier of Fortune *magazine.)*

9
BOB DOLE'S NIGHTMARE OF DEPRAVITY

Last May, Bob Dole made his famous attack on the Hollywood filth factory, or what around my house is called "Daddy's meal ticket." In the speech he divided motion pictures into two categories. Movies, according to Dole, are either "Friendly to Families" or "Nightmares of Depravity."

Forrest Gump, *The Lion King*, and *True Lies*, said Dole, are Friendly to Families, while *Natural Born Killers* and *True Romance* are Nightmares of Depravity. And he felt *very* strongly about this. Even though he hadn't actually seen any of the movies.

But the movies he mentioned have come and gone. How is a parent to know which category a film falls into when it's released? The last thing you want to do on a weekend is take your kids to what you think is a nice family film and have the whole experience turn into a nightmare of depravity. And believe me, it's happened to us. More than once. Pauly Shore's *Jury Duty*, for example.

Extrapolating from Dole's list, I've come up with a very brief . . .

Bob Dole Guide to Moviegoing

1. If there are multiple murders involving weapons on which the Republican party wants to repeal the ban, the movie is a Nightmare of Depravity.

2. Unless the movie stars Arnold Schwarzenegger.

3. Or anybody on the Republican donor list. Bruce Willis or Sylvester Stallone, for example.

4. If the plot of the movie involves an evil one-armed killer, as in *The Fugitive*, the movie qualifies as a Bob Dole Nightmare of Depravity. And the one-armed man doesn't have to be a killer; he need only be portrayed as "mean-spirited."

I apologize for that. It was wrong. Dole, of course, lost the use of his arm while defending my right to make a cheap, offensive, and not all that clever joke.

In his terrific book on the '88 presidential campaign, *What It Takes*, Richard Ben Cramer writes very admiringly of Dole's courage recovering from the nearly fatal wound he suffered in Italy. In one particularly jarring passage, Dole is sent home by train in a full body cast and met by his mother, Bina.

> Bina was there when he got to Winter General on June 12, 1945. Bob had the nurses take his arm out and lay it on his cast, so his mother could see it. She'd steeled herself, but the minute she came into the room, Bina broke down in tears. When she saw the way he looked at her, she told herself that was the last time she'd cry in front of Bob. And she sat down next to him and touched his face.
>
> She had to pick eight cigarette butts out of his plaster cast. She told her sisters: they'd used her boy for an ashtray on the train.

When I read that, I gasped. My wife was reading in bed next to me, and said, "What?" I handed her the book, and she read the passage. "My God," she said. "You'd think going through something like that would make a person very compassionate."

"Yeah," I said. "Or really angry."

I liked the Bob Dole I read about in Cramer's book, even though the ambition that made him an absentee husband and dad caused his first marriage to end in divorce. Frankly, I'm getting a little sick of cranky Republicans who can't keep their own families together telling everybody else about family values. Quick. What do Newt Gingrich, Bob Dole, Phil Gramm, and George Will have in common? Answer. They've all been married only one less time than Rush Limbaugh.

I spend time with my kids. And lots of it. I believe the best thing a parent can give his kid is time. And not just quality time, but big, stinking, lazy, non-productive quantity time. In fact, that's why this book is so badly written. Believe me, you'd be enjoying the experience of reading this book a lot more if I weren't so dedicated to my children.

Which me brings me back to movie violence. Personally I have a fairly low tolerance for movie violence. Especially as a parent. For example, a few years ago, I was concerned that *Bambi* might be too violent for my son, Joe. He was five at the time, and there's the scene where Bambi's mother dies. I took him anyway, but put a lot of thought into what I would tell him.

Sure enough, when the moment came, Joe turned to me and asked, "Where's Bambi's mommy?"

I was prepared. "Well, Bambi's mommy was shot by the hunters. And she's not going to be around anymore. But it's okay, because Bambi's father is going to take care of him, and Bambi's going to be fine. Also, your mom is fine. Hunters will never shoot Mommy. And Mommy is going to be around a long, long time. So don't you worry."

Joe seemed to understand. In fact, he enjoyed the movie so much that we went again the next weekend. And at the same point in the movie a little four-year-old girl in the row in front of us turned to her dad and said, "Where's Bambi's mommy?"

And Joe said, "She's dead."

So I don't worry about Joe.

10

THE INVISIBLE HAND
OF ADAM SMITH

Among Freud's least quoted statements, but to me one of the most comforting, is "The only thing about masturbation to be ashamed of is doing it badly."

Joycelyn Elders knows the power of the subject. When asked whether masturbation should be discussed in sex ed classes, her very reasonable response was immediately caricatured as a proposal to teach jerk-off techniques to schoolchildren. "High school seniors in Little Rock can masturbate at only a fifth-grade level. That is a disgrace!" was the joke we did the next night on SNL.

I don't want to get into the whole sex education (teaching abstinence vs. rolling-condoms-on-a-dildo-in-class) debate. I know I don't buy the Christian Coalition argument that sex education created promiscuity and thus today's alarming rate of illegitimacy. I believe promiscuity grew with the wide availability of the pill and smut like Newt Gingrich's novel *1945*.

I think most people agree that it's a good idea for adolescents to understand how our species reproduces. I recently heard William Bennett say that schools have to treat students as if they're children of God, not mammals in heat. I totally agree. But for those occasions when a 17-year-old child of God happens to become a 17-year-old mammal in heat, I think it's good for the mammal to have some clue about what's going on.

Of course, it's impossible to teach reproduction without discussing sex. And as I think Freud pointed out, sex is kind of a sore point with a lot of people. I knew when I sat down to write this book that I would have to discuss my own sexual history. Ever since Wilt Chamberlain's autobiography, it's become expected. So here goes.

Actually, I have had quite a sex life. Obviously it doesn't compare to Chamberlain, who had over 20,000 sexual encounters in his life (up to his book's first printing). But I have kept track, and I think you're going to be pretty impressed. I have had three hundred and twelve sexual encounters! All with my wife. And we've been married nineteen years. So not bad! Are you with me, fellas?!

Which brings me back to masturbation. And here's the point I wanted to make in the first place. America is a masturbatory society. Just register at any hotel that caters to businessmen, most of whom are angry white men, and check out the movie menu. For every *Forrest Gump* there are twenty *Romancing the Bone*'s.

Why? Supply and demand. Adam Smith's "invisible hand," so to speak. Is this good? Absolutely. Because the market unleashes the creative energies of people who create wealth and provide jobs.

Most people don't realize how many jobs are created by one porno film. Of course, we immediately think of the actresses and actors. But what about the technicians who do the lighting and sound? Porno films provide many of the crucial *entry level* jobs that are so important to expanding our workforce. And how about the fluffer? Don't know about the fluffer? Well, let's see. How do I put this? The fluffer is a woman, usually, who works off camera. Her job is to keep the male actor aroused. And she does this, I am told, orally. Hey. It's a job!

So next time Bob Dole starts bitching about casual sex in movies, ask him one question. How is it possible that he's crisscrossed this great country, stayed in two hundred hotels, and still hasn't seen *Forrest Gump*?

(Mr. Franken is a regular contributor to Juggs *magazine.)*

11
ADVENTURES IN POLITICS
NOVEMBER 8, 1988

Ladies and gentlemen . . ." The already very somber crowd grew silent. ". . . I've prepared two kinds of material. One in case we win this thing in a squeaker . . ."

It was about 8:45 P.M. Huge hotel ballroom. Hundreds of Dukakis workers. Men and women, mostly young, but some middle-aged and older, black, white, Democrats of all stripes, who had dropped everything in their lives for weeks, months, maybe a year or more to elect as president of the United States the shortest, swarthiest man ever nominated by a major political party.

By now they all knew he had lost. It wasn't official; the polls hadn't closed anywhere. But at this point we all knew. And I was supposed to entertain them for another four hours or so.

". . . and the other, in case . . . WE WIN BY A LANDSLIDE!!!"

Gallows humor. No one laughed, except a couple

members of the press corps who happened to be paying attention. It was a massive contingent of print and electronic journalists, now waiting to capture what was becoming a quadrennial ritual, the concession speech of a roundly defeated Democratic presidential nominee.

I decided to go with the conceit that I, the emcee, was the only person in the room who had no idea how badly we were doing. It seemed funny to me. I always love it when the very person who should know something is the only person who doesn't. Like when there's a punt in a football game and the receiver calls for a fair catch on his own one-yard line, and everyone in the stadium assumes he's going to let it go into the end zone so his team (the home team) will get the ball on the twenty. But suddenly everyone realizes that instead he's going to catch the ball. And there's sixty thousand people in the stadium and fifty million at home all thinking the same thought for a split second: "You're on the one-yard line, fuckhead! Let it go!"

See. This is why I'd make a terrible politician. No, not that I used "fuckhead." It's the tortured sports analogy. Any decent politician knows the key to a good sports metaphor is simplicity. When John Kasich described his approach as chairman of the House Budget Committee last spring, he said, "They gave me the bat, and I'm going to swing it. I may strike out, but I could also hit a home run." That's a sports analogy anyone can understand. "It's fourth and goal and we're gonna punch this thing in." I've heard Bob Dole use that. But me, I've taken a situation that occurs in football maybe once every five years and used it to explicate a comic conceit. And one that didn't work, at that.

As the polls closed in the East, the networks started delivering the bad news. Pennsylvania goes for Bush. Ohio goes for Bush. But I would just say things like, "Hey, we won Rhode Island! That's good. As Rhode Island goes, so goes the nation. Right?! Huh, everybody?!" Blank faces. Well, not blank really. There were a lot of tears.

So I decided to abandon the conceit pretty early in the evening and moved on to old material. This is one I always do at campaign events: "I've been asked by the *(candidate's name)* campaign to announce that the views I express tonight are mine and not necessarily those of the *(candidate's name)* campaign. Okay, now that that's out of the way . . . isn't *(widely respected person)* a *(wildly inappropriate epithet)*?" Thus, when I emceed fund-raisers for Mark Green's '86 Senate race against Al D'Amato, I'd open with: "I've been asked by the Green campaign to announce that the views I express tonight are mine and not necessarily those of the Green campaign. Okay, now that that's out of the way . . . isn't Cardinal O'Connor an asshole?" It would always get a nice laugh, mainly because a lot of Green supporters did think O'Connor was an asshole. Mark kept asking me not to do it, but I always would, and when he took the podium Mark would have to take a minute to emphasize his tremendous regard for the cardinal and his strong ties to the Roman Catholic community in the state of New York.

"The Dukakis campaign has asked me to announce

that the views, etc. . . . . Okay, now that that's out of the way, isn't George Bush a dink!" Now this gets a big cheer. And I think, "Oh, no! What have I done!?" I'm thinking ABC's taped this and they're going to air it without the disclaimer part, and it's going to look like I just said the newly elected President of the United States was a dink and the Democrats were all cheering. Which is basically what happened, except that the disclaimer part, in my mind, made it a joke, thus mitigating . . . oh, never mind.

Fortunately, Robert Klein had arrived, and I brought him on. Now, I love Robert Klein, and think he's done some of the classic stand-up routines. Many of which he did that night.

Nobody's laughing. They're just staring at him, and he does his José Feliciano singing the "Star-Spangled Banner" bit. And since Robert is basically dying, I decide that that's a good place to get him off. So I join Robert onstage to suggest that we all sing the "Star-Spangled Banner" as kind of a patriotic gesture to honor America and the free democratic process we've all been privileged to be a part of. Let's show America that Democrats are patriotic, too!

So we sing it, a couple thousand people singing our national anthem, a cappella, which you never hear. And it's really moving. People are weeping, holding each other. Even some of the press are singing. OH SAY DOES THAT STAR-SPANGLED BA-A-A-NER YET WA-AVE? Everybody's got goose bumps. Somehow, now it's all okay. O'ER THE LAND OF THE FREEEEE . . . Lee Atwater and Roger Ailes could walk in at this moment

and everyone in the room would hug them . . .
AND THE HOME OF THE BRAAAVE!!! The
cheer is deafening! And it doesn't matter whether the
TV cameras had captured it for America to see. We in
that room were all sharing an amazing moment. People were sobbing, flushed with patriotic fervor. It was
really something.

Then Robert went into his Pope at Yankee Stadium
routine.

The comic high point of the evening was going to
be an appearance by my colleague Jon Lovitz. Among
the highlights of that SNL season, of any season, was
the Bush-Dukakis debate sketch, in which Dana Car-
vey played his peripatetic George Bush to Jon's emo-
tionally inert Michael Dukakis.

The plan was to announce Dukakis over the P.A.
and have Jon enter to the driving, pounding beat of
Neil Diamond's awful song "America," which was, in
fact, how the candidate always made his entrance.
WE'RE COMING TO AMERICA! TODAY! The
song had been chosen to underscore, literally,
Dukakis's status as the son of Greek immigrants. And
the idea here, as it had been during the campaign, was
to pump enough energy into the room to build the
excitement of seeing Michael Dukakis (in this case,
Jon Lovitz playing Michael Dukakis) to a frenzy. I
checked with a young Dukakis staffer to make sure
they had the music. He said yeah, and I figured the
one thing the Dukakis campaign had to have together
was the "America" cue.

It was almost midnight and the polls were closing
on the West Coast, so people were expecting Dukakis

to make his concession at any moment. Jon was off-stage, ready, which is to say in his Dukakis suit, wig, and eyebrows.

I told the staffer to get ready to cue the music and went to center stage and the microphone. "Ladies and gentlemen, it is my distinct honor to introduce the Governor of Massachusetts, the leader of our party, Michael S. Dukakis!"

I could hear the music under the cheers. It was "America," but not the thumping chorus that I and millions of other political junkies had long since grown sick of. It was the *beginning* of the song, which I'd never heard before or since. All I remember is that it has a long, tepid opening followed by a longer, tepid verse that Neil Diamond sort of croons.

Jon and I looked at each other. I signaled for him to wait, and ran over to the staffer. It turned out he had gone out and bought a *CD*, and that's what we were hearing. State of the art. Except that you can't fast-forward a CD, or at least you couldn't on this guy's deck in 1988. The crowd was still cheering, but the music was sucking the energy out of the room, and as the intro went on and on, people started wondering what was happening. We really had no choice, and Jon made his entrance.

They did get a kick out of seeing Jon, who walked around the stage, smiling, winking, picking out people in the crowd and pointing like he knew them. Mainly, I could see Jon hoping Neil would stop crooning. Jon kept vamping, but the crowd died down before the chorus kicked in.

As flat as his entrance had been, it was pretty much

all downhill from there. On the flight up to Boston I had offered to help Jon with his remarks, but he insisted on writing them himself. Jon is a tremendously funny guy, but not a political satirist, and he was really shooting blanks. Some of the jokes were just inappropriate, especially considering that the real Dukakis was going to be out in just a few minutes. The only joke I remember was about how old Barbara Bush looked. "If he did that to Barbara, think what he'll do to the country."

By the time Jon got off, I had only one real remaining fear. That Michael Dukakis would walk on that stage and that before he was able to concede defeat, he'd slip on the collective flop-sweat of Robert Klein, Jon Lovitz, and myself and break his neck.

Jon and I were flown back to New York that night on a very small jet. We had a show that week and had to get back to write for the Wednesday read-through. As Jon and I sat alone in this tiny two-man cabin, I looked out the window down to the lights glowing from the New England towns below. I thought that in a small way we had taken part in American history. I thought about our country and the majesty of our system. And even though I was heartsick by the outcome of the election, I felt that the people had spoken, and, honestly, said a prayer for the man I had jokingly called a dink earlier that evening. I turned to Jon and saw that he was very upset. "I know," I said, "it's a big disappointment."

"Yeah," he said. "Now fucking Dana gets to play the fucking president for the next four years."

12
PHIL GRAMM, GUN LOVER

I was watching the news last May, and Phil Gramm said something interesting to the NRA convention. He said, "I own more shotguns than I need. But less shotguns than I want."

When I heard that I thought to myself, "Wow. He and I are very different people." His line got a lot of applause, so I guess I'm very different from most of the folks who belong to the NRA. But you know my motto, *Vive la différence!*

I also wondered what exactly he meant by this. For starters I tried to figure out how many shotguns Phil Gramm owns. I guess you'd have to begin by estimating the number of shotguns Phil Gramm thinks he needs. I think he thinks he needs three, one for each domicile. (A home in Texas, an apartment in Washington, and a summer house on Chesapeake Bay.) But remember, he owns *more* than he needs. But less than he wants.

Why would you want more shotguns than you

need? Probably convenience. How many times have you been in the living room, needed the shotgun, and said to yourself, "Nuts, I left the shotgun in the kitchen." I'll bet it happens to Phil Gramm all the time.

Seriously, I guess people collect shotguns. Which is great. I used to collect baseball cards. You know, when I was a kid. The thing about baseball cards is that each one is different; you get a Don Mattingly or a Frank Thomas. Is there that big a difference between shotguns? Somebody enlighten me because I'm operating out of ignorance here.

See, I've never owned a gun. I won't allow one in the house. According to a study in the *New England Journal of Medicine*, guns kept in the home for protection are forty-three times more likely to kill a family member than an assailant. Forty-three! "Hey, honey, I've brought something into the house that's forty-three times more likely to kill one of us than to do us any good." Maybe if the number was only thirty-three, I'd take my chances.

Among my more morbid diversions is collecting stories of tragic gun accidents in the home. There are some common threads. If you do have a gun in the house, here's some really bad advice:

1. *Keep the gun loaded.* When there's an intruder you don't want to be fiddling with bullets. (According to a 1991 Gallup poll more than half of handgun owners with guns in their house said their guns were currently loaded.)

2. *Put the gun in an unlocked drawer.* Who's got time to find a key when Mr. 1-in-43 comes calling?

3. *Rest assured.* Once you teach your kids gun safety, they can show their curious friends the gun while you're at the supermarket.

While I don't have precise figures, the anecdotal evidence leads me to the following conclusions:

• Grandpa is twenty times more likely to be shot by your seven-year-old nephew than by a drug addict trying to steal your VCR. The number goes up to thirty-six if Grandpa is barbecuing in the backyard.

• The odds are slightly better that a neighbor's kid will accidentally blow your kid's face off, than the other way around.

• A bullet fired by a six-year-old through a ceiling is twelve times more likely to lodge in your testicles than any other part of your anatomy. If you're a man, that is.

This, of course, covers *accidental* gun death. In a household with a gun, even more dangerous than the curious child is, of course, the angry spouse. That's really the reason why I won't allow a gun in the house. PMS. Remember that three out of four homicide victims are killed by a spouse, family member, friend, or acquaintance. Which is comforting for all of us who fear random violence.

Now again, I've just been talking about *death* from gunshot wounds. Tragic. But not as damn expensive as the pesky four to six non-fatal gunshot injuries that occur for every fatal shooting and crowd our emergency rooms. Maybe that's why the American Academy of Pediatrics supported the Brady Bill and has called for the ban of handguns and assault weapons.

Gunshot injuries cost 14 billion dollars a year. Who foots the bill? Right now, 80 percent of the cost is paid for by public funds. But I have a good idea. Let's get the money from people like Phil Gramm. Let's put a little extra tax on every shotgun he doesn't need.

And remember:

> You are three times more likely to shoot a Japanese exchange student who has knocked at your door by mistake than a Swedish exchange student who is trick-or-treating on the wrong night.

13
AFFIRMATIVE ACTION: THE CASE FOR THE MUSHBALL MIDDLE

Jonathan Alter of *Newsweek* recently made the compelling argument that debate on affirmative action has become so polarized that there is no room for those of us in "the mushy middle."

That's right. I said "us." I consider myself a moderate.

See. I hope it's clear to you by now that this book is a *satire* about the breakdown in the civility of public discourse. I'm making fun of meanness in public debate by being mean myself. It's called "irony." Perhaps you've heard of it?

And I know that I've been a little harsh about a few public figures. That's what I'm supposed to do as a satirist. But I want you to know that I admire everyone I'll be making fun of in the book. Except Pat Robertson. He's a lunatic.

And I really don't like Limbaugh. And Pat Buchanan, let's face it, is a racist. Ralph Reed, I have no use for. And Gingrich just plain scares me.

You know what I dislike most about these guys? They're always so certain. They're always 100 percent sure of what they're saying. Even if it's wrong. It must be a great feeling for a guy like Rush Limbaugh. To be able to sit there and say, "There are more Indians alive today than when Columbus landed," and really believe it.

This is why I like being a Democrat. When we see a complicated, seemingly intractable problem, we have the only really genuine, authentic human reaction you can have: we're confused.

Fortunately, I believe that "confused" is a majority position in this country.

I am not talking about stupid, uninformed confusion. I'm talking about intelligent, over-informed confusion. The kind you get from watching *MacNeil/Lehrer*, C-SPAN, and *Nightline*, listening to three experts from the Cato Institute, four from the Heritage Foundation, two each from the Urban Institute and the Progressive Policy Institute, then reading eleven different newspaper accounts that cite six different polls and four studies. And after all that, you *still* don't know what to think about grazing fees on federal lands.

Affirmative action is an issue that stirs more passion than grazing fees. And it has certainly been hotly debated. On the one hand, those in favor of it believe affirmative action is essential in overcoming the inherently racist nature of our society. I definitely agree with that.

On the other hand, those opposed say that for

America to be truly color-blind we must eliminate group entitlements which set one race against another. That also makes sense.

There are horror stories on both sides. You've heard them; you're sick of them. So am I. And it gets even more confusing when the strongest opponents of affirmative action are among its biggest beneficiaries.

Justice Clarence Thomas, for instance, was admitted to Yale Law School under a 1971 affirmative action plan whose goal was 10 percent minority students in the entering class.

In remarks to his EEOC staff in 1983, Thomas said that affirmative action laws were the best thing that ever happened to him: "But for them, God only knows where I would be today. These laws and their proper application are all that stand between the first seventeen years of my life and the second seventeen years."

Something must have happened to Thomas in his third seventeen years, because the guy really did a 180. I don't know what it was. Maybe a high-tech lynching.

In his concurring opinion in the affirmative action case of *Adarand Constructors v. Pena*:

> There can be no doubt that racial paternalism and its unintended consequences can be as poisonous and pernicious as any other form of discrimination.

A mean person could interpret the change of heart

to reflect an "I've got mine" attitude. I'll leave that to a mean African American person.

One mean person who won't say it is Rush Limbaugh. In *The Way Things Ought to Be*, Limbaugh describes Thomas as "a man who has escaped the bonds of poverty by methods other than those prescribed by these civil rights organizations." Not true, but at this point, who's counting? Anyway, Thomas returned the favor two years later, performing the ceremony at Limbaugh's third wedding. I can't think of anything more romantic for a blushing bride than having Clarence Thomas perform your nuptials.

Of course, the first President to apply affirmative action to the Supreme Court was Ronald Reagan, who pledged to appoint a woman during the '80 campaign. When he nominated Sandra Day O'Connor, George Will was not happy:

> Reagan dug about as deep as any President ever has into the state judiciary for a nominee. But, then, his sexual criterion excluded about 95% of the law school graduates in the relevant age group.

Will seems to be applying a mathematical formula: that it was nineteen times more likely that a man would be the most qualified nominee. Forgetting that the women admitted to law school at the time were probably twenty times more qualified than the men, Will doesn't seem to understand or accept the value of diversity. Now, I don't know if the fact that Sandra Day O'Connor has two ovaries inherently makes her better able to interpret the law as it affects women. Actually, I'm not sure she has two ovaries. I'll ask my research assistant, Geoff, to look it up. (Sometimes my writing gets ahead of the research.)

While we're waiting for Geoff, I'd like to speak to an affirmative action program which, as a Harvard graduate, I do like. And that is affirmative action for the children of Ivy League grads. Here's how it works. All applicants to Harvard, say, have to meet certain minimum requirements: SAT scores, G.P.A., and (a new one) lack of murder convictions.*

The applicants who meet those requirements are thrown into a pool from which the next year's freshman class is chosen. At this point, they start looking at special abilities. Does the orchestra need an oboe? Does the Sanskrit department need a kid who is actually willing to study Sanskrit? Is there a point guard with 1200 on his SAT's who's not good enough to be recruited by Duke or Georgetown?

And: Is the kid a legacy? That is, the child of an alumnus? If so, the kid is in. There are all kinds of good reasons for this. Well, one really. Fund-raising. But as it stands, it's an affirmative action program for one of the most privileged groups in the country: the sons and daughters of people like me.

Now we're told that one of the "poisonous and

---

* Last spring Harvard had to rescind its acceptance of Gina Grant after the college learned she had murdered her abusive mother. Though she had served her time in juvenile prison, Harvard felt that there were other equally deserving applicants on the waiting list who had murdered neither of their parents.

pernicious" "unintended consequences" of affirmative action is that it taints the real accomplishments of qualified blacks who have earned their place at the table. I'm sure that's true. But I think that's just further evidence of the racism in our culture. All the time I was at Harvard, I never heard a Lowell or a Cabot remark, "I dare say, I despise this godawful legacy policy. It makes me so suspect in the eyes of my classmates."

A small digression. This is an absolutely true story. The first guy I met at Harvard was a legacy. I had flown in from Minneapolis, taken a taxi directly to Harvard Yard, and, lugging my duffel bag and electric Smith Corona, found my freshman dorm. In the entryway was a young man my age, but somehow older. Khakis, polo shirt, tortoiseshell glasses. He extended his hand in a friendly yet proper manner and said, "William Sutherland Strong. I'm from northern New Jersey, but my family moved from Massachusetts."

"When?" I asked.

"In the late eighteenth century."

It took a beat to sink in. I said, "Al Franken. I'm from Minneapolis. But my family moved from Kraków in the early twentieth century."

I returned to Harvard in 1992 to speak to a standing-room-only crowd at the JFK School of Government. The week before, the speaker had been the editor of the only opposition newspaper in El Salvador, and only six people showed up. I think that was because he had never worked with John Belushi.

Except for the Eddie Murphy years, *Saturday Night Live* has always had a reputation as a white male bastion, and during the Q&A period I was taken to task for it. "Why doesn't the show hire more women and people of color?" At the time we had two very talented African American performers, Ellen Cleghorne and Tim Meadows, and I pointed out that another cast member, Rob Schneider, is half Filipino. Was that of any help?

No. And after I gave what I felt was a sufficiently exhaustive and responsive answer, the questioner pressed further. Finally, as a joke, I said, "Well, another reason, of course, is that minorities just aren't funny." Everyone, including the relentless questioner, laughed.

The next day *The Harvard Crimson* reported that "Mr. Franken said . . . 'minorities just aren't funny.' " No mention of the good-natured irony or the warm wave of laughter.

So, having had someone imply (wrongly) that I'm a racist, and having myself accused (rightly) Pat Buchanan of the same, I think I have some perspective on both sides of this prickly issue.

That's why I was happy when Bill Clinton, the hero of the Mushball Middle and our greatest post-war president, decided to study affirmative action. And when he came down firmly on the "mend it, don't end it" side, it helped me make up my mind. That's what leadership is all about.

Geoff just came back with the research. Both of Justice O'Connor's ovaries are intact.

By the way, Geoff is black.

No, he isn't. He's a white guy from Harvard. But wouldn't it have been a great ending to this if he was?

But he's gay!

No, he isn't.

14
SOMETHING WE CAN ALL GET BEHIND

There was a time when Constitutional amendments did things like free whole races of people. Or enfranchise an entire gender. Now with the American flag-protection amendment it appears that we're really getting down to the short strokes.

So, as long as we're making amendments that create exceptions to the First Amendment, I thought I'd offer up a few of my own. Basically, they would ban certain acts that, I think we can all agree, have been considered protected "speech" for far too long.

Amendment XXIX—makes it a federal offense to take a whiz on the Statue of Liberty.

Amendment XXX—allows states to punish anyone "hocking a loogey" on a reproduction of the Declaration of Independence.

Amendment XXXI—makes it illegal for a tourist

visiting the Lincoln Memorial to take a picture of a nude child sitting on Lincoln's lap.

Amendment XXXII—makes it an offense to send that picture through the Internet.

Amendment XXXIII—makes it a felony to walk into the U.S. Capitol and spray that fake Popeil hair paint on the bald spot of the John Quincy Adams statue.

Amendment XXXIV—makes it a high crime to dip a replica of the Washington Monument in a vat of Andres Serrano's urine.

Amendment XXXV—allows states to prosecute anyone making a jockstrap out of the U.S. Constitution.

Amendment XXXVI—makes it an act of treason to dress up the soldiers of the Iwo Jima Memorial as the Andrews Sisters.

Amendment XXXVII—allows states to prosecute an exotic dancer who picks up United States currency with anything other than her hands.

15

APOCRYPHAL ANECDOTES: THE REPUBLICAN CONTRIBUTION TO PUBLIC DEBATE

Republicans have a very annoying habit of proving political points by telling horror stories that aren't even true to begin with. You know, things like "we should abolish seat belts because I know someone who got strangled by one once."

The master of the apocryphal story was Ronald Reagan, the most successful Republican politician of the last thirty years. Remember Reagan's welfare queen in Chicago? She had bilked the government for $150,000 by applying for benefits using eighty different names, thirty addresses, a dozen social security cards, and four fictional dead husbands.

Attempts to confirm the story yielded only one woman who received $8,000 by using two false names.

Now you might say, "Well, it's a good story, though. It made the point, didn't it?" That's exactly what Reagan's press secretary said after he learned that another one of Reagan's stories was untrue. This one about England, where "if a criminal carried a gun, even if he didn't use it, he was tried for first-degree murder and hung if he was found guilty." Not true. But wouldn't it be cool if it was!?

Reagan told so many whoppers that the press basically held him to a lower standard. And that's a shame. Because the man felt so strongly about the importance of telling the truth. I know this because he used to tell a great anecdote about telling the truth.

I first ran across the anecdote in an article written by award-winning Reagan biographer Lou Cannon. The story was from his days on his high school varsity football team in Dixon, Illinois. It was during his senior year, and, as Reagan tells it, his team was behind in the last few seconds of the fourth quarter. Just as the final gun went off, Reagan caught a pass in the end zone for the winning touchdown. Only trouble was, Reagan had been offside. So he did the only thing he could. He went to the ref and told him about the infraction. "I told the truth, the penalty was ruled, and Dixon lost the game." The punch line of the story was that none of Reagan's teammates was upset. After all, he told the truth.

Cannon went back to Dixon, and no one could recall the incident. In fact, in the only varsity game in which Reagan played, Dixon lost 24–0. Well, it's a good story though. It made the point.

Reagan, of course, was a B-movie actor. So nobody really expected him to be authoritative on complicated facts and such. But Newt Gingrich, you'll recall, has a Ph.D. in history. That's why it's particularly puzzling when the Speaker of the House turns into the fellow I like to call Bizarro Newt.

See. In Superman's Bizarro World, everything is the opposite of things on Planet Earth. So if you like a hot dog in Bizarro World and would like another one, you would say, "Me hate hot dog. Me want more, me hate them so much." It's a little confusing, but believe me, so is Bizarro Newt.

Bizarro Newt: "Most people don't know that it's illegal to pray. When they learn that a ten-year-old boy in St. Louis was put in detention for saying grace privately over his lunch, they think that's bizarre. . . ."

Planet Earth: According to the school's superintendent, the boy in St. Louis was *not* disciplined for praying. Prayer is not illegal in school. *Organized* prayer is prohibited.

Bizarro Newt: Gingrich complained in December 1994 that a heart pump that was "invented in Denmark increases by 54 percent the number of people given CPR who get to the hospital with a chance to recover. The Food and Drug Administration makes illegal [a product] that minimizes brain damage, increases the speed of recovery, and saves money."

Planet Earth: The pump was invented in the United States. The Danish company which licensed the pump had yet to apply to the FDA for approval. Initial field tests conducted by the University of California, San Francisco, have "unfortunately showed the pump to be of absolutely no value."

Bizarro Newt: Gingrich claimed, also in December 1994, that 800 babies a year were being left in Dumpsters in Washington, D.C.

Planet Earth: In this case Bizarro Newt was off by 796 babies. The four babies found in Dumpsters in 1994 were rescued and cared for by government bureaucrats.

Bizarro Newt: In February 1995, Bizarro Newt told members of the National Restaurant Association that a federal shelter in Denver had 120 beds and cost $8.8 million a year to operate, while a similar-sized but private shelter in the same area costs only $320,000 a year and saves more lives in the process. Members of the audience gasped, "Oh my God!" and "Wow!"

Planet Earth: The "federal" shelter doesn't exist. What Bizarro Newt was apparently referring to is a rehab clinic run by Arapahoe House, Colorado's largest drug and alcohol treatment program, which operates its multiple clinics and 16 school-based counseling programs at a total cost of $11 million, of which $4.3 million is federal money. The "private shelter" is a homeless shelter which offers some drug counseling but no formal treatment or detoxification program.

Bizarro Newt told the restaurateurs that he wanted to discuss Denver's shelter to show "how totally different our vision of the world is from the welfare state. . . . Twenty-five times as much money to ruin lives. This is why we don't believe the big-spending theory of what liberal compassion is."

In fact, all reliable studies on Planet Earth show that for every dollar spent, good drug rehabs like Arapahoe House save society approximately seven dollars in medical expenses, crime, and lost productivity. They don't "ruin" lives, they save them.

If Newt's apocryphal anecdotes and Reagan's share a certain carefree indifference to the truth, Newt's usually lack the warm personal touch that Reagan could bring to his. That's why my favorite new Republican Apocryphal Horror Story is House majority leader Dick Armey's warm yet tragic tale of Charlie, the semi-retarded janitor.

Armey tells the story often. Charlie, it seems, swept the floors of Wooten Hall, the building where Armey worked as a professor at North Texas State University. Armey took a liking to Charlie and they talked a lot. (That's the warm part.) Well, one day Armey noticed that Charlie was gone. A few months went by before Armey ran into a degraded Charlie on the checkout line, buying his groceries with *food stamps*. "What happened, Charlie?" Charlie told him. The federal government had raised the minimum wage, and the university could no longer afford to pay his salary. (That's the tragic part.) From that moment on, Armey tells his audiences, he swore his undying hostility to the federal minimum wage.

(Here comes the truth part.)

Washington Post reporter David Maraniss spoke to four different professors who also worked at Wooten Hall during that period. None could remember a janitor named Charlie. The current chancellor of the university told Maraniss that, as state employees, university janitors are paid well over the minimum wage, and so Armey's story doesn't make sense. When pressed, Armey changed the tragic, moving story. He said that the head of the university's physical plant ("his name was Dale something") told him Charlie was fired because they could no longer afford him.

Still, there's nothing like a really dumb apocryphal horror story. Republican congressman David McIntosh of Indiana claimed on the House floor and in hearings before the Senate Judiciary Committee that the Consumer Product Safety Commission had issued a guideline requiring that all five-gallon and larger buckets used on worksites be built *with a hole in them* to "avoid the danger of somebody falling face down in the bucket and drowning."

You have to admit. Requiring a hole in a bucket would be really stupid. It would defeat the entire purpose of the bucket! I mean, why have a bucket if you're going to have a hole in it?! And, let's get real. What hardhat is going to fall face down in a bucket and drown?! Man, the federal government is stupid!

Do I even have to finish this one? Okay. Here goes: The CPSC never issued such a guideline. It did study the issue of small children—not adults, as McIntosh implies—drowning in such buckets (228 died in this manner between 1984 and 1994), but closed the investigation after the bucket industry agreed to put warning labels on the buckets and spend money for an information campaign regarding the problem.

Are there badly written, unnecessary, stupid government regulations? Yes. Are there enough of them that the Republicans don't have to make them up to give interesting examples? Evidently not.

Here's a good one. House Republican whip Tom Delay tells of a dentist who refused to give a child's baby teeth to his parents because the teeth were classified as toxic waste.

I didn't bother to check that one.

Instead I thought I'd spend my time trying to make up my own Democratic apocryphal story. Something really touching and horrible. Here goes.

There's this kid named Jason on my son's Little League team for which I'm the assistant coach. Hell. Let's make me the coach. Jason has Attention Deficit Disorder. No, wait. He's semi-retarded. And we play on a beautiful field that was once a Superfund site. Some corporate polluter had put carcinogens in the groundwater and the EPA forced them to pay for the cleanup, which was a huge success.

Anyway. Jason is semi-retarded. As coach, I've kind of taken him under my wing, and taught him the intricacies of the game. So, one day we're playing a game against a team of bullies. They're a better team, but we're only down by one run in the bottom of the sixth with two outs and the bases loaded. Jason is up and the entire game is on the line. It's the league championship! And the count is three and two. So Jason gets hit in the head with a pitch. He's fine, because he's wearing a helmet, which is a government regulation. And our team is cheering because that forces in the tying run. Only Jason stops everyone and says his head was in the strike zone, and he should be called out. So the umpire calls him out, but everyone on our team is happy because Jason told the truth. He didn't really; his head wasn't in the strike zone. He just thought it was because he's semi-retarded. But everyone's happy anyway.

So we all go out for hamburgers. I buy because that's the kind of guy I am. Jason's burger is undercooked. It's got the *E. coli* bacteria, because the Republicans deregulated meat inspection, and Jason dies.

I forgot. When he got hit in the head, he was okay, except the shock knocked out two of his baby teeth. And on his deathbed he gave them to his parents and told them to put them under his little sister's pillow so the tooth fairy would give her a quarter.

Unfortunately, she also died from eating an *E. coli* hamburger. As did every kid on the team. And a pregnant woman. And three tourists from Kansas. It was real tragic.

16
THIS BOOK IS NOT PART
OF A CONSPIRACY

I just want to assure the reader that this book was not written in the service of some conspiracy to form a one-world government. *Rush Limbaugh Is a Big Fat Idiot and Other Observations* is really meant as an entertainment to provide a few laughs, force my political opinions down your throat, and maybe even get you to think a little bit. But *not* about conspiring to form a one-world government!

There are, I can assure you, no encoded messages anywhere in this book. For example, if you took the fourteenth letter of each page in reverse order, they wouldn't spell out instructions to occupying U.N. soldiers or indicate the sites of future concentration camps for fundamentalist Christians who refuse to surrender their guns in a coming federal crackdown.

That information is already written on the backs of highway signs. Or at least that's what I've been led to believe.

And when I go on my book tour, the order of the

cities I visit will be of no special significance. If I spend a couple days near Groom Lake, Nevada, it will be because Delacorte feels I can sell a lot of books there. I will not, and I repeat, *not*, be visiting the defense facility in Groom Lake where scientists and CIA agents are working with six hundred space aliens. If some of the aliens come to the book signing and buy books, I'll sign them. But that's it. Come to think of it, maybe I'll have the aliens sign my copy of *Behold a Pale Horse*, the book by William Cooper, the Worldwide Christian Radio host, who says that President Eisenhower signed a treaty with space aliens in the 1950s allowing humans to be abducted in exchange for technological advice.

If Delacorte hires a black helicopter to fly me around, don't start jumping to conclusions. The logistics of these book tours can be pretty complicated, and sometimes you have to charter your own flights. So let's say I have to get from a signing in Missoula, Montana, to one in Coeur d'Alene, Idaho. My wife doesn't trust those Buddy Holly–Jim Croce puddle jumpers, and a black helicopter manned by Bureau of Alcohol, Tobacco, and Firearms agents might just give her a little more peace of mind.

And if I have really good weather on my tour, it will be just a big coincidence. It will *not* be because I was the beneficiary of government weather-tampering devices, which were designed to starve millions of Americans as part of the new world order's plan to take over the country. Frankly, I didn't know this technology existed before I started the book. Fortunately, I asked my research assistant, Geoff, to watch the Senate militia hearings in June where Robert Fletcher, a Militia of Montana founder, made a very convincing argument to Senator Herbert Kohl of Wisconsin:

> . . . If somebody had told me that equipment even existed ten years ago, I would have thought they were nuts, sir. And at this point in time, we have all the documents to prove it. And if you think that eighty-five tornadoes take place in the middle of our growing area by simultaneous accident, I'm sorry.

The Militia of Montana, by the way, is the source of a lot of good, solid information. In 1994, for example, the militia's newsletter, "Taking Aim," disclosed that a secret government plan to replace the lower forty-eight states with nine zones was spelled out in an illustration on the back of Kix cereal boxes.

Why Kix? At first I suspected that it was because "Kix are for kids" and that the government knew that kids could never break the code on the back of the box. But then Geoff reminded me that *Trix* are for kids. So I'm back to square one.

Not to upset anybody, I'd like to give a little credit to other militias. A few months after the Oklahoma City bombing, Commander Norman Olson and Colonel Ray Southwell of the Northern Michigan Regional Militia explained the whole thing. Turns out that a band of rogue CIA and FBI agents working for the Japanese blew up the federal building in revenge for the Tokyo subway gas attack by U.S. Army agents who were retaliating for the Japanese bugging of White House communications.

Angered by the left-wing, pro-government media's refusal to investigate the theory, Olson and Southwell fired off a fax to news bureaus across the country. Addressed to "COWARDS," the fax read: "We have cast pearls of truth before swine. Damn you all!"

Speaking of damnation, I'm very upset with the people at Delacorte. I *begged* them not to put the Universal Product Code on the back of the book. They argued that every retail item these days has to have the UPC bar code, and I said, "Exactly! That's *why* the UPC is the Mark of the Beast!"

Of course, the Delacorte people *pretended* not to know what I was talking about. So we had to go through this little charade where I showed them the passage in Revelation: "No man will be able to buy or sell without the Mark of the Beast." And they acted like they had never seen it before. And then I pointed out the passage in Pat Robertson's book *The New World Order*:

> . . . Can any of us doubt the truth expressed in the Book of Revelation that all credit could one day be controlled by a central one-world financial authority and that no one could buy or sell without its approval?

And the charade continued. They acted like I was crazy, and finally I just said, "The man went to Yale!"

Long story short, the back cover bears the Mark of the Beast. I'm sorry.

17
I GET LETTERS

The last time I appeared on C-SPAN I did a call-in show during which I talked about *Saturday Night Live* and political humor for about a half hour. A few days later, I received this letter:

To the Jew Franken:

I saw you on C-SPAN, and I always knew you were a fag Jew. You fucking faggot. I know you spend all your faggot time on your hands and knees getting fucked in the ass by fellow Jew faggot Barney Frank while you suck off that faggot Gerry Studds.

And I thought to myself, "He could tell all this from one little interview?"

18
ADVENTURES IN POLITICS
DECEMBER 31, 1993

Renaissance Weekend. Hilton Head. I Meet
Wolf Blitzer and Play Touch Football with
the President, and Fool the Greatest Minds
in the Country with "The Play"

It is a rule of thumb that people like me who
write about politics should not hobnob with the
people we're writing about.

For example, I have said that President Clinton is,
without a doubt, our best post-war president, and, if
not for Roosevelt, the greatest of this century. Do I
feel this way because I played touch football with
him? Maybe.

The occasion was Renaissance Weekend, an annual
get-together on Hilton Head Island. Founded fifteen
years ago by businessman Phil Lader, the Weekend
brings together people of "achievement" for four
days of *off the record* exchanges of ideas "in the Renaissance spirit." I emphasize *off the record* because I'm
not supposed to be telling you any of this.

The Clintons have been Renaissance regulars. So
have people like Admiral Bud Zumwalt, Justice Harry
Blackmun, Art Buchwald, various corporate CEO's,
academes, governors, mayors, and U.S. senators.

How did I get invited? Phil was my freshman proctor at Harvard. He had been inviting my family for years, but just the name *"Renaissance* Weekend" had kept me away.

The Weekend has been called "elitist" by many in the press, or at least by those who have never been invited as participants. It's just the kind of crowd Rush Limbaugh would feel most uncomfortable with.

First of all, it's predominantly liberal, with a few token right-wingers like former *Conservative Digest* publisher Richard Viguerie. But more than that, Renaissancers are the wrong type of achievers. If Limbaugh believes in nothing else, he believes that personal success comes from "self-reliance, risk-taking, hard work, and the courage to believe in yourself." None of that counts, however, if you're a liberal. Then you're a socialist who believes success comes from "relying on government handouts and affirmative action." Socialists like Microsoft billionaire Bill Gates come to mind.

For Rush, successful people fall into two basic categories: achievers in the "real world" to be emulated, and pointy-headed elitists to be resented. Thus, in *See, I Told You So* he writes, "Tell me something, friends. If you wanted to become a major-league baseball player, whose advice would you value more— baseball star George Brett's or Donna Shalala's?"* (See bottom of page for answer.)

To be embarrassingly honest, the main reason I decided to spend my New Year's in Hilton Head was

* George Brett.

the touch football game. I had seen the clips on TV the year before, the young Kennedyesque President-elect frolicking with windswept Renaissancers, while the Frankens shivered on 84th and Broadway in the movie line for *Beethoven's 2nd*. So this year, the Frankens accepted.

Sometime in November, with the big Weekend about a month away, I was throwing the football in the park with my eight-year-old, Joe. That's when the play came to me in a flash. It was beautiful!

That night, getting ready for bed, I proudly explained the play to my wife. Franni put down her book. "Honey," she said, "you're not going to play touch football with the President."

"I *might*."

"I just don't want you to be disappointed." The concern sounded a tad patronizing.

"Honey, you don't understand. It doesn't *matter* whether I play touch football with the President. The point is the beauty of the play. I've designed *the perfect* misdirection play!"

"It's just that I know you, and I don't want you to get your hopes up."

"You're not listening. I *know* this isn't going to happen. It's just the concept, that's all. I just wanted to share the joy of the concept."

"I know." She patted me. "I just don't want you to be disappointed."

The football game was scheduled for Day Three at low tide. About sixty other Renaissancers also wanted to play football with the President, and before he arrived, we were divided into four unwieldy teams, comprised mostly of university presidents, policy wonks, jurists, data processing entrepreneurs, heads of non-profits, journalists, and me. And our kids, some of whom were college age, fast, and tall.

The captain of our team, a well-connected Washington lawyer, had noticed during warm-ups that I had a better arm than anyone from the Brookings Institute, and I humbly accepted the quarterback duties. As we started playing, sans Bill, it quickly became apparent that there wasn't going to be a lot of scoring. It was a blustery day, but more than that, the game was just chaos. Once I'd get the hike, I was looking at thirty or more people, none of whom I knew except my son and Howard Fineman of *Newsweek*. I completed a few short passes to tall college students and a nifty little toss to the 13-year-old son of an American Enterprise Institute fellow, who had cut across the middle . . . well, now I'm just trying your patience.

Our team was on the sideline when the President arrived, trailed by an entourage of about fifty: Secret Service, the press corps, cameras. Our well-connected captain managed to snare him, and suddenly I found myself in a huddle with the President of the United States. Two things really struck me. The first was that up close he really does look like a Bubba: red-faced, jeans and a sweatshirt, and a gut.

The other was that the President, any President, has to be *in charge*. It's expected of him, and he knows it's expected of him. So now President Clinton was calling the plays, for really no reason other than he's the President. Which was good enough for everyone. We were all thrilled.

Mainly, the President wanted to get the little kids involved. Which is great, except it's no way to move the football. After two quick incompletions, we were facing a third and fifty. Back in the huddle, the President knelt down to draw in the sand, but before he could open his mouth, I said, "I have a play."

Everyone just kind of looked at me. . . . "Mr. President, I'd like to use you as a decoy."

A beat before, ". . . Okay."

We had all been instructed to call him "Mr. President." Some of the Renaissance regulars knew him as "Bill," but everyone was supposed to call him "Mr. President" as in:

"Mr. President, go out ten and cut to the right."

I told everyone else to stay short or block, except for one of the fast, tall college kids, who I told to go deep left. When we got to the scrimmage line, I made an announcement. I shouted, "The President wants everyone to know that whoever blocks a pass intended for the President on this play will get to spend a night in the White House."

The President turned to me and said, "What?!" That got a laugh, and, I think, sold the play. Then he shrugged with another, "Okay."

It couldn't have worked more perfectly. After the snap, the President went out ten and cut to the right sideline. That's when I made the *PUMP FAKE*.

They *ALL* went for it. It was embarrassing really. Fifteen people each thinking the same thing: "Lincoln bedroom." By the time I put the ball in the air, the college kid was, literally, thirty yards behind the defense.

After the touchdown, there was a lot of high-fiving. The President ran to the end zone and hugged the college kid. I ran up for my hug, but didn't get one. That was all right, though. I had played touch football with the greatest president of the twentieth century. And proved my wife wrong.

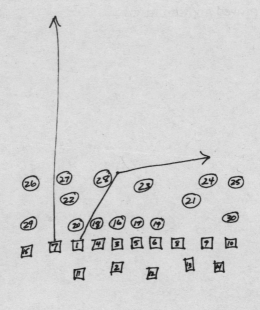

1. President of U.S.
2. Me
3. Pointy-headed liberal
4. Sandal-wearing liberal
5. Eggheaded liberal
6. Howard Fineman
7. Son of pointy-headed liberal
8. Wacko-feminist
9. Enviro-fascist
10. Daughter of feminazi
11. Poverty pimp
12. Ira Magaziner
13. Compassion fascist
14. Pro abortion militant leftist
15. Hollywood filth merchant

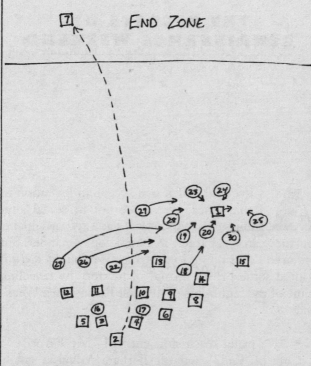

END ZONE

16. Beancurd eater
17. Wolf Blitzer
18. Lawyer
19. Draft dodger
20. Secular humanist

21. Son of enviro-fascist and feminazi
22. Ted Sorensen
23. Militant vegetarian
24. Smooth-talking, Ivy League-educated, Armani-clad class warrior
25. Treehugger

26. Zoë Baird
27. Modern statist
28. Ugly feminist
29. Diabolical Rodhamite
30. Token Conservative Richard Viguerie

19
THE SECRETS OF
RENAISSANCE WEEKEND

As I've said, when you accept an invitation to Renaissance, you agree not to reveal anything you see or hear. That way, participants feel they can speak freely in a frank, open manner. But I figured I'd be doing Renaissance Weekend a favor if I lifted some of the shroud of mystery by revealing some of the highlights of my first Renaissance Weekend:

- At a panel discussion entitled "My Favorite Cuts of Veal," Senator Barbara Mikulski got drunk and kneed neo-conservative Ben Wattenberg in the groin.

- At the Renaissance volleyball game, former *Conservative Digest* publisher Richard Viguerie taunted Justice Harry Blackmun, repeatedly yelling "Show me your serve, baby killer!"

- President Clinton used the four days out of

the public eye to undergo a series of painful liposuction procedures.

• At a panel on health care reform Ira Magaziner announced that the comprehensive package would cover people with the willies but not those suffering from the heebie-jeebies.

• Fed Chairman Alan Greenspan was seen leaving dinner sneaking shrimp back to his room.

• At a panel entitled "You're Only as Sick as Your Secrets," Wolf Blitzer admitted that his real name is Leslie Blitzer.

• Zoë Baird screamed at the kitchen help.

20
STOP THIS MAN BEFORE
HE KILLS AGAIN

That's me shaking hands with the President at the White House Correspondents Association Dinner. The photograph is real. It hasn't been put together digitally like that *Forrest Gump* footage. It's not a composite. How I wish it were!

Had I known at the time that the man was a murderer, I would never have shaken his hand. I have never *knowingly* shaken the hand of a killer. Once I did a fund-raiser for Pol Pot, but that was before I'd seen *The Killing Fields*.

Unfortunately, I spoke at the Correspondents Association Dinner before I had a chance to see "Bill Clinton's Circle of Power." According to the video, as governor and then as president, Clinton has been connected to the murders of "countless people."

The video has sold over 100,000 copies thanks to regular advertising on Jerry Falwell's *Old Time Gospel Hour*. Which means the information is getting to the right people.

The tape was so successful that its producers, an organization called Citizens for Honest Government, made a sequel called "The Clinton Chronicles," which Falwell promotes as "far more damaging, far more indicting" than the original. Says Falwell:

. . . Now on this brand-new video exposé, "The Clinton Chronicles," these brave men and women have stepped forward to tell what they know about the dark side of Bill and Hillary Clinton. Even in the face of alleged constant intimidation, threats, physical abuse, and even, some say, mysterious, violent acts of murder.

Basically, the tape tells a sinister tale of murder, adultery, Whitewater, and . . . cocaine:

An unidentified voice: [Drug smuggler] Barry Seale . . . had to find a state that had a sleazy governor hooked on cocaine, and everybody knew it. Bill Clinton was hooked on cocaine.

Narrator: Clinton had integrated a number of

corrupt cops, judges, and politicians into high-level positions to ensure the continued success of the drug smuggling, money laundering operation.

It gets worse. Much worse. A woman named Linda Ives says her son and a friend witnessed the smuggling and were murdered. But state officials, led by a political appointee of Clinton's, covered it up.

Ives: I was outraged that protecting a political crony of Clinton's was more important than the fact that two young boys had been murdered.

Narrator: A number of people approached the police about Don and Kevin's murders and were subsequently murdered themselves.

Wow! We're talking *dozens* of murders. As Florida talk radio host Chuck Harder, who is broadcast on 300 stations, has put it, "The difference between Watergate and Whitewater is a very, very big pile of bodies."

And who are these murder victims? One, obviously, was Vince Foster.

I'm embarrassed to say that for quite a while I bought the party-line "suicide" explanation. Just shows that I've been getting my information from all the wrong sources.

Had I been listening to Rush Limbaugh on March 10th, 1994, I would have heard this:

Okay, folks, I think I got enough information here to tell you about the contents of this fax that I got. Brace yourselves. . . . What it is is a bit of news which says . . . there's a Washington consulting firm that has scheduled the release of a report that will appear, it will be published, that claims that Vince Foster was murdered in an apartment owned by Hillary Clinton, and the body was then taken to Fort Marcy Park.

Limbaugh had actually botched it a little. The fax he received had said nothing about a murder and nothing about Hillary's apartment. But the point is still the same. Which is that Vince Foster was murdered in Hillary's apartment.

Had I been watching the *700 Club* around that time I could have heard Pat Robertson say, "Was there a murder of a White House counsel? It looks more and more like that." And more recently, Robertson's guest was James Dale Davidson, chairman of the National Taxpayers' Union, who told *700 Club* viewers that Foster's death was clearly a murder and that top people in the news media know that a cover-up was taking place.

If only I had known all this before I had shaken the Murderer's hand. Come to think of it, I could have used the occasion to say something. After all, there were a lot of top people in the media at the din . . . Wait a minute! Maybe it's good I didn't say anything.

In fact, maybe I shouldn't be writing this.

21
MONETARY POLICY: A TICKING TIME BOMB

This was going to be a hell of a chapter on the danger of monetizing the debt. Geoff did hours and hours of research and tells me the stuff is pretty frightening.

Unfortunately, I just haven't had a chance to look at it. Which is only the first step in writing these little essays. I have to read Geoff's research, then have him explain it to me, then reread it, and *then* try to think of three or four jokes that I can tie together in some lame, half-assed way so I can call the thing an essay. It's hard work. And time-consuming.

But that's what an artist owes his audience. This book is, in a sense, my gift to you the reader. It is a gift of my talent and my dedication. It is a solemn pact, as it were, between you and me. You keep your side of the bargain by buying the book. I keep my side by investing every fiber of my being into the work.

The thing is, I've got kids. And, sometimes, in life you have to set priorities. It would be nice to invest every fiber of my being in this whole monetary policy thing, whatever it is. But dammit, if this book is about anything, it's about how the family is the building block of a healthy society. And since the book is not about that, I guess it isn't about anything.

Which leaves me free to pitch batting practice for the West Side Little League all-star tournament team. You see, my son, Joe, made the team. In fact, he got the game ball from yesterday's 6–5 victory over Kingsbridge, the Bronx team that usually wins our district. Joe made this amazing throw that nailed the tying run at the plate. Joe got his arm from me. At least the accuracy. Which is why I pitch batting practice. I throw a meatball that any 10-year-old can hit.

The whole tournament has become a real production. Mainly because we keep winning. We now have about fifty-five parents, siblings, and grandparents who come along to the games, after which we eat. My wife is the team parent, so she's on the phone constantly making arrangements for minivans and Gatorade. That's put a lot of pressure on me to be a hands-on parent. Unlike some Republican officeholders I know.

And believe me, monetary policy isn't the only casualty of West Side's post-season juggernaut. If we had been eliminated in the quarterfinals, I would have been able to write a great chapter on campaign finance reform. If it hadn't been for Jake Seltzer's two-run triple against East Harlem in the opening round, you'd know a lot more about our trade deficit. The point is, your loss is my son's gain.

And if we win tomorrow, I probably won't get to

the Reagan years. That'd be too bad. Because I think Geoff has some really good stuff on the subject. Blows Limbaugh right out of the water.

But in the long run, I think the country will reap greater dividends from the added investment in my children, who will grow up to be much happier, more productive members of our society. As opposed to Reagan's kids.* Who, let's be honest, seem kind of screwed up.

* In his autobiography, *On the Outside Looking In*, Michael Reagan, the adopted son from Reagan's first marriage to Jane Wyman, tells this story: It's a beautiful June day in 1964. Reagan is the commencement speaker at an exclusive prep school outside Scottsdale, Arizona. Reagan is standing with several of the seniors, who have been invited to pose for pictures with him. He chats up each of the graduates, and to one of the boys says: "My name is Ronald Reagan. What's yours?" The boy says, "I'm your son Mike." "Oh," says Reagan. "I didn't recognize you."

22

THE REAGAN YEARS: RUSH LIMBAUGH IS A BIG FAT LIAR

As Rush Limbaugh likes to say, "words mean things." Which is why I probably should have called this book *Rush Limbaugh Is a Big Fat Liar.* But that just seemed so confrontational.

Rush lies about a lot of stuff. Some of the lies I don't really hold against him. These are the ones where he's been on the air for an hour or so, and he's really on a roll. He's hunkered down in the booth, probably sweating a lot; he's done a couple Billary jokes, and he's just ranting like there's no tomorrow. He's so far in the zone that he's left objective reality behind and entered this parallel universe where things are true because Rush wants them to be—where the Way Things Ought to Be is the way things are, even if they aren't. This is the place where Styrofoam becomes biodegradable, Hillary has Vince Foster rubbed out, and cigarettes stop causing cancer.

Other lies bug me a lot. These are the rational, carefully constructed, deliberate lies of a man running a giant propaganda factory dedicated to two things: convincing people who were screwed sideways by Reaganomics that it was actually good for them, and encouraging the people who turned the screws to feel good about themselves.

Reaganomics worked. This is the jewel in Rush's crown of bullshit. This is the big lie—the one he desperately needs the working-class members of his audience to believe. If Reaganomics worked, Rush is a straight-talking champion of the little guy on a populist crusade to take the country back from those pointy-headed liberals who think they know what's good for everybody and are drunk with the power of sending out welfare checks.

If Reaganomics didn't work, Rush is the carnival clown hired to distract the crowd while paramedics carry the mangled bodies from a derailed roller coaster. He does a little juggling, pulls some flowers out of his hat, and when the crowd begins to get a little anxious about the rising body count, he starts shrieking hysterically that this never would have happened if it weren't for those goddam liberal safety inspectors.

So the stakes are pretty high for Rush when it comes to Reaganomics. Which is why he devotes long statistic-riddled chapters in both of his books to proving that Reaganomics not only *didn't* cause the national debt to explode, but *did* result in an era of unprecedented economic growth from which all classes benefited. Especially the poor.

Take this bald assertion, straight from page 128 of *See, I Told You So:* "don't blame that [the deficit] on

Reagan. . . . He tried his best to reduce spending, but every one of his budgets was pronounced 'dead on arrival' by the Democratic Congress." That's Rush's party line. That Reagan submitted a whole lot of lean, fiscally conservative budgets to the Democrats in Congress, who fattened them up with a bunch of wasteful, "liberal" programs.

Here's a funny thing. In 1985, the midpoint of what Rush calls "full-blown Reaganomics," Reagan submitted a budget of $588 billion to Congress. The budget that Congress sent back for him to sign was $583 billion, five billion dollars smaller than Reagan wanted. Over the eight years of the Reagan presidency, the Gipper asked Congress for $16.1 billion *more* in spending than it passed into law. If Reagan was really "trying his best" to reduce spending, he must have been using some kind of reverse psychology I don't understand.

Either way, Rush has a point when he calls Ronald Reagan "a man to whom we Americans owe a debt that we will never be able to repay."

The second leg of the three-legged coffee table that is the Big Lie About Reaganomics is that Reagan's massive tax cuts were directly responsible for what Limbaugh calls "unprecedented growth and prosperity." This gets to the heart of supply-side economics: the less you tax the rich, the faster the economy will grow.

Take, for example, the fifties. We taxed the shit out of the rich. The top marginal rate was 88 percent. And the economy grew at an annual rate of just over 4 percent. Then look at the eighties. Reagan knocked the top rate down to 28 percent, and the economy grew at a yearly rate of just under 2.5 percent.

So cutting the marginal tax rate didn't give us "unprecedented" growth. What it did give us was "unprecedented" deficits.

But that's not the Way Things Ought to Be. So rather than admit that supply-side economics was kind of a dumb idea, Rush tries to drown his readers in a flood of impressive-sounding statistics, most of which he's twisted like a balloon animal.

Which brings me to the Chart. The Chart is Limbaugh's big attempt to prove the third leg of the Big Lie: that Reagan's economic policies were just as good for the poor as they were for the rich. And maybe even better.

In 725 pages of opinion-barfing spread over two books, only once does Rush consider a point important enough to trot out a visual aid. To prove that "all income groups paid less taxes as a percentage of their income during the Reagan years, but *the poor received the most relief, the middle class the next, and the rich, the least*" (my emphasis), Rush conjures up the Chart.

The Chart purports to use U.S. Census data (actually, they're Congressional Budget Office numbers) to make the argument that the poor received a *540 percent* tax cut during the Reagan years, while the tax cut for the rich was just 7.9 percent.

"What?" say the liberals in the media. "That can't be true."

"But it *is*!" reply the Didiots. "Look! He made a chart!"

RUSH'S CHART

REDUCTION OF TAX RATES				
Income Quintile	Top Income in Bracket	1980 (% of Income Paid As Taxes)	1992 (% of Income Paid As Taxes)	1992 (% of Taxes Cut)
Poorest 20%	$20,300	-0.5%	-3.2%	-540%
2nd Lowest 20%	$36,800	4.5%	2.8%	-37.8%
Middle 20%	$64,500	7.9%	6.2%	-21.5%
2nd highest 20%	$82,400	11%	8.7%	-20.9%
Richest 20%	....	17.2%	15.6%	-9.3%
Richest 1%	....	23.9%	22%	-7.9%
Source: U.S. Bureau of Census*				

what a dick!

Actually, these are Congressional Budget Office numbers.

Wow! That is pretty convincing. Until you realize the numbers have been cooked like the income statement for Don Corleone's olive oil import business.

First of all, you'll notice that Rush uses the years 1980 and 1992. This is interesting, because the Chart is supposed to be about tax rates "during the Reagan years," while two pages earlier, Rush says, "Reaganomics died in 1990" with George Bush's tax hike. In fact, this is the *only* statistic where Rush defines the Reagan years to include any year after 1989.

Why does he do this? Because including Bush's tax hike makes the size of Reagan's tax break for the rich seem smaller. So why doesn't Rush use 1990? Because it wasn't until the next year that Bush increased the Earned Income Tax Credit for the working poor. Which makes the apparent tax break for the poor seem much larger. So Rush includes the tax hike of 1990 (which he despised) and the increase in the E.I.T.C. of 1991 (which he also despised) in order to create a distorted picture of Reaganomics, which he claims was over by 1990 anyway. Those of you who are thinking, "What an incredible hypocrite!" just keep reading. It gets worse.

He leaves out payroll taxes! That's right. He leaves out payroll taxes, the taxes for Social Security and Medicare that come out of your paycheck before you even see it. Now, remember. Most Americans pay *the majority* of their taxes in payroll taxes. And since payroll taxes only apply to the first $61,000 of income, they are a much bigger burden on the poor than on the rich.

And guess what? While income taxes were going down during the Reagan years, payroll taxes were going up. For the lowest quintile in 1980, payroll taxes were 5.2 percent. By 1989, that number was up to 7.6 percent. The top one percent, on the other hand, paid only 1.5 percent of their income in payroll taxes in 1980. That went up to 1.6 percent by 1989.

So here's what an *honest* chart showing the change in federal tax rates during the Reagan years would look like:

AN HONEST CHART ON TAX RATES DURING THE REAGAN YEARS

Income Quintile	Avg. Income 1989	1980 Total Fed Tax Rate	1989 Total Fed Tax Rate	1989 % of Tax Increase/Cut	1989 Tax Increase Cut in $'s
(1993 Dollars)					
Poorest 20%	8,642	8.1	9.3	+15.0%	+104
2nd Lowest 20%	20,743	15.6	15.7	+0.6%	+21
Middle 20%	33,659	19.8	19.4	-2.0%	-135
2nd highest 20%	49,347	22.9	22.0	-7.6%	-444
Richest 20%	112,700	27.6	25.5	-7.6%	-2367
Richest 1%	576,553	31.9	26.2	-15.0%	-32,864

See? He's a dick

Source: 1992 Green Book, Congressional Budget Office (same as Rush)

So basically, tax rates *rose* for the poor by as much as they *fell* for the rich: 15 percent. And this came during a period when average wages went down, while the incomes of the richest 1 percent more than doubled.

Now let's look at these numbers as bar graphs. (By the way, I think I'm really breaking new ground here.

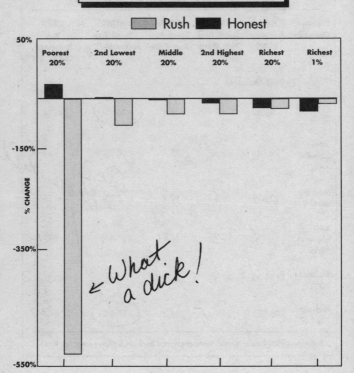

% CHANGE IN TAX RATES
DURING THE REAGAN YEARS

I mean, did you see bar graphs in Jerry Seinfeld's book? In Tim Allen's? Hmmmmm?)

And just for the hell of it, let's add another Rush quote: "Reaganomics did work, and . . . the gap between rich and poor was narrowed rather than expanded during those years."

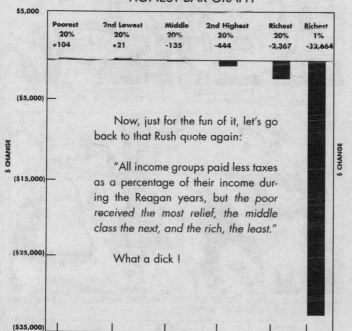

$ CHANGE IN TAX
DURING THE REAGAN YEARS

HONEST BAR GRAPH

	Poorest 20%	2nd Lowest 20%	Middle 20%	2nd Highest 20%	Richest 20%	Richest 1%
	+104	+21	-135	-444	-2,367	-32,664

$5,000
($5,000)
($15,000)
($25,000)
($35,000)

$ CHANGE

Now, just for the fun of it, let's go back to that Rush quote again:

"All income groups paid less taxes as a percentage of their income during the Reagan years, but *the poor received the most relief, the middle class the next, and the rich, the least.*"

What a dick !

Now let's listen to an economist, Paul Krugman from Stanford: "The widening of inequality is beyond doubt. It has been as firmly established by evidence as the fact that smoking causes cancer."

Then again, Rush docsn't believe smoking causes cancer, either.

TRACKING A TRICKLE-DOWN DOLLAR

Uncle Sam gives a $1.00 tax break to a Beverly Hills plastic surgeon...

Plastic Surgeon and his wife go to a fancy restaurant and order the foie gras...

Foie gras dollar goes to Farmer Jacques who force-feeds his geese in France...

Jacques spends dollar at EuroDisney...

Dollar, along with 200 million others, goes to Michael Eisner...

Eisner takes his wife to dinner. They order the foie gras...

Dollar goes back to Jacques...

Jacques goes back to EuroDisney...

Dollar goes back to Eisner. Takes
Cher to lunch. Cher orders foie gras...

Plastic surgeon performs liposuction
on Cher's thighs...

Fat from Cher's thighs used in celebrity lava lamp.

23
NEWT'S LOOT

I have to confess that techniques I've been employing in this book are taken directly from Gingrich's political action committee, GOPAC.

GOPAC trains Republican candidates to beat Democrats, providing them with strategies and tactics, audiotapes and videotapes, and the occasional infusion of cash. GOP candidates learn lessons like "Go Negative Early," "Don't Try to Educate," and "Never Back Off." They're told to "use minor details to demonize" their opposition.

Which is why I bring up the first wife, cancer surgery, deadbeat dad stuff as often as possible.

But there's so much more about Newt. Let's start with the money.

Most people know that Gingrich used to teach a course called Renewing American Civilization at a college in Georgia, and that the course was beamed by satellite to about 100 other locations. I say "used to" because he recently dropped it from his roster of activities. I guess he figured that, what with being the Speaker of the House, a shadow presidential candidate, a bestselling author, a cable TV talk show host, and a deadbeat dad, his plate was pretty full.

But what most people *don't* know about the course is that Gingrich financed it by soliciting contributions from various corporations. For example, for $50,000 a corporation could become a "sponsor" and "work directly with the leadership of the Renewing American Civilization Project in the course development process."

It seemed odd to me that a Ph.D. in history would seek the advice of corporate executives in preparing lesson plans. But it seems to have resulted in a real intellectual synergy. The course draws on the works of the Federalists, de Tocqueville, and the marketing department at Hewlett-Packard, which put together a spiffy promotional video that Newt showed his class.

Professor Gingrich also plugs "a very powerful, revolutionary" health insurance plan offered by the Golden Rule Insurance Company of Indiana, which didn't actually give a dime to the course. Instead, it acts as the sole sponsor of Gingrich's cable show on National Empowerment Television, and its executives and employees have donated $117,000 to GOPAC, $42,000 to Gingrich's campaign committee, and over half a million dollars to the Republican party.

Gee, I'd plug a company too, if they'd stuff that kind of money up my bum.

Hmmmm.

24
LEXIS-NEXIS

THE POWERFUL, REVOLUTIONARY
DATABASE TECHNOLOGY

In the last chapter you may have noticed that I cited quite a few facts, statistics, and whatnot. Now, a smart person like yourself might be wondering how I found all this information. Did I go to the library? No. A university research facility? Nope. The fact is, I didn't even have to leave my apartment.

That's right. Thanks to Lexis-Nexis, the powerful, revolutionary database technology, I was able to access literally thousands of different information sources, almost all of which provided documentation of at least one instance of questionable behavior by Newt Gingrich.

Yes, thanks to Lexis-Nexis, my book has entered the Third Wave! And unlike other database companies, many of which are weird, bizarre, and even grotesque, Lexis-Nexis is user-friendly and breathtakingly up-to-date.

Is Lexis-Nexis paying me to say this? It's none of

your business. But even if they weren't, I'd still be a satisfied Lexis-Nexis customer.

And while we're talking about state-of-the-art, user-friendly products, I'd like to say a little something on behalf of the good people at Hanes underwear. You know, when you sit in front of a word processor all day attacking right-wing ideologues, it's important that your briefs don't bunch up. Hanes, the underwear of satirists.

25
BACK TO NEWT'S LOOT

Now that I've paid for my kids' orthodontics, let's get back to Newt, Inc.

Besides GOPAC, there's the tax-exempt Progress and Freedom Foundation, "a non-partisan idea center" which has spent over $600,000 on Newt's course and cable TV show. The think tank gets a lot of its money from pharmaceutical and telecommunications companies. Which explains why a large part of the think tank's agenda is devoted to deregulating telecommunications and ridding America of the FDA. (See "apocryphal heart pump story," page 114.)

Philosophically, the foundation apes a lot of the futuristic mumbo jumbo of Alvin Toffler. As does Newt, who tends to gush when he talks about the Third Wave. Many of us, like Newt, have acknowledged smoking dope and reading Toffler in the early 70s. But after reading Gingrich's bestseller, *To Renew*

America, I think Newt's dirty little secret is that he smoked dope and watched *The Jetsons:*

> Imagine a morning in just a decade or so. You wake up to a wall-size, high-definition television showing surf off Maui. (This is my favorite island*—you can pick your own scene.) . . . When you are sick, you sit in your diagnostic chair and communicate with the local health clinic. Sensors take your blood pressure, analyze a blood sample, or do throat cultures.

And when it's time to take Astro out for a walk, you just hop on the space treadmill.

Back to the diagnostic chair:

> The results are quickly relayed to health aides, who make recommendations and prescribe medicine. . . . If you need a specialist, a data bank at your fingertips gives you a range of choices based on cost, reputation, and outcome patterns. . . . Health care has become more flexible and convenient—and less expensive.

Here's my question. If Medicare costs are already spiraling out of control, how exactly is providing every American with a *Blade Runner* diagnostic BarcaLounger going to bring down the cost of health care?

Also, if company comes over to watch the game,

---

* (Gee, I wonder why.)

what happens when someone tries to sit in the diagnostic chair? Do you yell: "Don't sit there! It'll give you a throat culture!"

I'm sorry, but if Newt Gingrich thinks our nation's health care problems are going to be solved by the diagnostic chair, then I've got to agree with the Unabomber on this one:

> "Oh," say the technophiles, "science is going to fix all that! We will conquer famine, eliminate psychological suffering, make everybody healthy and happy." Yeah. Sure.

Of course, when we talk about issues like technological development and its role in solving social problems, some pretty fundamental questions come up. Questions about how society can best marshal its limited resources, about the nature of government and its role in contributing to the well-being of its citizens. Unfortunately, the people who are currently deciding the answers to these questions are the same ones who "go negative early" and "never back off."

Which brings us back to GOPAC. Thirty-three members of the House Republican Class of '94 are what a less objective commentator might call "GOPAC Zombies." As such, they are the recipients of large volumes of GOPAC training material and are well versed in "the five key mechanisms of control," one of which is "language."

Fortunately, a copy of the GOPAC memo "Language: A Key Mechanism of Control" has fallen into my hands. According to the memo, it was prepared in response to the "plaintive plea" of candidates across the country: " 'I wish I could speak like Newt.' "

"That takes years of practice," the memo warns. "But, we believe that you could have a significant impact on your campaign and the way you communicate if we help a little. That is why we created this list of words and phrases."

There are two lists, actually. One contains "Optimistic, Positive Governing Words," which the candidate is told to use to "describe your vision for the future of your community (your message)." The other, a list of "Contrasting Words," which the candidate could use to defame, slander, and otherwise impugn his/her opponent.

"The words and phrases are powerful," the memo says. "Read them. Memorize as many as possible."

So for the benefit of any readers who may be considering a run for office, here they are, courtesy of the GOPAC memo "Language: A Key Mechanism of Control."

Optimistic Positive Governing Words

Use the list below to help define your campaign and your vision of public service. These words can help give extra power to your message. In addition, these words help develop the positive side of the contrast you should create with your opponent, giving your community something to vote *for*!

share liberty preserve
change principle(d) pro-(issue)
opportunity precious flag, chil-
challenge care(ing) dren, envi-
truth listen ronment
moral help workfare
courage lead eliminate good
reform vision time in
prosperity empower(ment) prison
children citizen strength
family activist fair
active(ly) dream protect
we/us/our freedom incentive
candid(ly) peace hard work
humane rights common sense
pristine proud/pride

Contrasting Words

Often we search hard for words to define our opponents.
Sometimes we are hesitant to use contrast. Remember that
creating a difference helps you. These are powerful words
that can create a clear and easily understood contrast. Apply these to the opponent, their record, proposals, and their
party.

decay crisis pathetic
failure(fail) destructive lie
collapse(ing) destroy liberal
deeper sick they/them

"compassion" is not enough	greed	shame
traitors	ideological	disgrace
hypocrisy	anti-(issue)	punish
radical	flag, family, child, jobs	(poor...)
devour	pessimistic	bizarre
waste	welfare	cynicism
corruption	corrupt	cheat
incompetent	insensitive	steal
permissive attitude	status quo	machine
impose	taxes	bosses
self-serving	spend(ing)	criminal rights
		red tape

Now, in case you're still a little unclear on how best to make use of these lists, let me offer the following example.

Let's say you're locked in a tight race against Colin Powell. You might want to insert the following into your stump speech: "Colin Powell is a sick, pathetic, corrupt, incompetent, bizarre, selfish traitor whose incompetent, destructive, shallow, cynical, self-serving conduct during the Gulf War was a disgrace." Chances are you'll see a big change in the polls!

Or take an example from Newt's own lips. During the 1990 budget debate in Congress, Newt criticized Democrats involved in the talks as being "sick, pathetic, liberal, incompetent, tax-spending traitors." Sounds like *he* sure memorized the list.

Finally, since these words seem to be so successful

for the Republicans, I thought I'd come up with a list of my own. So as a special treat for those of you who wish you could "talk like Al," here's a short list of powerful words and phrases you can use when contrasting your normal, healthy-looking body with Rush Limbaugh's grotesque girth:

fat	porker	lard-ass, lard-
fatso	oinker	butt, tub of lard
fat-ass	piggly wiggly	thunder thighs
fatboy	porcine	obese
meat show	flab(by)	chunkster
waddle	blubber-butt	Ailes-like
wide load	beached whale	balloon butt
hippo	two-ton tessie	cholesterol colony
gutbucket	walrus	fatty fatty two-
enormous	huge	by-four
suet-boy	butterball	elephantine
soo-eeey!	jelly belly	sow

ten pounds of shit in a five-pound bag

26
ADVENTURES IN POLITICS
APRIL 23, 1994

I Am Brilliant at the White House
Correspondents Association Dinner

Of all the social events in Washington, the annual White House Correspondents Association Dinner is probably the largest. About twenty-five hundred Washingtonians, men and women from the news organizations and their sources, which include congressmen, high-level bureaucrats, administration officials, and Pentagon bigwigs, put on tuxes and gowns for an inside-the-Beltway evening of fun. The only thing comparable that I've been to in Hollywood is the Emmys, although the Hollywood crowd is a lot better-looking.

The highlight of the dinner is supposed to be the entertainment. And over the years they've had the best. Frank Sinatra, Danny Thomas, Jimmy Durante, Fanny Brice, and Danny Kaye all performed for President Truman. During the Eisenhower years they had some tremendous legends: Nat King Cole, Dizzy Gillespie, Bob Hope, James Cagney. Performing for Jack Kennedy were Barbra Streisand, Benny Goodman, and Duke Ellington. In 1969, at President Nixon's request, the entertainment was Disneyland's Golden Horseshoe Revue.

Since 1983, the entertainment has been a comedian —Mark Russell, Rich Little, Jay Leno—on the bill with the President of the United States. I went in 1988 as a guest of the *Washington Post* and saw President Reagan and his favorite comedian, Yakoff Smirnoff. Both were very funny, but Reagan was unbelievably good. The man may have tripled our national debt, but he was a great after-dinner speaker. "I thought the Fourth Estate was one of Walter Annenberg's *homes.*"

It had become my goal after '88 to do the Correspondents dinner. Basically, for a comedian, the gig is comparable to doing a trade show. When a trade group like the scrap metal industry has a convention, they'll hire a comedian to do his act. If the comic can work in a few scrap metal jokes, they go nuts. Only in Washington, the industry is politics. So I imagined doing the White House Correspondents dinner would be like working a scrap metal convention if I knew an awful lot about scrap metal. "I don't want to say Pete Siezmasko is doing a lot of *volume* this year, but Arnie Zimpkin is thinking of moving his operation to *Cleveland*!"

I got a call in March from George Condon, the president of the White House Correspondents Association. George told me that Wolf Blitzer and Andrea Mitchell had reported to him in January that I had been very funny when I spoke at Renaissance Weekend and that I should do this year's dinner. George said that he thought that I would be absolutely *perfect* for the job, but that he had put off calling me until he had heard back from Garry Shandling. I thanked George for the compliment and tried to guess who had turned him down before Garry.

I was glad that Robin, David, Jerry, Tim, and Garry had better things to do.

Before the dinner, there's a whole bunch of cocktail parties thrown by the various news organizations. The best one is for the dais, which meant I got to have cocktails with the Gores and the Clintons. This is something you'd ordinarily have to pay the Democratic National Committee about $110,000 for, but I didn't enjoy it as much I should have because I was a little nervous. Frankly, I was worried about a couple of jokes.

I got Tipper alone in a corner. "I got this joke about your husband, and my instinct is that it might be over the line. I was wondering if I could run it by you."

She laughed and said, "Okay. Let's hear it."

"Okay. Here's the joke: Vice President Gore continued to show his commitment to the environment by announcing today that he's going to change the policy on the stick up his butt. Instead of replacing the stick every day with a *new* stick, the Vice President will keep the *same* stick up his butt for the rest of the Administration. Evidently, this will save an entire rain forest."

Tipper just kind of looked at me. And then said, "I'd go with your instinct."

The Marine band made me even more nervous.

They were behind us on the stage. After the rest of us on the dais had taken our seats, the band played the Gores on with the official vice president's march, which I didn't know existed, and then the President and First Lady entered to "Hail to the Chief." Then they announced the honor guard, which was comprised of servicemen from each branch of the military. Bearing the colors and marching in step down the center aisle, they were a somber, imposing presence. Watching them, all I could think about were the men and women who died defending our country. Then the Marine band played the national anthem, which everyone sang with patriotic solemnity. "I'm fucked," I thought. This wasn't exactly warming up the crowd. As we sat down, I turned to Tipper, who was next to me, and said, "This is kind of heavy."

She nodded with a knowing "Yeah."

Fortunately, the Marine band and honor guard left, and we ate dinner. I used the time to study my cards and make a monumental decision: whether to do a Nixon joke. Nixon had died the day before, and I was of two minds. On the one hand, it seemed like too significant an event to ignore. On the other, there was the danger of offending everyone and crashing and burning. Fortunately, I have a lot of friends who know Washington. Jonathan Alter of *Newsweek* told me everyone would be *expecting* a Nixon joke, and I'd be crazy not to do one. Norm Ornstein of the American Enterprise Institute said I'd be insane to take the risk.

"Ladies and gentlemen, I'm a little scared tonight. See, I was feeling pretty good a week ago, because I had about twenty minutes of dynamite Nixon material."

That was the joke I decided *not* to do. The whole honor guard thing had spooked me. Instead I started like this:

"Thank you. Thank you very much. First let me just say what a tremendous honor it is to be asked to speak at the White House Correspondents dinner. To be able to perform for the President, the First Lady, the Vice President, Mrs. Gore . . . Wolf Blitzer . . . a dream come true."

That got a nice laugh. Proving my theory that Wolf Blitzer is a funny name. I followed with about thirty minutes of non-Blitzer material. And, I don't know how to say this without seeming self-serving and egotistical, but I *destroyed*. What I did early on was brilliant, really, laying down the groundwork for the possibly offensive jokes to come:

"Before I go any further, a small caveat. I've never really performed for a Washington crowd like this, and I don't know your sensibilities. Now, there are a couple jokes in here that might be a little risky. So, if I do a joke tonight that offends anyone, if I say something completely out of line, if I make a total jerk of myself, I will simply apologize and move on. I mean, it seems to have worked for Alan Simpson." Big laugh.*

---

* During the previous year, Simpson had been forced to apologize to Nina Totenberg, the women of America, and Peter Arnett. A little inside, but remember, this is a scrap metal convention.

So I went right into a potentially offensive joke:

"I was doing some Washington star-gazing at the pre-dinner cocktail parties. I saw Ed Rollins. I like Ed. Though he does brag a lot. At the party I overheard Ed bragging that while in college he paid a prostitute five hundred dollars to do nothing." Big laugh.

"Now, tonight's dinner is being aired live on C-SPAN. Those of you watching at home might want to flip back and forth to C-SPAN 2, because there's a fascinating panel discussion from the Shorenstein-Barone Center on the Press, entitled 'Constant Self-Reevaluation—Useful Exercise or Giant Wankathon?' I can't wait to see what side Marvin Kalb comes down on. I think Wankathon. Don't you?"

Huge laugh. Now I'm cooking. I go right into:

"By the way, for those of you listening on radio. Seated at the head table are . . . Terrance Hunt of the Associated Press; David Brock of the *American Spectator;* Lani Guinier of Philadelphia, Pennsylvania; the President of the United States; to his left, Zoë Baird of New Haven, Connecticut; Hector and Consuelo Vasquez, Ms. Baird's driver and nanny, also of New Haven and Tegucigalpa, Honduras; Arkansas state trooper Bobby Fortenberry; to his left, the MacDougals of Little Rock, Arkansas; the First Lady; businessman Nyungen Binh Hac, who I understand is a friend of Ron Brown's, of Ho Chi Minh City and Los Angeles; his wife Mai Kao Hac, and their four children. Admiral Bobby Ray Inman is expected momentarily."

Huge laughs. Rolling laughs. The President's laughing, Hillary is *shaking*. I'm almost embarrassed, frankly, describing how well I did. But it was really something! In fact, you know what? I think it might be less embarrassing if I didn't describe it myself and just let you read some of John Podhoretz's review from the *New York Post*.

> . . . if you happened to be channel-zapping Saturday night and stopped on C-SPAN, you would have seen some dazzling comedy from the man who ought to be the next post-midnight star . . . as his brilliant and utterly fearless monologue proved, he has exactly the hard edge and political sophistication that could make the "Late Late Show with Al Franken" a cultural phenomenon . . . The cleverness of these Beltway barbs was to be expected from the man responsible in part for some of the most brilliant political satire of our time . . .

I mean I was cooking! In comedy terms, I strode the Earth as a colossus.

Go ahead. Read it again.

> . . . if you happened to be channel-zapping Saturday night and stopped on C-SPAN, you would have seen some dazzling comedy from the man who ought to be the next post-midnight star . . . as his brilliant and utterly fearless monologue proved, he has exactly the hard edge and political sophistication that could

make the "Late Late Show with Al Franken" a
cultural phenomenon . . . The cleverness of
these Beltway barbs was to be expected from the
man responsible in part for some of the most
brilliant political satire of our time . . .

That. Is a hell of a review!

*(The full text of Mr. Podhoretz's review can be found on
the Internet via ftp at nypost.com, under the file podhoretz/
reviews/sycophantic/franken.)*

27
PHIL GRAMM: EVERYBODY'S FAVORITE BASTARD

So far, every bit of polling evidence seems to suggest that the more people get to know Phil Gramm, the less they like him.

As I write this in August, he's slipped from double to single digits in the national polls and is down to 5 percent in New Hampshire. Talking to Judy Woodruff on CNN's *Inside Politics*, Gramm ascribed his slippage to the statistical inadequacies of the polls themselves. "These polls, you've gotta remember, Judy, have a margin of error of seven points."

Which conceivably could put him at negative 2 percent.

It's not surprising that people aren't taking to him. Gramm himself admits that he sometimes rubs people the wrong way. "I didn't come to Washington to be loved," he likes to say, "and I haven't been disappointed."

That's the bravado of an anti-government budget hawk. But it also exhibits a hint of the sort of self-deprecating humor that voters like so much in their politicians. "I'm going to test whether, in the age of television, someone as ugly as I am can get elected President."*

That's likeable. But consider for a minute that Gramm wasn't referring to mere *physical* ugliness.

Here, after all, is a man who wants to cut food stamps because: "We're the only nation in the world where all our poor people are fat."

Here, too, is a fellow who started off a meeting of his Senate reelection campaign by telling his staff, "I can do any one of your jobs as well as you, but I don't have the time."

During a floor debate on social security, another senator argued that the legislation under consideration would hurt people over 80. Gramm's response: "Most people don't have the luxury of living to be 80 years old, so it's hard for me to feel sorry for them."

And there was the time that an elderly black widow approached Gramm after a speech in Texas. When she told him that his proposals to cut social security and Medicare would make it difficult for people like her to remain independent, Gramm replied, "You haven't thought about a new husband, have you?"

Basically, Gramm is a big jerk.

But I get the feeling that he considers this his biggest strength. Gramm has been counting on his reputation as the Senate's Angriest White Male, plus his huge campaign war chest, to carry him to the nomination.

* No.

Why isn't it working?

Some say it's because Gramm is the biggest hypocrite in the race. Gramm told the last Republican convention: "In all the world, only in Cuba and North Korea and in the Democratic party in America do we still have organized political groups who believe that the answer to every problem is more government." Yet Gramm himself has lived off the government his entire life. David Segal of the *Washington Monthly* writes:

> The government helped bring him into this world (he was born in a military hospital), funded his upbringing (his father was an army sergeant), paid for him to attend private school (with GI insurance money Gramm's mother received when her husband died), and even picked up the tab for graduate school (thanks to a National Defense Fellowship). After getting his Ph.D., Gramm got a job at Texas A&M, which is state-run, was elected to the House of Representatives, and then to the Senate. In sum, Phil Gramm joined the government rolls the first day of his life and has never left.

And being anti-government hasn't stopped Gramm from backing ridiculously expensive projects like the Superconducting Supercollider that bring federal money back to Texas. "I'm carrying so much pork, I'm beginning to get trichinosis," he once bragged to a local paper.

But I don't think Gramm's lack of physical charisma, his general nastiness, or even his blatant hypocrisy are to blame for his failure to catch on with Republican voters. I think the real problem is his boob fetish.

Bear with me a minute. I can support this.

Let's wade in slowly. When Larry King asked him last March if he'd consider a woman as his running mate, Gramm replied, "Sophia Loren is not a citizen." Okay. So far, so good.

In June, I was watching a CNN report on Gramm in which he discussed his use of the local library as a schoolboy: "We always went there eagerly awaiting the arrival of the next edition of *National Geographic* to look at all those ladies from faraway places who were topless in the magazine." Mighty incriminating. In fact, I could probably rest my case there. But I haven't even played my high card yet.

Much has already been made of Gramm's $7,500 investment in a soft-core porn movie in 1974. First of all, it's worth mentioning that many people call soft core movies "tit" films. But even more damning is the account offered in the *New Republic* by Gramm's former brother-in-law, George Caton, with whom Gramm invested the money.

Caton describes the moment that Gramm's interest in the investment potential of nudie films was first piqued, viewing rushes from the work-in-progress *Truck Stop Women:* "It really got Phil titillated because there was frontal nudity in it." Pow! "Really puts the nail in the coffin, don't you think?"*

---

* I've since found strong empirical support for my theory. Most incriminating was a January 29, 1996, article in *The New*

So Gramm's got a boob fetish, which is why the religious right doesn't trust him. And without their support, Gramm has no chance of getting the nomination. But that hasn't stopped Gramm from doggedly pursuing his party's nod. So doggedly, in fact, that he's working his poor wife, Wendy, nearly to death.

Mrs. Gramm was hospitalized with heatstroke in July after Rollerblading a hilly fifty-mile leg of the Cycle Across Maryland Tour in sweltering ninety-plus degree heat. According to the Associated Press she had been "combining her love of skating with efforts to boost support for her husband." Most of the participants rode bikes, but Mrs. Gramm chose to Rollerblade, I guess because it's harder to wave to crowds when you're holding on to handlebars. Also, none of the other participants were scheduled to attend a series of campaign lunches and evening events along the route.

Barbara Bush was never asked to do anything like this.

But if you get beyond the fact that Gramm is ugly, mean, hypocritical, mammario-fetishistic, and drives

---

Republic. During the New Hampshire primary season, writer Michael Lewis accompanied Gramm on a visit to the home of Matt and Kate Conway, two undecided voters. Lewis describes his post-visit conversation with the couple as follows:

"I ask Kate if she noticed that Gramm looked her in the chest as he spoke to her. She did; it was one of the things she noticed most about him. Her husband seemed slightly shocked. "I didn't want to tell you," she explains.

his wife like a mule, he does have a certain folksy charm. Take, for example, Gramm's hardworking little buddy, Dickey Flatt, a printer from Mexia, Texas. According to Gramm: "Whether you see Dickey Flatt at the PTA or the Boy Scouts or at his church, try as he may he never quite gets that blue ink off the end of his fingers."

Gramm's respect for Dickey Flatt is so great that he's devised a philosophy of governance based on the man. Gramm claims that he won't support any government program which fails the "Dickey Flatt test"; namely, "Is it worth taking money from Dickey Flatt" to pay for the program?

Back in 1994, Gramm-watcher David Segal actually called Dickey to ask whether several programs Gramm had proposed or supported passed the Dickey Flatt test. Dickey's responses ranged from "No, that would not pass the test" to "That is just an *awful* idea, absolutely *awful*."

I'm sure a number of Gramm's proposals would pass the Dickey Flatt test. One of these might be welfare reform, where Gramm has led the charge to get rid of Aid to Families with Dependent Children, make cuts in Medicaid and turn it into a block grant, cut home heating allowances and food stamps, and deny assistance to welfare moms who can't find work. He admitted on *Meet the Press* that there would be some pain: "And I know, when we begin welfare reform, you'll have every horror story imaginable brought up. You can't change this mammoth system without hurting some people."

Gramm seems to be saying that the big challenge in

reforming welfare will be to ignore these horror stories of pain and suffering. I agree. In fact, I think the larger challenge here is not just to ignore these stories, but to *laugh* at them.

That's why I've come up with my own Dickey Flatt test. I call it the Stewey Moss test. Stewey's a guy I went to grade school with. Now, just about every third-grade class in America has one kid who thinks it's funny to blow up a frog with a cherry bomb. Stewey was that kid.

I decided to construct a welfare horror story based on the Gramm cuts, but not to print the story unless it passed the Stewey Moss test. That is, unless it made Stewey laugh.

I looked Stewey up. When I reached him at his printing shop in Canadia, Minnesota, I said, "Stewey, do you still derive perverse pleasure from laughing at the misfortune of others?"

"Did Rose Kennedy own a black dress?!" he chuckled. Same old Stewey.

I explained the premise of the Stewey Moss test, and I must say Stewey was flattered and eager to participate.

"Okay," I said. "It's 1997, and the Gramm welfare reform plan has gone into effect. Let's say there's this housewife and she has two little kids, and her husband, who makes about $38,000 a year, suddenly dies."

"That's funny. How did he die?"

"I don't know, Stewey. Maybe a car accident."

"How about some teenager drops a bowling ball off a highway overpass? That's funny."

"Fine. Anyway, the husband had no life insurance, so the wife is left with almost no money. And what she does have is quickly dissipated by mortgage payments."

"Why doesn't she get a job?"

"Well, she does. But there's a lot of unemployment in her area, so the best she can do is a job at a fast-food place."

"Who's taking care of the kids?"

"You're ahead of me. Actually, she can't afford child care, so the kids sort of take care of themselves. So, one day, her little girl gets sick."

"Funny."

"So, the mom stays home from work to take care of her daughter, and she gets fired. And now she's considered an able-bodied adult who refuses to work, so she's ineligible for any cash assistance."

"And this could happen?"

"Yes. Under Gramm's plan."

"Well, then I'm laughin'!"

"Wait. So the girl's really sick, and the mom takes her to the hospital. But it's late November and the state's run out of its block grant for Medicaid. They can't spend any money on Medicaid cases till January, so she's out of luck."

"What's wrong with the kid?"

"We're not sure. In fact, she has something that requires a lot of investigative work. So the mom spends her last four hundred dollars on tests, only to find out they need to do more tests."

"That is fucking hysterical."

"So there's no money, and the bank repossesses the house."

"I'm on the floor."

"Wait, wait. So now she and the kids have to sleep in the car, except that they also repossess the car, so they go to a shelter."

"That's good! A lot of crazies in a shelter!"

"Right. And mom and the kids are totally freaked out. The girl's still sick, and just when they're thinking life couldn't possibly get any worse, the shelter gets closed down for lack of funds."

"Stop, I'm peeing my pants!"

"So, they have to sleep on the street. And there's a cold snap, so during the night the sick little girl freezes to death. What do you think?"

"I love it. But could the girl be frozen in some kind of weird position?"

"Hmmm. How 'bout she's frozen like Rodin's 'Thinker'?"

"That is fuckin' *hi*larious!"

"So it passes the Stewey Moss test?"

"Absolutely! But one thing. Under the Gramm plan, is there any chance the government might just mow down destitute kids with machine guns?"

"No, Stewey."

"Just asking."

28
FUN WITH NEXIS

One more obnoxious thing about Gramm that I didn't cover in the last chapter: he's a famous publicity hog. In fact, he's the absolute worst. And I can prove it too.

Here's how. You've probably heard this joke construction:

> The most dangerous place in *(blank)* is between *(blank)* and a camera.

It's used a lot. I first heard it as: "The most dangerous place in Washington is between Phil Gramm and a camera." That doesn't prove much. Since then I've also heard: "The most dangerous place in the capital is between Newt Gingrich and a camera" and "The most dangerous place in the world is between Alan Dershowitz and a camera."

So I asked Geoff to do a Nexis search. For those readers not familiar with the latest advances in database technology, a Nexis search is something that allows us, at no small expense, to search hundreds of magazines and newspapers for articles which mention a certain person, subject, or key phrase.

For example, let's say you wanted to look up all references to Gingrich's first wife. You would type in: Gingrich AND geometry teacher. Or you might type in: Gingrich AND deadbeat dad. Or: Gingrich AND cancer surgery.

Gingrich AND geometry teacher yielded 33 stories.
Gingrich AND deadbeat dad yielded 188 stories.
Gingrich AND cancer surgery yielded 91 stories.

You get the idea. Well, I wanted to test my theory that it is more dangerous to stand between Phil Gramm and a camera than between anyone else and a camera. So I asked Geoff to perform this search:

dangerous w/10 [within ten words] between w/ 15 camera.

Nexis spat out 64 stories, which Geoff went through very painstakingly. The results were fascinating. Most important, they proved me right.

Twenty-three stories had nothing to do with the line: "the most dangerous place to stand is between *(blank)* and a camera."

The remaining 41 stories, however, all contained that joke construction. Here's how it broke down:

Phil Gramm—19

politicians—4

Newt Gingrich—3

congressmen—2

O.J. trial legal experts—2

O.J. lawyers—1

Alan Dershowitz—1

Bill Bennett—1

Jesse Jackson—1

Chuck Schumer—1

Stephen Jones (Tim McVeigh's lawyer)—1

Dallas mayor Steve Bartlett—1

Senators—1

Pat Leahy—1

professional mediator Bill Usery—1

"a certain congressman" (probably Phil Gramm)—1

The evidence clearly indicates that it is at least six times more dangerous to stand between Phil Gramm and a camera than between anybody else and a camera.

A couple of interesting sidelights. As I thought, the joke *was* originally used in reference to Phil Gramm. It first appeared in a 1982 *New York Times* article entitled "Texan Irks Colleagues on Budget."

The Nexis also kicked up a 1994 syndicated column by Molly Ivins in which she writes of Gramm: "I swear to God, he once nearly trampled me and Marilyn Schwartz of the *Dallas Morning News* to get in front of a lens at the Republican national convention in '88."

So it's not just a clever joke. Apparently, it really *is* dangerous to stand between Phil Gramm and a camera.

This whole exercise was actually a lot of fun. And since we had Nexis up and cranking, I thought we'd just go to town. Really kick out the Nexis jams. It cost me not a few simoleons, but Geoff and I were having a great time. And it was certainly easier than actually sitting down and writing something.

And so we spent the rest of the day typing in search requests:

Packwood AND tongue	336 stories
Gingrich AND grotesque	432
Specter AND hopeless	452
Pat Robertson AND crazy OR nutty OR lunatic	677
Gingrich AND bizarre	992
Limbaugh AND fat	1,084
Buchanan AND racist	1,089

D'Amato AND corruption	
OR crooked	1,310
Gingrich AND frankly	3,908
Clinton AND sex	33,948
Dole AND mean	53,695
Al Franken AND egomaniac	2

I'm thinking of doing a whole book of these. If you have any good search ideas please send them to the same address listed for the death threats.

29

ARLEN! ARLEN! ARLEN! AND OTHER THOUGHTS ON THE '96 ELECTION

When I hear pundits handicap the '96 Republican race, I'm always surprised that they leave Arlen Specter out of the first tier of candidates.

He has so much going for him: he's from a big state with a large number of delegates and electoral votes. He's been a U.S. senator for fourteen years. He got a lot of name recognition from the Clarence Thomas hearings, where he attacked Anita Hill for making accusations about sexual harassment. Speaking of the women's vote, he's pro-choice! And best of all, he's Jewish, with access to a lot of pro-Israel money.

If I were Arlen Specter, I would assign a transition team right now.

But first things first, I guess. Planning his coronation at the Republican convention. I've been trying to envision it since Specter announced his candidacy, and I've decided it will look something like this:

First of all, lots of signs. But they won't say "Specter." Focus groups will show that the name "Specter" scares people. So the signs will read "Arlen." And when Wyoming puts him over the top, there'll be thousands of grassroots Republican loyalists who have worked years just for this moment, all chanting at the top of their lungs, "Arlen!" "Arlen!" "Arlen!"

The theme of the Arlen Convention, as it will come to be known, will be "The Big Tent." Or perhaps, "The Huge Tent." Or maybe, "The Extraordinarily Large Tent." There'll be a big Christian Coalition press conference on the eve of the convention, where Ralph Reed will back off from his threat to oppose any ticket with a pro-abortion nominee. Instead, Reed announces he'll support any Republican ticket that doesn't include a nominee who has actually *performed* an abortion.

I've been giving this a lot of thought. As I see it, there are two possible scenarios that could lead to an Arlen Convention. The first is a plane crash. A 747 carrying Dole, Gramm, Buchanan, and Alexander crashes . . . on top of Newt Gingrich and Colin Powell.

The second is a bus crash. It plays out kind of the same way.

WHAT IN GOD'S NAME IS ARLEN SPECTER THINKING?

REALLY. What is he *thinking*?

Forgetting he's pro-choice in today's Republican party. Forgetting that the women for whom that would be attractive mostly remember him as the man who accused Anita Hill of committing perjury. Forgetting that he's humorless and pasty-looking. He's Jewish!

See, I've been following the whole Colin Powell phenomenon, and it's led me to one indisputable conclusion: The first Jew to be elected President of the United States will have to be a four-star general.

That gave me the idea of looking for a Jew in the military that we could start grooming for a run at the White House. So I had Geoff do some research. Unfortunately, it turns out that the highest-ranking Jew in the armed forces right now is Comptroller of the Coast Guard.

As I write this, we have no idea of what General Powell will do in '96. Perot showed us in '92 that Americans are yearning for a figure who can rise above the partisan bickering of our two national parties. Someone who can inspire us and move us forward together. Polls show, however, that this time Americans would prefer someone who hasn't claimed that he and a guard dog once fought five mysterious intruders on his front lawn.

Of course, if Powell doesn't run every Republican candidate has the general at the top of his short list for running mate. All except for Alan Keyes. As if Keyes doesn't have enough disadvantages. In addition to being unknown and unemployed, he's the only Republican candidate who might actually *lose* points by putting Colin Powell on the ticket.

I have given a lot of thought to the composition of the '96 Republican ticket. The danger of writing a book like this is that by the time it comes out everything will have changed. In politics a month can be a lifetime, and books take a lot of lead time. You've got to write the book, pose for the cover, then wait. You should know that, as I'm writing this, it is March 1978. So at the risk of looking foolish, here are some thoughts.

Assuming Dole wins the nomination, and there's no reason not to assume that, other than no one in the Republican party seems to really want him . . . assuming he wins the nomination, he has to use the second spot on the ticket to address the age problem. He has to pick someone young enough to represent a different generation and yet experienced enough to take over if, God forbid, Dole only reaches normal U.S. life expectancy.

Dole's been joking about the age issue in his speeches lately: "I'll put Strom Thurmond on the ticket for age balance." Actually, I didn't start worrying about Dole's age until after I heard that joke. Maybe he's lost it.*

By the way, for the record, I like Strom Thurmond because he's the only senator who still refers to a microphone as "the machine."

I think New Jersey governor Christine Whitman would make a good running mate for Dole. True, she's pro-choice and the Christian right already doesn't trust Dole, so they might take a hike. But the Republicans need women, and she's smart and tough.

---

* During the Reagan Administration, Dole was present at a ceremony that included every living ex-president. Looking at a tableau of Ford, Carter, and Nixon, Dole said, "There they are: Hear No Evil, See No Evil, and Evil."

Plus, I have a theory about Christine Whitman that I've never heard anyone else articulate. Here it is: Americans love royalty. No couple represents royalty to Americans more than Prince Charles and Princess Di. Christine Whitman is a dead-on cross between Prince Charles and Princess Di.

So I think Christine Whitman would be a good addition to any ticket. For other vice presidential possibilities, you have to look first to the field of presidential candidates. Since the Eagleton debacle in '72 and the Quayle draft-deer-in-headlights near-disaster in '88, it's become clear that it's safest to pick someone who's already run for the nomination and lost. That way the media have already, supposedly, investigated the person, and they're afraid to come up with any new bombshells because it would make it look like they didn't do their job during the primaries.

So let's say Gramm wins the nomination. You could have a Gramm-Lugar ticket. Although Lugar is considered unlucky. He announced his candidacy the day of the Oklahoma City bombing. So . . . Gramm-Buchanan. Wow! Or . . . Buchanan-Gramm! No, wait! Buchanan-Dornan!

By the way, I talked to Bob Dornan yesterday. We met a couple years ago on Bill Maher's *Politically Incorrect*, and we talk occasionally. After the White House Correspondents dinner he called me, sounding annoyed: "Someone told me you did a rough joke about me. What was it?"

I told him the joke, which you've read already: "Having Al D'Amato lead an ethics investigation is like getting Bob Dornan to head up a mental health task force."

There was a beat on the other end of the phone, then, "Oh yeah, that's fine."

Anyway, yesterday I told Dornan I was trying to envision an Arlen Specter convention. So I asked if he had any idea what a Dornan convention might look like. I said I thought it would be very militaristic. He said, "Right. We'd have a parade of tanks and an overfly of B-2's."*

Back to vice presidential possibilities (of which Dornan is not realistically one, because he's a crazy homophobe).

Jack Kemp. He's an economic conservative. He ran for president in '88. And he has demonstrated, more than any other Republican, a desire to expand the party to include more blacks and minorities. Which is why no Republicans actually voted for him in '88.

But in a general election, many political observers believe Kemp would attract millions of black votes. Mainly, this is about his support of ideas like empowerment zones and tenant ownership of low-cost housing. But on more than a few occasions, I've heard pundits say that minorities are comfortable with Jack Kemp because he's a former NFL quarterback. As Newt Gingrich once said admiringly, "Jack Kemp has

---

* Here's a funny thing I read about Bob in *Newsweek*. Apparently, during his brief career as a fighter pilot, he crashed three jets and a helicopter. I'm not sure how much that cost taxpayers, but I'm pretty certain it's more than he's going to get in presidential matching funds.

probably showered with more blacks than most Republicans have shaken hands with."

I've heard the same kind of thing said about Bill Bradley, and it always strikes me as odd. But I suppose there's something to it. So as a service to my readers, a short list:

Politicians Who Have Showered with Blacks

Sen. Bill Bradley (D–N.J.)—New York Knicks— showered with Walt Frazier, Willis Reed, and Earl Monroe

Rep. Jim Bunning (R–Ky.)—Philadelphia Phillies—showered with Dick Allen, Curt Flood, and Ferguson Jenkins

Jack Kemp (former Sec. HUD)—Buffalo Bills— showered with Haven Moses and O.J. Simpson

Rep. Steve Largent (R–Okla.)—Seattle Seahawks—showered with John L. Williams, Curt Warner, and Ken Easley

Rep. J.C. Watts (R–Okla.)*—Oklahoma Sooners—showered with Billy Sims

This is obviously not a complete list. I'm guessing, for example, that Congressman Mel Reynolds has showered with at least one underage black woman.

* Is himself black

The point is that if Jack Kemp had stayed in the league one more year, he could have also showered with Al Cowlings. That has no relevance to anything in particular, but it would have made my list more interesting.

30
PAT BUCHANAN: NAZI LOVER

In case you've reached this point in the book and are saying to yourself: "Why should I listen to this guy? He doesn't know anything. The only stuff he *pretends* to know comes from his research assistant. *And* he just wasted forty-five seconds of my life, which I will never get back, making me read a list of politicians who have showered with blacks." In case you're saying that to yourself, let me show you a little something from the 1992 year-end issue of *Rolling Stone* magazine:

> Comedy Central aired its own live coverage of both conventions alongside the sober networks, with comedian Al Franken anchoring . . . But Comedy Central could get serious, too. Franken sensed—and said—that the ugly tone of Pat Buchanan's speech was a mistake for the Republicans, that it would backfire. It wasn't until days or even weeks later that the traditional pundits

called the speech the beginning of the end for the Bush campaign. It was disorienting to watch a comedy broadcast that almost incidentally told more truth and offered more insight than most networks and newspapers and at the same time was so much more comfortable to watch.

Yep. That's right. I was the only one. Not Dan Rather, not Tom Brokaw, not Peter Jennings, not even Cokie Roberts, none of them understood what I, the guy you're doubting, understood: that Pat Buchanan was scaring America and guaranteeing that George Bush would receive the lowest percentage of popular votes of any incumbent president in American history.

Please understand that I called it *during* the speech. See, our Comedy Central convention coverage, which by the way was sponsored by Mentos, was comprised largely of live, simultaneous commentary on the speeches. This requires a quick wit and a commanding knowledge of the broader sweep of world history insofar as it applies to contemporary American politics. Also it's good if you can get an advance copy of the speech and have a small team of writers feeding you lines.

Unfortunately, we didn't get an advance copy of Buchanan's speech. If we had, I could have looked like a genius by predicting that he would make not one, not two, not three, but four attacks on homosexuals.

Maybe I should have expected this from a man who had once said about AIDS: "The homosexuals have declared war upon nature and nature is exacting an awful retribution." But why *four* attacks? This was, after all, the first prime-time speech of the 1992 Republican convention. America was watching, and America got the message: Pat Buchanan really hates gay people.

But the high point was when Buchanan announced that "there is a religious war going on in our country." I'm sorry, but when you're Jewish and you hear "religious war," you get nervous. We haven't done well in religious wars. At least, not before 1949.

Back to Buchanan's speech. "And in that struggle for the soul of America, Clinton and Clinton are on the other side, and George Bush is on our side." And the Republicans on the floor were screaming with delight. Fists were in the air! It was really something.

So I said, "Is it just me, or is Pat Buchanan making a big mistake? Isn't he just scaring people?" And it *was* just me. Everywhere else on TV, analysts were saying that this was just the kind of "red meat" needed to energize the right and get them working for George Bush. And I was saying, "Wow! Aren't the Bush people upset? This is going to cost them California. And the Rust Belt states of Ohio, Illinois, and Michigan. Why, if Perot decides to reenter the race, I'll bet Bush doesn't get more than 38 percent of the popular vote and only picks up 168 electoral votes to Clinton's 370." Or something like that; I can't remember my exact words.

And so, in keeping with my record of fearless, ahead-of-the-curve punditry, I'd like to make a little prediction right here.

He's going to do it again.

Only this time it will be worse. Because this time the people screaming will be his delegates. In fact, I believe that Pat Buchanan may very well win the nomination. That gives you some idea how low my regard is for Republican primary voters. I know that's an ad hominem attack on millions of people I've never met. But let me tell you a little about Pat Buchanan.

Where to begin?

First of all, he's the only man running for president who has assaulted a cop. Or at least bragged about it. In his autobiography, *Right from the Beginning*, Buchanan spends a number of pages relishing what was "among the great, dumb deeds of my life." It occurred two weeks before his twenty-first birthday and involved, basically, getting pulled over for speeding, cursing out two police officers, resisting arrest, and then kicking one of them in the ass: "I put a size $10\frac{1}{2}$ cordovan where I thought it might do some good."

As the *New Republic* put it in their 1990 review, "Much of his memoir is a gleeful recounting of brawls, including ones in which he and his brother Hank ganged up on single victims, or 'sucker-punched' guys who deserved it. The book is suffused with a thug's love for combat."

Evidently, Buchanan's love for combat had its limits. After being expelled from college for the assault, he received a 4-F for a bad knee (presumably not the one used to kick the cop's butt), and never served in the military. In case you're concerned, the knee healed nicely, and now Buchanan's daily jogs keep him fit and trim.

Buchanan's beliefs were shaped by his father, William Buchanan, an accountant whose heroes included Joe McCarthy and Francisco Franco. The Buchanans were of Irish and Scotch-Irish ancestry, not Apache as Pat's current "no-immigrant" policy might suggest, and were devout Catholics. "We lived in a world of clarity and absolutes."

One of those absolutes is the belief in the superiority of Christianity. When asked about that earlier this year, Buchanan said, "I believe that Jesus Christ is the son of God and is actually God and that that is the path to salvation, so quite obviously I believe it's superior to Buddhism and Taoism and other faiths, yes." I'm fine with that, I guess. But, not to be flippant, will someone explain to me how Jesus can be both the *son* of God and also God. Does it have something to do with the Holy Trinity? Help me here; I'm from an inferior religion.

This superiority appears to extend mainly to *white* Christians. As a speechwriter in the Nixon White House, Buchanan was a vehement opponent of integration. In a memo obtained from the Nixon archives, Buchanan called Martin Luther King, Jr., "one of the most divisive men in contemporary history" (remember, this is a memo to *Richard Nixon*), and later wrote the president that "the ship of integration is going down. It's not our ship."

Not surprisingly, Buchanan saw no problem with apartheid, and in another memo to Nixon referred to South Africa's 1960 Sharpeville Massacre, in which sixty-seven blacks were killed, as "whites mistreating a couple of blacks."

In fact, Buchanan admired the white regime in Pretoria so much that after Nixon resigned, he made a bid to become Gerald Ford's Ambassador to South Africa. I don't know why Ford turned him down. It would have been just so *perfect*.

By 1990, Buchanan was still defending apartheid, mocking those who believe "White rule of a Black majority is inherently wrong."

> . . . where did we get that idea? The Founding Fathers did not believe this. They did not give Indians, who were still living a tribal existence, the right to vote us out of North America. When they created the republic, they restricted the franchise to property-owning males, believing that not every man was qualified to rule, nor every people prepared for self-government. If the past 30 years taught us nothing else, it has surely taught us that. To elevate "majority rule" to the level of divine revelation is a heresy of the American idea.

Buchanan has repeatedly expressed disdain for what he called "the one man, one vote Earl Warren system," and once suggested "improving" the Bill of Rights to restrict voting to those who have paid at least $300 in taxes during the previous year. I wonder if there would be an adjustment for inflation on that.

Today, as America's preeminent nativist, Buchanan continues to spout this kind of racist and undemocratic piffle, to borrow a word from George Will. On restricting the immigration of Third World types, Buchanan made this point: "If we had to take a million immigrants in—say, Zulus—next year, or Englishmen, and put them in Virginia, what group would be easier to assimilate?" I think the Englishmen, don't you? But I think the million Zulus would do better than a million Pygmies.

Buchanan's point can be found in his rhetorical question, "Who speaks for the Euro-Americans, who founded the U.S.A. . . . Is it not time to take America back?"

Sure. Let's take it back! How? Buchanan proposes a literal Fortress America erected with border walls and trade barriers. A fierce opponent of NAFTA and GATT, Buchanan blames free trade for the loss of good-paying American jobs. That didn't stop him from buying a Mercedes-Benz and calling American cars "lemons" in 1992. When the Bush campaign criticized him for owning a German car, Buchanan said that his wife made him buy it.

Now, before I get into the Nazi stuff, I have a horrible confession. I've met Pat Buchanan. I spent some time with him over a four-day period. And I liked him very much.

It was during the 1988 Democratic convention in Atlanta, and I was there doing commentary for CNN. And of all the CNN people, Buchanan was the most accessible and unfailingly good-natured and charming. When I told my friends back in New York, I would invariably get a response like: "Yeah, well, Goebbels was charming."

That is so unfair. First of all, Goebbels wasn't charming. He was known as an ill-tempered backbiter.

Also, Goebbels was part of a small group that presided over the most horrible genocide in the history of man. Buchanan, on the other hand, has merely devoted a large part of his career to *defending* people like Goebbels.

Since the early 80s Buchanan has attacked "the hairy-chested Nazi hunters" in the Justice Department's Office of Special Investigations (OSI). "Why not devote those sources to going after organized crime . . . instead of running down 70-year-old camp guards."

John Demjanjuk was one of those 70-year-old camp guards. For years, Buchanan has defended Demjanjuk against charges that he was the infamous Ivan the Terrible of Treblinka and called him "the victim of a greater miscarriage of justice than Alfred Dreyfus." Dreyfus, of course, was guilty of nothing. Buchanan's defense of Demjanjuk was simple. He was a guard at a *different* concentration camp.

> The Soviets took testimony . . . from one Ignat Danilchenko, who said Demjanjuk was a member of his guard platoon at Sobibor . . . Yet at Demjanjuk's trial the witnesses against him all testified he was at Treblinka . . . Can a man be at two places at once?

Good point. What were the chances of someone like Demjanjuk being a guard at *two* camps? I'm guessing that this is why Buchanan supported the "Three Strikes and You're Out" part of Clinton's crime bill. He thought it meant that to put a Nazi war criminal away, he had to be a guard at three separate camps.

Today Buchanan is fighting Demjanjuk's deportation, even though the former SS volunteer lied on his original visa application. By the way, did you know that to become a citizen of this country, there are different rules for ex-Communists and ex-Nazis? It's true. You can't get citizenship if you've *ever* been a Communist. You can't get citizenship if you were a Nazi *from 1939 to 1945*. It's probably a good policy. I'd trust a guy who became a Nazi in 1946. You know he's not a fair-weather friend.

Buchanan has proven that he, unlike most other politicians, is no fair-weather friend. Particularly if you're an accused former Nazi. But in a way, I trust Pat Buchanan. He is a man who stands by his principles. And the more repugnant and dangerous those principles, the smarter I'm going to look next summer when Pat Buchanan single-handedly scares the country into reelecting Bill Clinton.

31
THE MIDDLE-CLASS
SQUEEZE

This was going to be a fairly exhaustive chapter on how life is getting harder and harder for middle-class Americans. How real wages are going down, how most couples now have to work at two jobs to make ends meet.

I even had an especially obnoxious Limbaugh quote to start the thing off. In *The Way Things Ought to Be* he writes: "Why is it that whenever a corporation fires workers it is never speculated that the workers might have deserved it?" I've had the same thought about plane crashes.

Unfortunately, I just haven't been able to concentrate this week. See, over the weekend we drove up to my fourteen-year-old daughter's camp. As you already know, the book has suffered considerably because of my commitment to hands-on, always-there-for-you, sensitive-dad parenting. Which is why the Frankens serve as much better role models for the

American family than the Doles, the Gingriches, the Reagans, the Wills, or the Wilsons.

Most of the time it's fun. But not this weekend. We drove up to Thomasin's camp to see her in a play. See, it's an arts camp. The kind that liberals send their kids to so they can get in touch with their creative sides.

Well, she got in touch all right. About halfway through the play, this six-foot, sixteen-year-old kid from Long Island with a ponytail planted one right on her lips. And two scenes later she kissed another guy. And then at the end of the play her character died of a drug overdose.

I've been having trouble dealing with it ever since. Frankly, it's been pretty tough to work with the image constantly running through my head of some long-haired punk from Long Island stealing the innocence of my only daughter.

My shrink said this is a normal part of the father-daughter relationship. He suggested I channel my emotions into a chapter on teenage promiscuity, illegitimacy, and AIDS.

That's when I decided to change therapists. The new one says I need to let go of this chapter and move on to something lighter and more fun.

32

RUBBERNECKING ON THE INFOTAINMENT SUPERHIGHWAY

We are now living in an era where the wall between news and entertainment has been eaten away like the cartilage in David Crosby's septum.

That's why the Information Superhighway means different things to different people. To Al Gore it means out-of-work aerospace workers accessing a video classroom to retrain themselves for the transition from a cold war economy to an information economy. To Clarence Thomas it means 24-hour-a-day pornography.

That's why I think the Information Superhighway should more accurately be called the Infotainment Superhighway. And why all of us who work in the media should be called "infotainers." Dan Rather is an infotainer. Maybe more info than tainer. Connie Chung is about half info, half tainer. Her husband, more tainer than info. Rush Limbaugh is a disinfotainer. (See rest of book.)

More Americans get their news from ABC News than from any other source. At least that's what they say on ABC News, which is where I got all the information for this book.

That's why the Disney–ABC deal had me so worried. You might remember Disney's proposed America Amusement Park in Virginia. Disney was going to pave over a Civil War battlefield to put up a theme park about American history. No irony there. Anyway, the park was going to have an attraction "simulating" the experience of being a slave. I looked into the plans for the attraction, and all I can say is that it is a gross distortion of history to have the Underground Railroad loop the loop.

With the mainstream getting more and more monolithic, thank goodness we've got the alternative media. Like C-SPAN. Which is all info and no tainment. Except that I did see an unexpectedly engrossing *Booknotes* interview last week with the author of the definitive analysis of sliding pay-scales for G-S level federal employees. The guy had visual aids and everything.

Sometimes I worry, though, that on the Infotainment Superhighway, a lot more people are driving on the tainment lanes than the info lanes. Either that or we've always been a nation of idiots. Because I've seen some polling statistics lately that are really scary. For example: Only 64 percent of U.S. adults know that when it's winter in New York, it's summer in Australia. Only 53 percent know that Arabs and Jews "have been in conflict over Israel." More Americans can name the judge in the O.J. Simpson trial than the Speaker of the House.*

Speaking of the Speaker, during the '94 House race between Tom Foley and George Nethercutt, a third of the voters in their district believed that whoever won would become Speaker of the House.

My favorite, though, comes from a focus group survey done by Mark Mellman, one of the few Washington pollsters who bothered to return my call. When asked what they thought having dinner at their congressman's house would be like, a majority said they thought they would be served by uniformed servants and eat food that they had "never heard of before." Just out of curiosity, I called my congressman and asked him what he'd serve if I went to his house for dinner. He said, "Probably chicken." But who knows? Maybe it would be "chicken fandango" or something.

So I'm worried that a lot of people just aren't really thinking much about things these days. Which is kind of scary, because with all this new technology, there are a lot of big issues out there that aren't being discussed.

For example, there is one aspect of the Infotainment Superhighway that actually frightens me very much. In fact, I'm a little loath to discuss it publicly. But maybe if it's out in the open, the Senate could hold a hearing on it or something. Because it's a real potential nightmare.

It involves the Internet. No, it's not pornography.

* Lance Ito and Tom Foley

It's something much more frightening. And that is the possibility, I think probability, that before long we will be seeing a new form of terrorism. Mark my words: one of these days you're going to turn on the news and hear some grisly report about a terrorist whom the media will dub "The E-mail Bomber."

Now, I don't know much about the Internet or how it works, but I imagine the E-mail bomber thing would happen this way. Some guy at a university or maybe a big computer company will log up or boot on or whatever. And he'll see a thing saying he has some E-mail. So he'll try to retrieve it, and KABLAM!!!

Pretty frightening, huh? That's why I don't go in for this Internet stuff. Way too dangerous.

33
ANOTHER FEARLESS POLICY INITIATIVE FROM ME

There are some developments along the Infotainment Superhighway that I do find encouraging. As the father of two, I was delighted when the Senate approved a proposal that would give parents a tool to deal with television violence. The tool is the v-chip (v for violence), and it would be installed inside all TV sets 13 inches or larger. A panel would assign each show a rating, which would then be encoded into the show's signal. Parents could then program their TV's to block out shows that are rated as violent.

The beauty is that the chip now only costs about five dollars, and that price will come down until it costs only cents per TV set. The question is, since we have the technology, why not give parents more options?

That's why I'm proposing a twenty-six-chip system that will *really* give us the tools we need to protect our children:

a-chip: blocks out any program containing the word "asshole."

b-chip: blocks out any program about Leona Helmsley.

c-chip: blocks out any program about Leona Helmsley.

d-chip: blocks out all docudramas.

e-chip: blocks out all programs explaining evolution.

f-chip: blocks out farting.

g-chip: blocks out Geraldo.

h-chip: blocks out all programs portraying whores. (Research shows most people believe "whore" starts with an "h.")

i-chip: blocks out all programs that have ironic content.

j-chip: blocks out Jerry Seinfeld, Ted Koppel, Billy Crystal, Paul Reiser, and me.

k-chip: kickboxing.

l-chip: blocks out all commercials for lawyers.

m-chip: blocks out Madonna.

n-chip: blocks out all news.

o-chip: blocks out all news about O.J. Simpson.

p-chip: either "pornography" or "politicians" —still under consideration.

q-chip: would block out programs with Harvey Fierstein, Barney Frank, and Bob Dornan.

r-chip: blocks out programs in which a woman's bosom is referred to as a "rack."

s-chip: blocks out all sitcoms.

t-chip: would block out all toilet humor, particularly "shit" jokes.

u-chip: blocks out all shows explaining the function of the uterus.

w-chip: blocks out all references to "wetlands."

x-chip: blocks out *The X-Files.*

y-chip: blocks out sex scenes where someone yells "yahoo!"

z-chip: blocks out zombie movies that contain adult language or where the zombies eat people.

34
ADVENTURES IN POLITICS
APRIL 29, 1995

WASHINGTON, D.C. WASHINGTON HILTON,
WHITE HOUSE CORRESPONDENTS
ASSOCIATION DINNER.
I CHARM THE SOCKS OFF ARIANNA HUFFINGTON,
MEET NEWT GINGRICH, AND
OFFEND AL D'AMATO

Conan O'Brien gave me a call. He had agreed to perform at the White House Correspondents dinner, and he was nervous. Conan said that the woman from the White House Correspondents Association had told him that the President was scheduled to speak first. Conan told her that he was a little apprehensive about speaking after the President. And she informed him that speaking first had been the President's request, but suggested, "Why don't the two of you work this out between yourselves?"

Conan was nervous because of what had happened a few weeks earlier at the TV and Radio Reporters dinner, where the audience had jeered comedian Bill Maher. Like at the Correspondents dinner, the speaker at the TV and Radio dinner shares the dais with the President. Maher ran afoul of the audience, who felt he crossed the line with jokes like "Phil Gramm is so worried about immigration that he's thinking of deporting his wife." But they were particularly shocked when, discarding a joke, he said something like "fuck this one." In front of the President! A week later Garry Shandling, appearing on Maher's show *Politically Incorrect*, gave Bill some reassurance. "You were part of a long tradition of comedians offending presidents that started when Will Rogers said to FDR, 'Oh, yeah? Well, if you don't think that's funny, you can get out of your chair and blow me.' "

Conan ran through his material. He had a lot of great jokes, including this one: "Evidently, there was quite a disturbance when Pat Buchanan made his announcement for president. Some people jumped onstage and shouted that he was a racist. And those were his supporters!"

There was a joke that referred to a recent shooting incident. Al D'Amato shooting himself in the foot. A few weeks earlier, Senator Pothole had been on the Imus radio show and done an over-the-top Japanese stereotype impression of Judge Ito. It was real Jerry-Lewis-bucktooth-Coke-bottle-glasses stuff, particularly weird since Ito actually has a very strange accent that is not in the least bit Japanese. It created a big flap, and D'Amato had to apologize, but his apology was so weak (an "I'm sorry if anyone was offended" type of thing) that he had to apologize a second time. A couple days later he was rushed to the hospital with heart palpitations, which friends said had been caused by "stress." Conan's joke was, "The entertainment tonight was either going to be me, or Senator D'Amato doing impressions." I suggested a refinement: ". . . me, or Senator D'Amato doing an impression of a Japanese guy having a heart attack."

Conan felt reassured after we talked. I did, too. I thought he had enough strong material to do very well, but not to do better than I had done.

I had been invited to the dinner by Josette Shiner, managing editor of the *Washington Times*, which most liberals outside the Beltway think of as "the Moonie paper" because it's owned by the Unification Church of the Reverend Sun Young Moon. But the *Times* has become a very well respected conservative paper, and for many in Washington a welcome alternative to the *Post*. Moon, I am told, is very hands-off in the day-to-day operation of the paper. For example, staffers are allowed to marry whomever they choose.

I had met Josette a few months before at the Renaissance Weekend, where we hit it off. See? Conservatives like me. And I like conservatives. As people. I'm a people person. The last night of Renaissance, Josette asked me if I had any questions for Newt. This was January 3rd, and she had an exclusive with Gingrich the next day, his first print interview since the '94 election. So I said, "Yeah. Why don't you ask him if he got the idea of churches filling in for government from his personal experience. From when he was a deadbeat dad, and his ex-wife's church had to take up a collection for his ex-wife and kids." Josette thought she might not have time to ask that.

Instead, she thought she might ask him about a discussion my wife, Franni, and I had had a few days earlier. Newt had called a press conference to announce that he was going to give up his 4.5-million-dollar book advance. I told Franni I thought he was

going to admit he had made an error in judgment.
Franni said, "No, he's not that smart."

I said, "No, honey, he's really smart. He's unbelievably smart. He's going to apologize. He's going to
say something like, 'It was wrong of me as the newly
elected Speaker of the House to take a 4.5-million-
dollar advance. It sent the wrong signal. We in Congress are here to serve the people, not line our pockets, and to the extent that I've undermined the
public's trust, blah, blah, blah . . .' Something like
that."

Franni said, "Well, if he's smart enough to apologize, I'm really scared."

At the press conference Gingrich did announce
that he was taking a one dollar advance and a royalty
in lieu of the 4.5 million. But instead of apologizing
he just sprayed invective like a skunk. "We're about to
have the first Republican Congress in forty years, and
I did not want to walk in next Wednesday and give the
embittered defenders of the old order something that
they could run around and yell about." I hate it when
my wife is right.

About a week before the Correspondents dinner,
we received our tickets along with a seating chart,
which had my wife next to the undersecretary of defense and me between Josette and Dr. Ruth West-
heimer. When I called to give my wife's regrets
(because of Little League, not the undersecretary of
defense), Josette's assistant said, "Don't you just love
who we put you next to?!" This is one of the curses of
being a comedian. They think it's magic to put you
next to somebody like Dr. Ruth.

I said, "Well . . . uh, yeah . . ." as diplomatically as possible, while still trying to bring home the point. Which I guess I did.

"Well . . . now that your wife's not coming, we will be rearranging the seating. Is there anyone you see on the chart who you'd like to sit next to?"

"Arianna Huffington."

Arianna (I call her Arianna now) is the wife of Michael Huffington, the oil heir who spent thirty or so million dollars in a losing bid for Dianne Feinstein's Senate seat. The Huffingtons had been the subject of a couple of particularly mean articles in the press. Sidney Blumenthal of the *New Yorker* had called Arianna "the most upwardly mobile Greek since Icarus," and in *Vanity Fair* Maureen Orth accused her of being a New Age cult priestess who yelled at her Mexican help.

Pretty horrible stuff. And I'd get to sit next to her! I called a few people in Washington who might know something about her, including Blumenthal. The consensus was this: When it comes to the Huffingtons, she's the brains of the outfit—and not merely by default.

She was educated at Cambridge University and was the first woman president of the Cambridge Debating Society. Also, she's quite striking, a Greek-born blonde (though not, strictly speaking, a blonde-born Greek), and incredibly charming. She'll do a Pamela Harriman on you. Rivet her attention, gaze into your eyes, make you feel like you're the most enchanting person in the world. Flatter you, laugh at your jokes.

Boy, do I like Arianna Huffington! Man oh man!

Dinner was great. Although I can't remember what they served, Arianna was so fascinating. Or really, I was. Mainly I ragged on Newt. A number of people had told me that she had been raising money for his Empowerment Network, so I thought it'd be fun to tear into him. I guess I did it in such a funny and utterly charming way that she didn't take offense. Lines like, "What kind of sleazebag doesn't support his kids?" Witty stuff like that.

Josette, who was joining in when not engaging the undersecretary of defense, would occasionally defend the Speaker. He's made some mistakes, but he's admitted them, that sort of thing. Arianna talked about a TV show she was developing called *Beat the Press*. The idea was to take on the press, which Arianna felt was getting more cynical and destructive. She said the show was to be produced by Four Point Entertainment, the producers of *American Gladiators*. "Oh, the Tiffany's of TV production," I said. She laughed. It was just delightful.

At one point we were talking about compassion. Arianna heads something called the Center for Effective Compassion. As opposed to ineffective compassion. Way too much of that going around. Republicans think that there has been a "tragedy of American compassion" this century, a phrase borrowed from the book by the same name.* The basic

* *The Tragedy of American Compassion* was written by Marvin Olasky with the financial support of the Heritage Foundation. At one point in the book Olasky seeks a "first-hand look at contemporary compassion to the poor," by dressing

thesis is that liberals' compassion for the underclass had the unintended, or maybe not so unintended, consequence of creating an addiction to dependency and the bureaucracy of the welfare state. I said something about how sad a commentary it is on my generation that we were the ones to coin the phrase "compassion fatigue." Arianna laughed again and talked about how charitable giving had gone up during the Reagan years. I said, "Yeah, but a lot of that was rich guys giving their hospital a colon cancer machine so it'd have one when they needed it." Arianna laughed.

Between dessert and the entertainment there was enough time to mill around and talk to people. I said hi to Wolf Blitzer, chatted briefly with the Israeli ambassador and then with Kennedy (the MTV VJ,

---

up like a street person and spending two whole days on the street. He comes away particularly disgusted with the treatment he received at a Congregational church:

A sweet young volunteer kept putting food down in front of me and asking if I wanted more. Finally I asked, mumbling a bit, "Could I have a Bible?" Puzzled, she tried to figure out what I had said: "Do you want a bagel? A bag?" When I responded, "A Bible," she said, politely but firmly, "I'm sorry, we don't have any Bibles."

For Olansky, this event epitomizes the misguided sense of compassion of modern America. They'll feed your stomach but not your soul. I guess in Olasky's perfect world, a hungry man would walk into a soup kitchen and say, "Could I have a bagel?" And instead he'd receive the King James Bible and a polite but firm, "Not until you've read Second Corinthians."

not the bloated senator). Then I left the ballroom to hit the bathroom, and there in the hallway was Arianna standing with Newt.

"Al, you must meet the Speaker!" Now as I said, I'm a people person. So I tried.

"It is an honor to meet the Speaker of the House." It was the best I could do.

"You guys really helped us out at the end of the hundred days," he said with a friendly smile. He was referring to a bit Chris Farley, who played Newt on SNL, had done a few weeks earlier at the Capitol. It was a little surprise that NBC whipped up for the Speaker.

"I had nothing to do with that," I said pointedly. He seemed a little confused.

"It was a real boost. I was caught totally by surprise."

"Yeah, well, I had nothing to do with that." I felt that I made that clear, and I didn't want to be an asshole about it. "But Chris really had a good time, and couldn't talk about anything else for the whole week." Why am I sucking up to this guy? "Could I say something?" He nodded. You're not supposed to talk politics at these things. But how often would I get this chance? "I believe in the market system. I think that, at the end of the day, what you're doing will lead to a situation where the states are forced to compete with each other to drive out their poor by lowering benefits."

"What's wrong with that?" That's what he said. He was serious too.

Then Dennis Hopper walked up. "You, sir, are a

great man. You are doing great things." He wasn't talking to me. Newt told Hopper how brilliant his performance was in *Blue Velvet*. How he loved Hopper's *intensity*. I started to feel like I was *in Blue Velvet*.

After Hopper left, Gingrich and I talked about Christina Jeffrey, the woman Gingrich had chosen as House historian. He dropped her like a hot potato when it was disclosed that she had once objected to a course on the Holocaust because it failed to present the Nazi and Ku Klux Klan points of view. He defended her, saying, "She's very anti-Semitic and very anti-racist."

"Can I quote you on that?" I wanted to know. Arianna explained to Newt what he had just said.

"I meant very anti-anti-Semitic." See, I get them mixed up all the time.

Conan did great that night. I was a little disappointed that he used his version of the D'Amato joke, but it got a big laugh.

After dinner, I headed over to what everyone considered the hip party, thrown by *Vanity Fair* magazine. When I walked in, I saw Al D'Amato standing in a corner. That's how hip this party was.

D'Amato's fiancée, former gossip columnist Claudia Cohen, recognized me, and when I approached, she introduced me to the senator. "He's from *Saturday Night Live*."

He looked a little agitated. "What was that thing about my sistah having sex with a donkey?"

A couple weeks earlier cast member Mark McKinney had done a piece in which Judge Ito responds to D'Amato's impression with an impression of

D'Amato's sister having sex with a donkey. "Oh datsa good! Oha I lika dat!"

I said, "Well, you know, I thought it was fair. It was Ito responding to something that you've admitted was a mistake."

"Well, I admit, I did think it was funny," he said, referring to McKinney's piece.

"Then deep down you probably thought it was fair."

"But my sistah?"

I didn't tell him that the NBC censors had made us change it from his mother having sex with a donkey to his sister. In the interest of good taste, I guess. "Okay. Maybe it wasn't fair to your sister. But it was fair to you."

"I don't know. My sistah having sex with a donkey?" Then he went on to say that he really didn't see what was so wrong with what he had done on Imus in the first place. And as long as we were on the general subject, I thought I'd take a little risk.

"I wrote a joke about you for Conan but he didn't use it."

"No, he used it. I thought it was funny."

"Yeah, well, I had a variation. It went, 'The entertainment was either going to be me or Senator D'Amato doing his impression of a Japanese guy having a heart attack.'"

The senator and his fiancée just looked at me.

See, I'm a people person.

35
MORE FUN WITH RUSH LIMBAUGH'S FACT CHECKER

It's August, and we hadn't heard from Rush's fact checker, Waylon, since June. Geoff left a couple messages on his voice mail, but we didn't hear back until yesterday. And once again, we got it all on tape.

Telephone ring

Geoff: Hello! Rush Limbaugh Is a Big Fat Idiot. How may I direct your call?

Waylon: Oh, I'm sorry. I thought I was calling Empower USA.

Geoff: Oh. You want the conservative think tank across the hall. Hold on a sec, I'll transfer you. *(Pause)* Hello! Empower USA. How may I direct your call?

Waylon: Geoff?

Geoff: Hi, Waylon! Haven't heard from you in a while.

Waylon: Yeah, sorry about that. I've been having a lot of trouble checking my voice mail. I keep forgetting my access code.

Geoff: Have you tried using your birthday?

Waylon: You can't really do that on this system. It only takes numbers.

Geoff: All-righty then . . . Why don't I put Mr. Franken on.

Al: Hi, Waylon! Megadittoes!

Waylon: What?

Al: Never mind. Listen, Waylon, we're preparing our annual report on the environment here at Empower USA, and we just wanted to run a couple of Rush's comments by you before we publish them as incontrovertible fact.

Waylon: I'm your man.

Al: Okay, let's jump right in. First of all, back in 1991, Rush claimed that Styrofoam was biodegradable and paper wasn't.

Waylon: Right. I remember that. That is . . . uh . . . that's totally wrong.

Al: Oh.

Waylon: Yeah, we caught a lot of flak for that one.

Al: Okay. How about this one? In his book, *See, I Told You So,* Rush writes: "There are more acres of forestland in America today than when Columbus discovered the continent in 1492."

Waylon: Wait. Is that Chapter Fourteen?

Al: Uh-huh.

Waylon: Yeah. Here's the thing. I didn't do Chapter Fourteen. We had a temp in that week, so I just farmed it out.

Al: Really?

Waylon: Yeah, good kid. Didn't have a whole lot on the ball though. Just out of curiosity, *are* there more acres of forestland now than in 1492?

Al: No. Turns out Rush was off by about a quarter of a billion acres.

Waylon: Wow! Don't tell the Sierra Club.

Al: Don't worry. Let me ask you a little something about global warming.

Waylon: Doesn't exist.

Al: Fair enough. But in 1992 Rush said it wouldn't be a big deal if did exist because "Even if the polar ice caps melted, there would be no rise in ocean levels. . . . After all, if you have a glass of water with ice cubes in it, as the ice melts, it simply turns to liquid and the water level in the glass remains the same."

Waylon: Well, that's just common sense.

Al: Except that most of the world's ice is on land.

Waylon: Hold it. You lost me there.

Al: Antarctica. It's a continent, not an ice cube.

Waylon: Your point?

Al: If the ice cap melted, sea level around the world would rise about two hundred feet.

Waylon: Holy cow! We'd all drown!

Al: Calm down, Waylon.

Waylon: Calm down?! I've got a basement apartment!

Geoff: Sorry to jump on. But, Al, James Carville is on line two.

Waylon: James Carville? Isn't he the guy who ran the Dukakis campaign?

Al: Uh, no, Waylon. Actually, he ran the Clinton campaign.

Waylon: The *Clinton* campaign?! Why is he calling Empower USA?!

Al: You know, Waylon, I might as well come clean. There is no Empower USA. We're actually writing a book called *Rush Limbaugh Is a Big Fat Idiot.* . . . Waylon? . . . Waylon?

Waylon: I . . . I feel so violated.

Al: Yeah, well, gotta go. Megadittoes.

Waylon: Yeah, *right.*

36
REPUBLICANS AND ENVIRONMENTAL REGULATION: LIKE MIXING OIL AND WATER. LITERALLY.

I hope you loved that Waylon bit as much as I did. Well, I didn't really. I think I've reached a point in this book where using Rush Limbaugh as a point of departure for discussing a topic has gone from being an amusing device to a sad reminder that millions of Americans are being lied to every day by an obese millionaire with a repugnant political agenda. But his views on the environment are so god-awful wrong that it would have been a disservice not to include them.

By the way, Rush says that his convictions are spiritual in nature. In *The Way Things Ought to Be*, Rush (or his ghostwriter, anyway) says:

> My views on the environment are rooted in my belief in Creation. . . . I refuse to believe that people, who are themselves the result of Creation, can destroy the most magnificent creation in the entire Universe.

I don't know. If God can allow genocides to occur on a more or less regular basis, if God can stand by while famine ravages large parts of the Third World, if God can permit Sonny Bono to sit on the House Judiciary Committee, why should we figure He's going to get off His Butt to stop Union Carbide from leaking polychlorinated biphenyls into the groundwater underneath Piscataway, New Jersey?

But that probably doesn't concern Rush. If God fails us, there's always the free enterprise system. For example, here's how Rush explains how Cleveland went about cleaning up the Cuyahoga River:

> Take the Cuyahoga River, which caught fire about twenty years ago because it was filled with so much junk and sludge. We set out to clean it up, we rolled up our sleeves and we did it. I'm sure some regulation was used, but the major factor was good old American know-how. . . . The key to cleaning up our environment is unfettered free enterprise.

I've looked into this and it seems that people who actually live in Ohio have a slightly different interpretation of what "some regulation" actually means. According to the Cleveland *Plain Dealer* of June 22, 1994, the $1.5 billion cleanup came about "as a result of federal regulations passed after the river last burned." (That's the funny thing about the Cuyahoga. It actually caught fire three times before the federal government finally stepped in.)

But don't take the *Plain Dealer*'s word for it. Listen

to what the *Dayton Daily News* had to say on May 8, 1995: "In 1969, before the federal government stepped in with its water pollution controls, the Cuyahoga caught fire as a result of the industrial waste that clogged it. The Cuyahoga no longer 'goes smoking through my dreams,' as songwriter Randy Newman once described it, largely because of the Federal Water Pollution Control Act passed by Congress in 1972."

The Federal Water Pollution Control Act, popularly known as the Clean Water Act, is currently being rewritten by the Republican Congress. Not to worry, though. House Republican whip Tom Delay, realizing how complex an overhaul of our nation's environmental policy might be, was wise enough to bring in people who "have the expertise" to make sure that the Clean Water Act will do exactly what they want it to do.

These people, undeniably "experts" in pollution law, include lobbyists from the chemical, mining, paper, petroleum, auto, and steel industries. But don't be alarmed. I can't imagine how any group that calls itself the Clean Water Industry Coalition could possibly have a hand in fouling our nation's water supply.

Their kindred spirits in the National Endangered Species Reform Coalition, which includes timber, ranching, mining, and utility interests,* have been

---

* Here's a fun little brainteaser. See if you can match the following special interest groups with their corporate sponsors.

1. National Wetlands   a. oil drillers, developers,
   Coalition   natural gas companies

busy improving the Endangered Species Act. All I can say, it's about time. As Rush said, "If the [spotted] owl can't adapt to the superiority of humans, screw it."

But the real E-ticket in Washington lobbying this past year was Project Relief, an all-star team of lobbyists representing 350 different corporate interests that was put together by Tom Delay. Delay, who was a Houston bug exterminator before he became a parliamentarian, has called the EPA "the Gestapo of government." (Which I bet left a lot of people in the ATF feeling unappreciated.)

Delay set up Project Relief to write the House regulatory moratorium bill. As written, the moratorium would prevent the federal government from issuing any more regulations on just about anything. Which in the case of environmental regulations is maybe a good idea. Because after they cut the EPA's enforcement budget in half, the agency won't have the resources to enforce the regulations already on the books.

Delay believes that working hand in hand with business lobbyists is equivalent to Democrats working with labor unions and environmental groups: "Our supporters are no different than theirs. But somehow

2. Citizens for Sensible Control of Acid Rain	b. coal and electric companies
3. Global Climate Coalition	c. coal, gas, and oil companies
4. Nevadans for Fair Fuel Economy	d. Detroit automakers

answers: 1,a 2,b 3,c 4,d

they have this Christ-like attitude what they are doing [is] protecting the world."

Delay's allies don't have the same attitude problem. Project Relief leader-lobbyist Gordon Gooch, who wrote the first draft of the legislation, proudly admits: "I'm not claiming to be a Boy Scout. No question I thought what I was doing was in the best interests of my clients," which include energy and petrochemical companies.

Project Relief is what you might call a dues-paying organization. The dues go directly to members of Congress. From 1989 to 1994, the one hundred and fifteen PACs associated with Project Relief contributed nearly $40 million to various representatives and senators. Last year the top recipient in the House was Newt Gingrich.*

During the debate on regulatory reform, Republicans set up a war room for Project Relief lobbyists in a small office directly off the House floor. As Democrats raised objections to the bill (such as "people will get very sick"), lobbyists with laptops spat out responses for use by Republicans on the floor.

So, in other words, lobbyists aren't just *writing* the bills, they're *debating* them as well. Personally, I think this is good. Because it frees up the members' schedules so they can spend more time fund-raising. In fact, I think government will run a lot more efficiently

* See also Gingrich's speech to Perot conference on evils of money in politics, pages 249–250. You'll particularly like the part about our freedom being "bought off in a wave of money."

once we figure out a way to let lobbyists do the voting, too.

Keep in mind that these bills have only passed the House. They have yet to get through the Senate, which is traditionally a more moderate, deliberative body. Unless, of course, some of the senators are running for President.

When Bob Dole took it upon himself to lead the Senate's charge for regulatory reform, he turned to many businesses and lobbyists for, well . . . "advice." And maybe even a little "encouragement."

The final product happened to reflect the regulatory concerns of a lot of Dole-for-President contributors, and was in some ways even more pro-industry than the House bill.

Basically, the Senate bill would require the government to prove through a bureaucratically tortuous process of cost-benefit and risk analysis that any proposed regulation is the cheapest way to protect the public. For example, improved meat inspection by the USDA that could save four thousand lives a year and prevent up to five million illnesses could be nixed, not just because it would cost the meat industry $245 million a year, but because the USDA couldn't prove that it's the "cheapest" way to protect the public.

This whole cost-benefit analysis business is very sticky, because it's hard to put a dollar value on some things. Like human life. At one point in the debate over regulatory reform, Ted Kennedy prepared an amendment which would have set the value of a human life at a minimum of $7.5 million. That probably made the Kopechne family perk up their ears. My guess is that when Congress finally gets down to setting a dollar value on a human life, it'll be closer to the buck ninety-five suggested by the Lawn Jart people.*

Dole's bill probably would have squeaked through the Senate if it weren't for a piece of good luck. Right in the middle of the floor debate, five kids in Tennessee got *E. coli* poisoning from eating bad hamburgers. Fortunately, none of them died, but they got sick enough to kill the bill. Temporarily.

Eventually, though, the Republicans will manage to push through a bill deregulating everything from motorcycle helmets to nuclear power plants. And if history's any judge, the results will be a tremendous disaster.

In October of '82, when Ronald Reagan signed the bill deregulating those poor, overburdened savings and loans, he remarked, "I think we hit the jackpot!"

I don't know who the "we" referred to. But with the taxpayer cost of the S&L bailout approaching $200 billion, *somebody* sure hit the jackpot.

---

* I'm sorry, I got carried away there. The Lawn Jart people never suggested that a human life is only worth $1.95. Everything else in this chapter is true.

37
THE LAW AND ORDER
PARTY: US!

Finally. We Democrats are the law and order party. We're for the ATF. The Republicans are for David Koresh, the militias, and guns. That's an oversimplification. But who's got time for a whole long thing?

It's just that we've been taking hits since the 60s on this issue, and I think we can make some headway if we show that we're on the right side.

I should say right off that I'm just a citizen who's been mugged once. I don't claim to be an authority on crime. For example, I seemed to be the only person I know who didn't follow the O.J. Simpson trial. For a while there, I thought O.J. was the black guy who kidnapped Susan Smith's kids. As I write this, I don't know what the verdict will be. But I will say this about O.J. The man has suffered enough.

Of course, both the O.J. and the Susan Smith cases underline the fact that most murder victims are killed by people they know. And if you believe Newt Gingrich, they also underline the importance of voting Republican.

As Newt put it right before the '94 elections: "I think that the mother killing the two children in South Carolina vividly reminds every American how sick the society is getting and how much we need to change things. . . . The only way you get change is to vote Republican."

I imagine that Susan Smith's stepfather, Beverly Russell, can also attest to "how sick the society is getting." As a member of South Carolina's Republican state executive committee, he's been very actively pushing the Republican agenda for years. Unfortunately, he was also pushing another agenda for quite some time. Russell, who also happened to be a local organizer for the Christian Coalition, has admitted to having molested his stepdaughter Susan from the age of fourteen, as well as to having had consensual sex with her up to two months prior to the death of her children. Russell has made very public expressions of guilt over this. Of course, as far as I know, he's still voting Republican.

But enough about this rather unsettling hypocrisy. Back to violence.

I don't know what makes people violent. Some experts say television. I'm sure it does. But I know that the Nazis didn't watch a lot of TV, and something tells me the Serbs weren't watching a lot of the *A-Team* during the 70s.

On the other hand, Senator Bill Bradley has quoted this statistic: By the time a kid's eighteen, he'll have seen 26,000 murders on TV. Well, that may seem like a lot, but if you do the math, it comes out to only four per day. So, I don't know what the big deal is.

Other experts say that the rate of violent crime is directly linked to the availability of guns. That's why I'm a big advocate of "gun buy-back" programs. In fact, I have a radical gun buy-back idea that I guarantee would be a huge success. Here's how it works: Hand in a gun, get a free vial of crack.

Of course, that would put more drugs on the street. And that is not good. Last year 78 percent of those arrested in New York City tested positive for cocaine, a drug which makes people very aggressive, and hostile, and violent. That's why heroin would probably be better for the gun buy-back program.

An uncomfortable subject that's not discussed enough is black on black crime. Jesse Jackson had the courage to talk about it in terms that most people can identify with. He said it pains him that when he's walking down the street at night and hears footsteps, he's relieved if it's a white man and not a black man. I know exactly what he means. I was leaving NBC late one night and heard some footsteps. When I turned around, I saw it was Jesse Jackson, and it scared the living daylights out of me!

A couple years ago, the Supreme Court ruled that it was constitutional to give perpetrators of "hate crimes" stiffer penalties than criminals who committed the same crime, only without the hate motive. I'm sympathetic to that. I think hate crimes are despicable. But at least there's a *reason* for the crime. What I fear is *random* acts of violence. I don't know. Something to think about.

One of the largest contributing factors to urban crime is unemployment. Among black teenagers looking for jobs, nearly 40 percent can't find work. I can't understand why anyone would be against midnight basketball, which provides these guys something to do *and* job training. Maybe the Republicans believe this is the kind of social welfare program that attracts undesirable immigrants. I do recall that a lot of the Haitian boat people mentioned they were looking forward to playing midnight basketball.

President Clinton's crime bill paid for a lot of new prisons, and that's good. The question is what to do with these criminals once they're behind bars. I think drug rehab is a good idea, and studies show that it's been a dramatically successful tool in decreasing recidivism. I read Newt Gingrich's chapter in *To Renew America* called "Violent Crime, Freedom from Fear, and the Right to Bear Arms." Nowhere in this, his only chapter on crime, is there any mention of drugs or of domestic violence (unless you count pointing out that Nicole Simpson was killed by a knife and not a gun), but he does touch on Willie Horton and spends quite a bit of space on the need to "eliminate all weight and muscle-building rooms and break down the cult of macho behavior in prison." I agree. My suggestion is to replace weight training with mandatory step-aerobics performed to Ace of Base.

Then there's the death penalty. The Democrats finally won the White House in 1992 because we ran a guy who's pro capital punishment. As governor of Arkansas, Bill Clinton carried out the death penalty many times. He even put a semi-retarded guy away.

Here I am of two minds. I have no moral qualms about executing someone who rapes and murders Kitty Dukakis. That is, as long as we know we have the right guy.

Consider this *New York Times* story from 1985 about a murder trial in Gainesville, Georgia. It appeared under the headline RACE AND BLIND JUSTICE BEHIND MIX-UP IN COURT. The key word is "mix-up":

> Here in Hall County last June one man was arrested as a thief and another as a murderer. And last week, when the murder defendant was summoned to stand trial, the other man was produced, and nearly convicted.
>
> . . . Both men are Vietnamese of about the same height and weight, and none of the white participants in the judicial process—not the prosecutor, the sheriff's officers, the defense lawyer, or the witnesses—noticed the difference.

Basically, what happened was this: The county jail was holding two Vietnamese immigrants, neither of whom spoke English. Hen Van Nguyen, age 21, had been arrested for stealing. Nguyen Ngoc Tieu, 27, had been accused of stabbing a woman to death.

Mr. Nguyen was brought to the courthouse to stand trial for theft. A court officer assumed he was Tieu and brought him into another courtroom to stand trial for murder. For a day and a half Nguyen repeated over and over again, "Not me, not me," but that didn't stop several witnesses, including the murder victim's roommate, from identifying him as Mr.

Tieu, who was, in fact, sitting three blocks away in jail.

Tieu's court-appointed attorney had interviewed Tieu through an interpreter a few weeks earlier for about an hour ("There wasn't a whole lot to talk about"), but didn't realize that Nguyen wasn't his client. The attorney, sure of a conviction, offered to plead his uncooperative client guilty to a lesser charge.

It all ended as it had started. With a coincidence. A witness who was there for the theft trial accidentally wandered into the wrong courtroom and recognized Mr. Nguyen as the thief.

Former Hall County District Attorney Jeff C. Wayne sort of summed up the whole mix-up this way: "It's like the colored race—most of them look exactly alike."

Again, I have no problem frying a murderer. In some cases I'd even wave the cruel-and-unusual prohibition. But a dead man can't appeal.

Maybe I'm being overly fastidious. I once heard Pat Buchanan's answer to this objection to the death penalty. He said that surgeons lose people on the table all the time. What's the big deal?

38
FAIR MEAN VS. UNFAIR MEAN

Those of us who make our living in what Calvin Trillin calls "the small joke trade" are keeping alive one of America's noblest traditions. By commenting in a humorous way on the events of the day, we bring laughter, and, perhaps, fresh insight to our grateful readers. Every now and then, however, we come up with something that's just plain mean, having our fun at someone else's expense. And that's fine. That's what high-minded satire like *Rush Limbaugh Is a Big Fat Idiot and Other Observations* is all about.

Now, I am not a mean person. Just ask my kids. But don't ask the guy at the Alamo Rent-a-Car counter that kept me waiting for two and a half hours. And to maintain my own image of myself as a nice person, I have tried to draw a distinction between "fair mean" jokes and "unfair mean" jokes. I can't define the distinction, but like the Supreme Court with pornography, I know it when I see it.

Below are a few mean jokes, some of which you've already read. See if you can tell which are fair and which are unfair.

1. We now live in an era where the wall between news and entertainment has been eaten away like the cartilage in David Crosby's septum.

Fair or Unfair?

2. I'd like a Gingrich-Gramm ticket. That way the president could write the pornography and the vice president could produce it.

Fair or Unfair?

3. Bob Packwood misunderstood the "three strikes and you're out" provision in the crime bill. He thought it was "three strikeouts and you're out."

Fair or Unfair?

4. Packwood used alcoholism as an excuse for his behavior. I say if you're a U.S. senator and you have a drinking problem, you should just say, "I've done some things I'm not proud of, I've acted in ways not becoming a U.S. senator," and then simply leave it up to the people of Massachusetts.

Fair or Unfair?

5. Sam Donaldson once said on *David Brinkley* that a sketch I wrote "just wasn't funny." I'll tell you what, Sam. You don't make rules about comedy, I won't make rules about hair.

Fair or Unfair?

6. Instead of "with talent on loan from God," Rush Limbaugh should open his show by saying "with fat on loan from the American Beef Council."

Fair or Unfair?

(for answers, turn to next page)

1. Unfair. He mainly freebased.

2. Fair. The first, uncensored version of Gingrich's novel *1945* made me hot. I gave it a six on the peter-meter. Gramm invested $7,500 in a soft-core porn movie. It was never made. But, then again, I don't like him.

3. Fair. But too easy.

4. Unfair. No one has ever *proven* that Ted Kennedy is an alcoholic. Also, two of his brothers were killed by assassins.

5. Extremely fair. His toupee is hideous. And he criticized me.

6. Absolutely fair. You cannot have too many "Rush is fat" jokes. This is only my eighty-third.

And while we're on Limbaugh and the subject of "fair mean" vs. "unfair mean," let's go back to 1993. On his TV show he put up a picture of Socks, the cat, and said, "Did you know there's a White House dog?" Then he put up a picture of 13-year-old Chelsea Clinton. But, you know, she asked for it.

39
ADVENTURES IN POLITICS
AUGUST 12-14, 1995

I ATTEND THE PEROT CONFERENCE IN DALLAS, TALK TO A LOT OF ANGRY WHITE RETIRED PEOPLE, LISTEN TO EVERY REPUBLICAN PRESIDENTIAL CANDIDATE, AND PERSONALLY GET JOHN KASICH TO ADMIT TO AN ACT OF INTELLECTUAL DISHONESTY

When you step off the plane in Dallas and enter the main terminal, you are greeted by a huge sign that proudly proclaims: WELCOME TO DALLAS—WE HAVEN'T HAD AN ASSASSINATION IN OVER THIRTY YEARS!

Not really. That's just what I was thinking as my cabdriver drove past Dealey Plaza on the way to the Hyatt.

I had come to Dallas for a panderfest. All the declared Republican candidates were scheduled to speak to a gathering of several thousand members of Ross Perot's organization, United We Stand America. I learned later from journalist Gerald Posner that the organization would be called simply "United We Stand" except for the fact that a lesbian group in San Francisco owns the name, and Perot was forced to add the "America."

The Hyatt lobby was filled with excited Perotistas, practically all of them white, most in their sixties or seventies. Jerry Garcia had died a couple of days before, but most of these people were still mourning Lawrence Welk.

In the elevator, a middle-aged woman wearing an orange pantsuit recognized me. "I didn't know you were one of us!"

"Well, I'm not actually." Everyone was staring at me. "But I do agree with a lot of Perot's views."

"Then why aren't you a member?"

"Well, um, he's a little . . . you know." Still staring. "Um . . . you know. He's a little . . ." Help me out here, everybody. "You know . . . a little . . . paranoid. Maybe?"

The rest of the ride was pretty quiet. But I had learned something. Which was to shut up. After all, these were people who cared enough about America to come to Dallas in August at their own expense to try to make a difference. I felt ashamed.

That wore off pretty early the next day. Not that I didn't have fun chatting up a lot of nice folks. It's just that for every friendly, intelligent, concerned idealist, there was an angry, horribly misinformed xenophobe. Sort of Capra on acid.

There was Elaine, a nice enough old lady from North Palm Beach, Florida, and a Buchanan supporter because of his stance on immigration. She told me she lives so close to the water that "you can practically see the Haitians getting off the boats." Then Elaine leaned in and whispered, "You know which ones because their pants are wet to the knees." She went on about the Haitians' big scam. According to Elaine, the boat people land in Florida, go directly to the Salvation Army, where they stock up on pots and pans and shoes, and then fly back to Haiti to sell them on the black market. Hmmm. I say if you're willing to brave shark-infested waters and third-degree sunburn for the profit margin on a few pairs of used Nikes and some Corning Ware, then more power to you. I mean, *that's* rugged individualism.

Then there was Heather, an "economist" from Citizens for a Sound Economy. She was at a booth beating the drum for Dick Armey's flat tax, an especially popular issue at the conference. Part of the attraction of the flat tax is that I can explain it in one sentence: You take your wages, subtract a personal allowance of $22,700 for a married couple or $14,850 for a single head of household and $5,300 for each dependent, and then pay a flat 17 percent on the difference. That's it.

A friend of mine in Hollywood makes about $3.5 million a year. When I first explained the Armey flat tax to him, he said, "What do I have to do to get this guy elected President?" We estimated that he'd save somewhere in the neighborhood of $600,000.

Heather told me she was for the flat tax because it was progressive. When I disagreed and suggested a Gephardt-like "It's a flat tax because I call it a flat tax" higher rate for people making over $200,000, I got the supply-side response. Heather told me that the greatest economic growth in this country has always been when the marginal tax rate on the top bracket was lowest. I asked Heather what the top marginal rate was during the Eisenhower administration, and she thought a minute and said, "About twenty percent, I think."

Fortunately, the Citizens for a Sound Economy booth had a book that contained the very information we needed. The top rate during the Eisenhower administration was 88 percent. Heather explained, "I'm an economist, not a historian."

And there was the commotion at the Alan Keyes for President booth, where Keyes volunteers showed an exceedingly graphic video of an actual abortion. This violated an agreement that presidential candidates would show only campaign videos. The Keyes people said the abortion video *was* their campaign video, but Perot staff and police came in to close down the booth.

A Keyes campaign worker, who was wearing a T-shirt with an American flag and a cross, started chastising the cops at the top of his lungs, calling their actions "an abomination against the Lord." He was going on and on, and I felt bad for the police, who were being accused of doing the work of Satan, so when the guy stopped for a breath, I shouted something about how the police were doing their jobs. A couple minutes later it was all over, and the guy who had been preaching came up to me and told me he liked my work. Then a friend of his spent ten minutes trying to convert me to Christ.

The presidential candidates weren't speaking until the second day, but Perot was happily emceeing a slate of important, if somewhat dull, political figures. After speeches like Senator Paul Simon's "The Importance of a Strong, Stable Dollar," the little Texan would take the stage with applause-inducing lines like, "Now, didn't that speech hit the bull's-eye?" or "Wasn't that a home run?" or "Was that a world-class presentation or what?"

Pete Petersen, a co-founder of the Concord Coalition, did hit a home run with a very sobering speech about what will happen if we don't reform social security. He was the first speaker to make use of charts, which were projected onto two big video screens, and as such, the first to make a joke about using charts at a conference hosted by chart enthusiast Ross Perot. I counted eight speakers during the conference who used charts and made the same joke. The last one was Pete Wilson, who seemed utterly bewildered that he didn't get a laugh.

It became apparent very quickly that this was a conservative crowd. Anti-immigration, anti-welfare, anti-tax, anti–big government, anti-U.N., anti–foreign aid, and anti–affirmative action. And, boy, do they hate Clinton! Their welcome for the President's stand-in Mack McLarty was so cold that as he took the stage, you could almost hear his balls shrivel up and recede into his body cavity.

More than anything, the crowd was anti-establishment. So there was a warm response to Jesse Jackson, although I did witness a domestic mini-drama featuring a retiree in a baseball cap who insisted on heckling the Reverend. Every so often the guy would cup his hands around his mouth and yell something while his poor wife sat there mortified. At one point Jackson was decrying the growth of our prison population, and the man yelled out, "Put them in camps!" as his wife buried her face in her hands. I wonder how their car trip home went.

I was really looking forward to Gingrich's speech. The *Vanity Fair* article had just come out. The one in which a former campaign volunteer said that Newt preferred oral sex so he could say he didn't *sleep* with another woman. Which I don't really understand. I mean, I *slept* with the woman sitting next to me on the red-eye down to Dallas.

I was especially interested in how Gingrich would justify his failure to honor his handshake with the President. The one in New Hampshire where they both pledged to form a bipartisan commission on campaign reform. Political reform is at the top of Perot's agenda. And here was Gingrich, perhaps the most egregious offender of the Washington money game. I mean, lobbyists are now *writing* legislation. So, after winning the crowd over by kissing Perot's ring, Newt had the nerve to say this about money:

> I think this is a topic too serious to play narrow, cheap political games with . . . our freedom as a country and our tradition of over 200 years is too important to let it be bought off in a wave of money from a variety of sources that we don't understand and can't even follow.

And as I watched him on the stage, my hands were clenched in fists of rage. As Don McLean might say, assuming he hates Newt Gingrich as much as he hated Mick Jagger.

But it just got worse. Gingrich went into this obnoxious thing he does about how the Republicans are not cutting Medicare.

> This year Medicare spends $4,800 per senior citizen. Under our plan, over the next seven years, Medicare will spend $6,700 per senior citizen. Now, most of you probably do math well enough that you know if you're at 4,800 here and you're at 6,700 here that's called an increase. Now I want to go real slow here for a minute because we've got a lot of reporters who are listening.

It was really nauseating. He was using his hands: 6,700 up here, 4,800 down there. I kept wondering, "Are these constant dollars?" But people around me were laughing hysterically. He went on:

> Now I don't want to be negative, but you might even have one or two liberals show up who claim that going from 4,800 to 6,700 is a cut. Now, this is not because they're bad people; this is an early sign of the educational dysfunction which has hit our society.

The crowd laughed, then broke into applause and cheers. No angel born in hell could break that Satan's spell.

But the big hit Friday night was something of a surprise. Bob Novak wrote it this way in the next Monday's *Washington Post:*

But out of all 36 speakers, the people's choice was somebody few here could have recognized before this weekend, Rep. John Kasich of Ohio, Chairman of the House Budget Committee. . . . Indeed, dozens of admiring Perotites— particularly the younger ones—separately approached Kasich after his speech to praise him and suggest that the presidency lies in his future.

The boyish Kasich, who spoke about his long, heroic, lonely struggle to put the country's fiscal house in order, *did* blow the place away. But he didn't hurt himself any by sucking up to Novak in the Hyatt cocktail lounge later that night.

I was there. At one point Novak asked him who a President Kasich would appoint as Fed Chairman, and Kasich said, "Why you, Bob!" Novak laughed heartily.

We were having a good time. Me, Novak, Kasich, and Margaret Warner. If you're a *MacNeil/Lehrer* fan, as I am, you'll know Margaret as the *Newsweek* reporter who took over for Judy Woodruff as the show's chief Washington correspondent.

At one point Novak was extolling Gingrich's "masterful" speech, and I objected, especially to the patronizing crap about the $4,800 versus the $6,700. So I turned to Kasich:

"By the way, are those constant dollars?"

Margaret jumped in. "It must be constant dollars. They wouldn't be that dishonest."

"Sure they would," I said. Turning back to Kasich, "*Are* those constant dollars?"

"Al . . ." Kasich's voice had a touch of annoyance, "we're *increasing* funding for Medicare."

"But the $4,800 to $6,700, has that been adjusted for inflation?"

"Al, the dollars are going up."

"I just want to know if those are constant dollars."

"Al, we're going from 178 billion to 283 billion." Kasich gave the others an exasperated grin. When will this guy stop?

"Look. Gingrich is going like, 'Hey, you're a *fucking moron* if you can't see that 6,700 is more than 4,800.' I just want to know how big a moron I am. Are those constant dollars?"

A pause. Then. "No, Al, they're not constant dollars."

Kasich slumped in his chair and admitted, "I guess we're being a little intellectually dishonest on this one." And I took a few victory laps around the table.

Margaret was slightly embarrassed and begged me not to repeat the part about her assuming it was constant dollars. I knew she was kidding, however. She's a terrific journalist and knows a good story.

Which brings me to the reason I came to the conference in the first place. Frank Luntz. Frank is Washington's latest *Wunderkind*, a pudgy 33-year-old pollster whose focus-group approach to political research has revolutionized the Republican party's ability to sell itself to the electorate. In fact, Luntz is the guy who produced the GOPAC list of "contrasting words." Which means Frank is evil.

He's also the guy who discovered that more people under thirty believe in UFOs than believe they'll get their social security. I'd been thinking of putting to-gether a chapter on how stupid people are, so I gave Frank a call.

Luntz is now a consultant to Phil Gramm's cam-paign. But he had worked for Perot in '92, and sug-gested I come down for the conference. He told me I could watch him conduct some focus groups of Perot supporters, and that I could even ask some questions. Which gives you some idea how systematic his re-search is. I asked him if I could be a wiseass, and he said, "Sure. They won't know."

I hooked up with Frank while he was taping a *Mac-Neil/Lehrer* interview with Margaret "it must be con-stant dollars" Warner. Part of the interview focused on the Contract with America, which was largely the result of test-marketing by the Luntz Research Com-pany. At one point in the taping, Margaret asked Frank whether the Contract was designed specifically with the Perot people in mind.

Frank answered, "The contract was de-signed . . ." He stopped himself. As GOPAC's num-ber one celebrity pollster, Frank knows better than anyone that "words and phrases are powerful." And "designed" was a powerfully bad word in this context.

"Well, it's not really designed," he continued, hopelessly thrown. ". . . The contract was effective in convincing . . . don't do that to me."

"What's wrong with saying the contract was de-signed?" Margaret wanted to know.

". . . Because . . . Because I don't want to say it on camera, that's why."

Margaret let him rephrase his answer, which was

some bull about how the Contract demonstrated to the Perot people that a group of elected officials could make a promise and then keep it.

I hung out with Frank on and off for the rest of the weekend, and, of course, actually grew to like him. He's extremely smart, and his boyish naked ambition is almost endearing. Also, he was a fountain of interesting insights. For example, Frank worked for Pat Buchanan in the '92 primaries, and he told me Buchanan's views were "getting crazier every year." And from the way he discussed Phil Gramm, I gathered that the Gramm campaign strategy at that point had come down pretty much to hoping that Dole gets sick.

Occasionally, I would bother to challenge Frank on something or other and he'd answer, "Do you think you have a really solid grasp on what people are thinking?" Which is a little like Julia Child asking if you think you really know how to make a soufflé.

In fact, Frank pretty much worships at the altar of public opinion. He believes that polling is not just the key to winning elections, but to governing as well. This puts him squarely at odds with Edmund Burke, the eighteenth-century British philosopher who said that a legislator should make decisions based not on the passion of the moment or the whim of the people, but rather on his conscience and best judgment. (I've never read Burke. I heard Cokie Roberts quote him.)

Frank told me that most people who take part in focus groups consider it a "license to whine." And the ten young men and women who bitched and moaned in the Generation X group I witnessed were no exception. They were all college-educated, and their biggest complaint seemed to be that there hadn't been a cushy, high-paying job waiting for them when they graduated.

Frank asked them questions like: "Overall, does Washington help or hinder your achievement of the American dream?" Their answers were bitter denunciations of everything from social security to the Goals 2000 program. David, a 26-year-old from California, suggested that "we let the Catholic Church educate everybody like they used to." I pointed out that the Catholic Church didn't educate my people. To which he replied, "I mean the Western World."

It turns out that Frank is working on a book about the American dream, so afterwards he asked me what I thought the American dream had become. I said, "Well, judging from this group, I'd say it's to have a very well-paying job and to live in an expensive house in a gated community."

A focus group of eleven retirees was more heartening. All of them were excited to be at the conference and were enjoying the speeches. As Bob from California said, "It's what you learn after you know it all that counts."

They all seemed financially comfortable (probably because of the social security "distrust fund" so reviled by their grandchildren), but were concerned with the world they were passing on to their heirs. They worried that the country was being destroyed by partisan bickering. As Myrtle of Florida put it, "I wish people would stop blaming each other for everything." I didn't tell her the title of my book.

The group hated Clinton and held a generally favorable view of the Republican party. Bob felt that they were there to "force the Republicans to do what they promised to do." And most of them didn't want Perot to run for president, wanting him "to be a kingmaker, not a king." But when asked who'd they vote for in a three-way race between Clinton, Dole, and Perot, all but two said Perot. They hated Dole almost as much as Clinton.

Dole knew that when he spoke. Of all the Republican candidates, he was the least craven in tailoring his speech to the Perot crowd. Maybe that's because he knew he wouldn't be fooling anyone. "So I would say right up front, yes, the federal government is big, but the federal government does a lot of good things."

The cold reception just seemed to irk him. At one point he said, "I am not perfect." Then he couldn't help himself, adding, "Maybe everybody here is."

Dole opened by talking about World War II, and ended by talking about leadership. He seemed to be saying that he deserved the nomination because it was his turn. "I have been tested and I have been tested and I have been tested." But he might as well have been saying, "I have been testy, and I have been testy, and I have been testy."

Phil Gramm fared better. The usual stuff about his momma, Dickey Flatt, and the people in the wagon getting out to help pull the wagon, all that was well received. He added something new, though. His vision. Gramm described what the country would be like on January 1, 2001, the end of his first term and "the first day of the new millennium."

That confused people. Almost everyone thinks the first day of the new millennium will be January 1, 2000. But they're wrong. Gramm is right. The first year of the first century was the year one, not the year zero, so the first year of the new millennium will be 2001, not 2000. I've been trying to explain this to people for years, but no one will listen. On New Year's Eve, December 31, 1999, I'll be there in Times Square, along with Phil Gramm and maybe George Will and perhaps Dick Cavett, telling people to calm down. A thankless job, but someone will have to do it.

Alan Keyes brought the crowd to its feet with his highly charged speech. Well, performance, really. I found it particularly disturbing, not so much for its content, which was disturbing enough (abortion, abortion, abortion), but for its canned emotion. See, I'd seen the speech before on C-SPAN. Now, it's one thing to give your standard stump speech over and over, but when it involves thrashing and sweating and dramatic pauses which signify that you've been overcome with emotion, and those pauses always appear at the same exact point in the speech, it's time to apply for your actor's equity card.

Arlen Specter, on the other hand, urged that abortion be taken "off the political table" and won an ovation, which isn't easy when most of the audience is walking out of the room.

Richard Lugar did himself no good whatsoever by concentrating on foreign policy, and Bob Dornan spent about 80 percent of his time ranting about all things military, at one point reminding us that it took four years to thrash "the Krauts." He did leave the battlefield long enough to call Bill Clinton "the most corrupt person to sit in the Oval Office in two hundred years."

Pete Wilson tried to pull a cheap standing O at the end of his speech by exhorting the crowd: "If you want to take back our government, stand up!" The crowd knew it was a ploy for the benefit of the TV cameras and resented it. But they also wanted to take back their government, so they stood up quickly and then sat down as fast as possible.

Lamar Alexander. What can I say about Lamar Alexander? Lamar, give it up.

Pat Buchanan stole the show. I counted six standing ovations, although it's hard to count when you're cowering under your seat. Like Dornan, Buchanan gave us a martial tour of American history, touching on Lexington and Concord, Paul Revere's ride, Robert E. Lee, Little Big Horn, Pearl Harbor, the Bataan Death March, Corregidor, Midway, the Coral Sea, Okinawa, Iwo Jima, his uncle losing a leg in the "European Theater of Operations," Vietnam, the Marine barracks in Beirut, and what he referred to as "that so-called friendly fire incident in Iraq." This from a guy who was 4-F.

Buchanan was almost totally in sync with the Perot crowd and drew his biggest ovations on their red meat issues. On NAFTA and the Mexican bailout: "Politicians of both parties sold us out up in Washington, D.C. They took Citibank and Chase Manhattan and J.P. Morgan and Goldman Sachs off the hook, and they put us on. Well, I'll tell you this, you've got my word, when I get to the White House, NAFTA will be canceled!"

International bankers caught it on the chin a few times, along with the U.N.: "So I want to say today to all the globalists up there in Tokyo and New York and Paris, when I raise my hand to take that oath of office, your new world order comes crashing down!"

On immigration: "I will build a security fence and we will seal the border of this country cold!"

On dress codes: "We don't need some character in the Department of Education in sandals and beads telling us how America's children should be educated."

Buchanan ended his speech with a Freudian slip. He meant to say, "We'll take back my party, and then together we're going up the federal road, and we'll take back Washington, D.C., and we will take America back to the things we believe in." He messed up just one word. So it came out: "we'll take *black* Washington, D.C." I swear. I saw it again later on *MacNeil/Lehrer*.

When Buchanan finished the speech, emcee Perot brought Buchanan's wife, Shelley, to the podium. "Can we agree on one thing? This guy married way over his head, didn't he?"

Now it was Perot's turn. He thanked his people for not being morning glories. "Remember, morning glories wilt by noon." He told his people that they were responsible for the Republican '94 victory. He complained that the Republicans had pilfered the Contract with America:

And that came right out of the back of one of our books. . . . Again and again, people have come to me and said, "Weren't you offended by the fact that they took . . . ?" And I said, no, no. That's the nicest compliment they could pay us.

Then he demanded another Contract. For campaign finance reform. ". . . and let's make all these government reforms in the next hundred days and give it to the American people as a Christmas present in 1995. Right?"

The implication was clear. I'll form a third party if Congress doesn't pass political reform in the next hundred days. Sooner, if Colin Powell sells a lot of books in September and starts to upstage me.

The irony, of course, is that Perot's is easily the most autocratic, least democratic organization in the country. And any candidate who gets the nomination of the Independence party or the Reform party or whatever it's called will really be getting the nomination of "The Lunatic Who Dropped Out Because the Republicans Were Going to Disrupt His Daughter's Wedding" party.

I'm guessing Lowell Weicker.

40
THE URGENT NEED FOR
HEALTH CARE REFORM

It was my original intention that this piece would be the linchpin of my book, much as health care reform was meant to be the linchpin of the first Clinton Administration.

My initial plan was to overwhelm you with facts, figures, and unassailable logic that would all lead to one inescapable conclusion: namely, that America urgently needs to adopt all of Ira Magaziner's proposals for a system of universal health coverage based on the principles of managed competition.

Unfortunately, we've run into a little difficulty here at *Rush Limbaugh Is a Big Fat Idiot*. It seems that my researcher, Geoff, is sick. Which has led to something of a bottleneck in the production of facts, figures, and unassailable logic.

So we . . . I mean "I" (he's really sick) have had to change tack. Instead of a rational argument in favor of health care reform, I've decided to take a cue from the congressional Republicans and prove my point anecdotally.

Which brings me back to Geoff's illness. Right now he is lying in St. Luke's with a shunt draining neural fluid from the lining of his brain. But don't worry. The doctors say that's under control. Apparently the head injury isn't as bad as it looks.

The real worry is the Lyme disease, which may have entered its irreversible phase.

Let me back up. I don't pay Geoff much. Basically, I pay him the going rate for researchers. Which, believe me, is a joke. So Geoff can't exactly afford his own health insurance. And since he's only a temporary employee, Lord knows I'm not going to pick up the tab.

Which is exactly why we need government-mandated universal health insurance.

You see, if Geoff had had health coverage, he would have gone to a doctor right after he was bitten by the tick. Or at least as soon as he developed the rash and fever.

We think the tick was a deer tick. They're pretty prevalent around my son's day camp up in Westchester. It was funny hat day, and my boy had left his funny hat at home. So, I sent Geoff up to the camp with it, and he came back with Lyme disease.

It's actually a very treatable disease. If you catch it in the early phase, before the heart palpitations and fainting spells set in. It's like Ira Magaziner says: A lot of unnecessary medical costs are incurred because people don't seek treatment until they're really sick.

That is so true! Had Geoff seen a doctor when he

was only running a 102 degree fever, a simple course of antibiotics would have done the trick. But when he asked me if I knew any good doctors, I couldn't think of a single one in his price range.

So Geoff stuck it out. The fever came and went. The rash pretty much stayed with him from the get-go, but we thought it was an allergic reaction to the laundry detergent he had been using, so we ignored it. Likewise, the arthritic condition of his hands, which we chalked up to carpal tunnel syndrome. See, he had been doing a lot of typing. You know, mainly research stuff. Well, actually, he *wrote* pages 91 to 143 while I was summering in Maine. I don't know why I'm telling you this.

When I got back from Maine, I noticed that his performance was getting a little spotty. Some of the research seemed kind of suspect. I don't think Richard Lugar was ever married to Elizabeth Taylor. And I'm *sure* Dick Armey never played third base for the Astros.

Then it happened. Geoff had been having dizzy spells for a while, but he'd never actually fainted until one day when I was out for a long lunch with my publicist. When I left, Geoff was doing a Nexis search on Limbaugh's third wife, and when I returned he was lying on the floor passed out cold. At first I was pretty ticked off, because he'd left the Nexis connection running and they charge by the minute.

The emergency room was a zoo. There were something like six or eight head injuries ahead of Geoff's, so we had to wait for hours. Finally, when they got to him, the doctors put him through all kinds of tests, including a CAT scan, and determined that Geoff had suffered a cranial hematoma when he hit his head on the desk or floor after he passed out.

It wasn't until he'd been in the hospital a couple days that they figured out he had fainted because of the Lyme disease. So now even though the doctors think Geoff will only need the shunt for a few more days, they're worried about possible Lyme-related heart failure. Which means Geoff may be in the hospital for weeks.

All of which you're paying for in two ways. One, this book is not nearly as well researched as it should be. And second, since Geoff doesn't have insurance, the hospital is passing on the entire expense, now approaching six figures, to your insurance company and mine. This is why you pay seven dollars for an aspirin when you get it in the hospital: because employers like me aren't required to cover employees like Geoff. It's an outrage!

And it's all the fault of the Republicans in Congress. All two hundred and . . . whatever, of them. Especially that guy, you know, the one who made that speech about how he didn't want his mom going to some government bureaucrat if she got sick. You know the guy. I could find out his name if I could just get this damn Nexis thing to work.

41

THE CRITICAL NEED FOR
LEGAL REFORM

It's been a tumultuous couple of weeks here at *Rush Limbaugh Is a Big Fat Idiot and Other Observations*. First, Geoff got out of the hospital. And he's made a miraculous recovery.

Now that we've settled the lawsuit.

When Geoff first returned to work, everything was fine. Except that one of us seemed a little bitter. Since I felt that we had covered health care, I decided to move on to the issue of legal reform.

You see, I'd always intended to put a chapter in the book about how we *don't* need legal reform. I've always felt that as cumbersome and unwieldy as our legal system is, we need to preserve the right of the little guy to seek redress for any injustice he may suffer at the hands of faceless corporate behemoths.

That was before I realized that in the eyes of the state of New York, I am, in fact, a faceless corporate behemoth. But I'm getting ahead of myself.

When I told Geoff to do some research on legal

reform, the first thing he did was to phone an organization called the Center for Legal Reform. The guy he talked to gave Geoff the usual arguments about frivolous lawsuits and ridiculously high awards for silly things like "pain and suffering." This struck me as very sloppy research, because what I really wanted were the arguments *against* legal reform. And I guess I came down a little hard on him.

I told him to call the American Trial Lawyers Association and then went out for a long lunch with my new publicist. When I returned, Geoff had a big smile on his face for the first time since he developed his rash.

Some shyster at the American Trial Lawyers Association had told Geoff that the whole Lyme disease thing was actionable and that he'd be happy to take the case for a third of the future settlement.

First I thought Geoff was bluffing. So I laughed at him. Which he tape recorded. Ultimately, my lawyer figures, that recording cost me about . . . well, I'm not allowed to discuss the terms of the settlement. Let's just say I chortled away about two years of tuition at a very good private college.

It was two days after what both parties now call "the laughing incident" that my lawyer received the letter from Geoff's new "counsel." In addition to restitution for his ongoing medical expenses, Geoff was seeking damages for pain and suffering, lost wages (I didn't pay him for the days he was in the hospital), incapacitation, irreparable emotional injury, and something called "loss of consortium," which I understand had something to do with his girlfriend. He also sought compensatory damages on the grounds that I had grossly deflated his ego.

Worse still, he was threatening a civil rights action against me, claiming that he was a member of a minority group (Generation X) which has been discriminated against by the Baby Boomers, of which I am a member.

Once I realized that Geoff was playing hardball, I fired him. But the next day he showed up for work with a court order which said I was legally prohibited from dismissing him while the case was still pending. In addition, he got a special injunction seeking additional monetary damages on the grounds that my attempt to fire him was retaliatory and constituted an attempt to prevent him from exercising his constitutionally protected right to sue me.

So Geoff continued to work for me. Sort of. Because his lawsuit was work-related, he was entitled to spend all of his time on Nexis doing legal research for his case against me. The cost of which he billed to me, in addition to time-and-a-half for overtime.

Work on the book ground to a halt once the court required me to comply with discovery requests made by Geoff's lawyer. I had to hand over all my papers, including my financial records, my diary, even my video rental records, which were very embarrassing. As were the numerous depositions, including one six-hour session which was devoted entirely to an argument I once had with a guy from Alamo Rent-a-car.

My lawyer kept assuring me that we had them cold on the civil rights complaint, ego deflation, and loss of consortium, and that we'd probably win everything else. Unless someone on the jury had ever had a problem with an employer.

Of course, my lawyer had also assured me that the other side would come down from its original settlement demand. Instead, as the days dragged on, the number multiplied like bacteria in an unflushed toilet.

By this time the aggravation and uncertainty were beginning to take their toll. Plus the deadline for the book was approaching, and Geoff hadn't written a line in weeks.

Finally, I caved. As I've indicated, I am not free to discuss the precise terms of the settlement. Let's just say that I have more mortgages now than when I started the book. Also, you'll notice that the next chapter is written by Geoff, who appears to have an ax to grind. All I can say is I have a new respect for the efforts of the Republican leadership in Congress to bring some common sense back to our legal system before it careens out of control and destroys us all!

One last thing. If you guys could make whatever you do retroactive, I'd appreciate it.

42

THE DESPERATE NEED FOR ENTITLEMENT REFORM

OR MY GENERATION IS HOPELESSLY SCREWED
BY GEOFF RODKEY, RESEARCH ASSISTANT

First of all, I would like to thank my attorney for negotiating the terms of the agreement under which I have been allowed to air my grievances against Mr. Franken. Since my ongoing medical expenses are likely to consume most of the financial settlement, I consider this chapter my only real compensation for the cruelty to which I have been subjected at the hands of this man.

I could, and perhaps may, write an entire book on the depth of Mr. Franken's self-centeredness. His shameless self-promotion knows no moral or ideological bounds. In Mr. Franken's universe, a fifteen-minute phone conversation with Arianna Huffington, during which the phrases "Greek goddess" and "preeminent social thinker of our time" pass his lips repeatedly, may well be followed by a series of plaintive calls to the White House social office in a pathetic attempt to wheedle an invitation to a dinner honoring Marian Wright Edelman.

While this may sound amusing, I can assure you that watching it at close range, day in and day out, is not. Neither is being forced to watch the videotape of the West Side–Kingsbridge Little League game in its entirety, twice daily, for six consecutive weeks. There is a school of thought which asserts that parenting is the ultimate form of narcissism. Having observed the inner dynamics of the Franken family, I find myself in full agreement.

But I have far too much self-respect to spend the balance of this chapter engaged in the sort of ad hominem attacks which Mr. Franken employs to mask his near-total lack of political insight. Besides which, I have bigger fish to fry.

It occurs to me that Mr. Franken's relentless self-absorption is symptomatic of his entire generation of Baby Boomers. Likewise, the atrocities which I have personally suffered at his hands are destined to be inflicted wholesale upon my entire generation in the not too distant future. I am talking about the looming crisis in the social security system.

The economic facts on this point are appalling. The federal government is currently engaged in a massive transfer of wealth from the young (me) to the old (Mr. Franken's mother). Contrary to the AARP-inspired propaganda that retirees only get out of the social security system what they put in, the average one-earner couple retiring this year will eventually receive a quarter of a million dollars *more* in present dollars than they contributed.

This national Ponzi scheme is currently scheduled to implode in a spectacular fiscal nightmare right about the time Mr. Franken retires. When I first explained this to him, he shrugged it off and suggested that my time would be better spent researching synonyms for the word "fat."

At first I assumed that Mr. Franken simply did not grasp the contours of the issue. Here, after all, is a man who to this day believes that the Education Department's Goals 2000 program actually has something to do with World Cup soccer. So I carefully explained that unfunded liabilities in the social security system already amount to about nine trillion dollars, a sum which is almost twice that of the current national debt.

Mr. Franken pondered this, then asked me to make a graph comparing that number to Rush Limbaugh's weight in pounds. When I informed him that such a graph, if scaled at one hundred pound/dollars per inch, would be over a million miles high, he dismissed the idea as impractical and recued the videotape of his son's game-winning throw against Kingsbridge.

Undeterred, I pointed out that if the social security problem were left to fester, his son's generation would face a lifetime tax rate of 84 percent. At this point Mr. Franken paused the videotape and, in a rare moment of intellectual honesty, admitted to me the reason he has refused to address the social security crisis in his book.

Mr. Franken, it turns out, is deathly afraid that if we reform the social security system, his mother will have to move in with him. It is exactly this fear that has led some eighty million Baby Boomers to make a Faustian pact with their political leaders to lay waste to our nation in exchange for another twenty years of relative peace.

This is in direct contrast to my generation. Most of us can't afford to leave home to begin with. And by the time we manage to get jobs that pay us well enough to strike out on our own, the Baby Boomers in the federal government will raise payroll taxes again, beating us back into our parents' basements with our spouses and children in tow.

By then the inevitable crisis will be upon us. Already denied the opportunity to own our own homes or send our children to college, what meager financial reserves we do have will be wiped out in the inevitable hyperinflation that will result when the government is forced to monetize the debt. Those of us who do not starve to death will die of easily preventable diseases because we *still* won't be able to afford health insurance.

The only alternative to this apocalyptic scenario is generational warfare. On this point let there be no mistake: in any conflict which pits Generation X against either the Baby Boomers or their parents, *we will lose*. We are poorly educated, Nintendo-addicted children of divorce, intermingled with the occasional crack baby. Those of us who haven't been lulled into a state of mild hypnosis by the Fox Network are mostly busying ourselves with discovering new and different parts of our bodies to pierce. And our generational representation in Congress is limited to Patrick Kennedy.

Collectively, our only hope is that the Baby Boomers experience some sort of spiritual awakening

—or at least a modicum of shame—that leads them to shoulder their part of the burden before it crushes us completely. If the track record of the "Me Generation" is any indication, this will not happen.

As for myself, I am possessed of the clarity of mind which only a near-death experience can provide. Consequently, I am well equipped to weather the coming "time of troubles" (to borrow a phrase from Pat Robertson) with serenity and resignation. For that, I have Mr. Franken to thank.

(Mr. Rodkey died of complications from Lyme disease in October 1995. He was 24.)

43

BILL CLINTON: GREATEST PRESIDENT OF THE TWENTIETH CENTURY

As you may have noticed, I haven't spent a lot of time talking about the Democrats. That's because we're in such good shape. We currently have the White House, the governorships of several middle-sized states, and a real shot at keeping the Republicans below a filibuster-proof sixty seats in the Senate.

I can't wait until August. We Democrats are going to have one rollicking good time in Chicago. Of course, there'll be some intraparty squabbles between competing factions. Hey, we're Democrats! We've got a big tent. And if we want to hold together that 43 percent of the electorate that voted the Big D last time, we're going to have to smooth over the rough edges in our coalition of dispirited liberals, confused moderates, government employees, working-class gays, the voting poor, and the nostalgic elderly. Oh yeah, plus labor.

And who better to forge these disparate elements

into a galvanized bloc of electoral steel than the Man from Hope? The man whom I like to call: The Greatest President of the Twentieth Century.

I know you're thinking, "Wait a minute, Al. Franklin Roosevelt was the greatest president of the century." And I suppose an argument *could* be made for FDR. Or Truman, I guess. Or Wilson, Kennedy, or Johnson. Or the other Roosevelt, if you're a Republican. Or Reagan, if you're a fucking idiot.

Well, I think it's time someone made the case for Bill Clinton. In fact, I believe one of the reasons we lost control of Congress in '94 was that he hasn't received anywhere near the credit he deserves.

Admittedly, some of that is his fault. Sometimes he gets off message. For example, in '93 he was off message for pretty much the whole year. And in large parts of '94. Whitewater was a big distraction. And they really ambushed us with that midnight basketball thing.

By mid-'95, though, he was right on message, delivering a balanced budget proposal against the wishes of just about every Democrat in Congress. But like I said, we've got a big tent, and you have to expect a little grousing sometimes.

That's why it's particularly important for someone to cut through all the political hype and set the record straight. Why me? Well, for one thing, I really want to get invited to dinner at the White House. And once this book comes out, the chances of my eating with a Republican president are going to be pretty slim.

So here goes. Bill Clinton, greatest twentieth-century President.

First things first. Gays in the military. Right out of the gate, Clinton proved he was willing to offend tens of millions of Americans to honor a commitment on an issue of relatively little consequence to our nation's future. Then he backpedaled, proving he's no straightjacketed ideologue.

Honoring another campaign commitment—to choose a Cabinet that "looked like America"—Clinton stocked his administration with an adulterous Hispanic, a couple of mildly crooked black guys, a six-foot-one woman whose mother used to wrestle alligators, and a four-foot-tall Jewish guy. Which doesn't look like America at all, but it's an exceptional model of diversity.

In a brilliant political maneuver, for which he's never received credit, Clinton used the nomination process as a tool to open a national dialogue on a festering social problem. I think I speak for every American when I say we're all much more aware of the problem of yuppies who don't pay social security for their domestic help than we were during the "hear-no-evil, see-no-evil" Bush administration.

Meanwhile, America was falling in love with the Clintons. Hillary's hairstyles were aped by women across the country. Journalists of all stripes swooned during Bill's press conferences. Huge popular demand coaxed a bashful First Brother Roger out of his shell to record an album of soulful R&B croonings.

And millions of kids across America begged their parents to send them to private school just like Chelsea.

Having conquered the hearts and minds of the country, Clinton set out to conquer Capitol Hill. Working with such bold visionaries as Dick Gephardt, Tom Foley, and Dan Rostenkowski in the House, as well as the gritty, take-no-prisoners George Mitchell in the Senate, Clinton pushed the 1993 Deficit Reduction Act through Congress by rallying a sizeable majority of his own party around the flag of slightly smaller government. Fifty senators and 218 Representatives marched in lockstep, providing a comfortable margin of one vote in the House and giving Vice President Gore the Constitutionally protected honor of breaking the tie in the Senate.

As the deficit plummeted to $161 billion a year, the Clinton juggernaut rolled on like a panzer through France: Family Leave. Americorps. Reinventing Government. Expansion of Head Start. The School-to-Work Program. NAFTA. GATT. The Brady Bill. The Assault Weapons Ban. The Crime Bill. A cease-fire in Northern Ireland. Democracy in Haiti. Peace in the Middle East. Six million new jobs. And both inflation and unemployment at near-record lows.

Jesus Christ. This guy really *is* a good President. And I was going to spend the rest of this chapter being sarcastic. There's a real irony at work here. I mean, here I was trying to write a scathing piece on

Clinton, and at a certain point it just became impossible.

Wow. This kind of thing never happened when I was writing the Phil Gramm chapter.

And you know who else is really great? Hillary.

(The White House social office can reach Mr. Franken via Delacorte Press.)

44
ADVENTURES IN POLITICS
SEPTEMBER 9, 1995

If the Road to Victory Conference convinced me of anything, it's that I wouldn't make a good journalist. A journalist's job is to observe and report. I observed and got a migraine.

I'd decided to go because the rise of the Christian Coalition amounts to one of the most astounding political stories of the last decade. Its founder, televangelist Pat Robertson, built the 1.6 million–strong coalition out of the ashes—or, really, the mailing lists—of his failed 1988 presidential campaign. Under the leadership of Robertson and made-for-TV Boy Wonder Ralph Reed, the coalition is now the single largest political action group in America and effectively controls the Republican party in at least twelve states, including Texas and Florida.

And six years ago the organization didn't even exist. Robertson and Reed have somehow managed to convert a group of Americans whose previous organized political activity was pretty much limited to picketing

Ozzy Osbourne concerts into a force that now runs school boards and legislatures all over the country. And now they were getting together for their annual blowout, and all the Republican presidential candidates (all the pro-life ones anyway) had signed on for the opportunity to snuggle up.

Unfortunately, I wound up missing a lot of the snuggling, because, basically, after a couple hours I had to lie down. In a dark, quiet room. So if my report is a little sketchy, please cut me some slack.

PAT ROBERTSON—FOUNDER, LEADER, LUNATIC

The person I really wanted to hear speak was Robertson, because I had done a lot of research on the guy. Research that, frankly, made me nervous. For example, I learned that Pat Robertson believes that a satanic conspiracy led by Jews has threatened the world for centuries.

Now I know you might be thinking: C'mon, Robertson's not a *nut*! He's a businessman, a reverend, a graduate of Yale Law School. Yeah, I guess you're right. I mean faith healing, that's pretty mainstream:

> There's a woman named Marcia who's got cancer of the throat and the Lord has just healed you . . . someone else who has a lung fungus has just been healed by God's power. . . . A hernia has been healed. If you're wearing a truss you can take it off. It's gone! Several people are being healed of hemorrhoids and varicose veins

> . . . in the center section here, somebody's just
> been healed of an ulcer.

That's from the *700 Club*, where faith healing has
been a regular feature. Kind of like Stupid Pet Tricks.

OK, you might say. So he's a little fervent. Maybe
even a nut. But what about this satanic conspiracy
stuff? C'mon, Al. Be fair.

> It may well be that men of goodwill like Wood-
> row Wilson, Jimmy Carter, and George Bush,
> who sincerely want a larger community of na-
> tions living at peace in our world, are in reality
> unknowingly and unwittingly carrying out the
> mission and mouthing the phrases of a tightly
> knit cabal whose goal is nothing less than a new
> order for the human race under the domination
> of Lucifer and his followers.

That's from Robertson's 1991 book, *The New
World Order*, the paperback edition of which begins
with a couple pages' worth of quotes in praise of the
book. Somewhat mysteriously, all of them are anonymous, including my favorite: "I hardly ever read or
even finish a book . . . I finished this one."

Well, I also hardly ever read or finish a book, but
Geoff read *The New World Order* and highlighted
some of the better passages with a yellow marker. I
had trouble reading the yellow and had Geoff
reunderline with a green marker. And I must say, after
reading the greenish yellow stuff, I was a bit unset-
tled.

It is reported in Frankfurt, Jews for the first time were admitted to the order of Freemasons. If indeed members of the Rothschild family or their close associates were polluted by the occultism of Weishaupt's Illuminated Freemasonry, we may have discovered the link between the occult and the world of high finance.

Actually, this was good to know. See, I've been looking for the link between the occult and the world of high finance for years, and wouldn't you know it, the missing link is a Jew. Uncle Baron. (I wish!)

Continuing on, I discovered that this secret cabal of Jewish bankers (usually referred to as "Europeans" or "Germans") had its hand in the "satanic carnage" of the French Revolution, the Civil War, Bolshevism, the Cold War, and most recently the Gulf War. And God help those who tried to stop them.

There is no hard evidence to prove it, but it is my belief that John Wilkes Booth, the man who assassinated Lincoln, was in the employ of the European bankers who wanted to nip this American populist experiment in the bud.

In other words, we Jews didn't just kill Christ, we killed Lincoln. Of course, Robertson admits he has "no hard evidence," and, in fact, he has little proof of anything. That's why the book is written in an annoying "can it be that . . . ?" style. . . .

Can it be that the phrase "the new world order" means something entirely different to the inner circle of a secret society than it does to the ordinary person. . . ?

. . . *is there not a possibility* that the Wall Street bankers . . . enthusiastically financed Bolshevism . . . for the purpose of saddling the potentially rich Soviet Union with a totally wasteful and inefficient system that in turn would force the Soviets to be dependent on Western bankers for their survival?

Is it possible that the Gulf War was, in fact, a setup?

Before the war [WWI], monarchies held sway. After the war, socialism and high finance held sway. *Was it planned that way or was it merely* an "accident" of history?

Can it be that the leader of American's most powerful grass-roots political movement is a raving lunatic? *Is there not a possibility* that Robertson himself is Satan and that the members of the Christian Coalition are, in fact, his unwitting dupes? *Is it possible* that the Republican party is in the thrall of Lucifer? *Was it planned that way or was it merely* an "accident" of history?* (See bottom of page for answers.)

By now I know some of you are thinking: "Wait a

* yes, no, yes, "accident of history"

minute. Robertson is a supporter of Israel. He can't be anti-Semitic!"

Let's take this one step at a time. I have not said that Robertson was anti-Semitic. I said only that he was a lunatic who thinks that a satanic conspiracy led by Jews has threatened the world for centuries.

Robertson *is* a big supporter of Israel. And if you read his interpretation of prophecy as put forth in his 1990 book *The Last Millennium*, you'll learn why. According to Robertson, Israel must exist so that when Armageddon rolls around, it can get wiped off the face of the Earth. At that point, says Robertson, "the Jews will cry out to the one they have so long rejected."

In a way, Robertson's words would prove prophetic. Two hours into the Road to Victory Conference, I was moaning, "Jesus! Have I got a headache!"

THE CONFERENCE—RALPH REED, EMCEE

Unless you make it a point to catch the *700 Club*, you don't see much of Pat Robertson these days. That's because the spokesman of the Christian Coalition is now its baby-faced executive director Ralph Reed. Reed is a self-professed practitioner of "stealth" politics.* "Every moment you disguise your position and your truth from the enemy," he has said.

But since the press was covering this event, the

---

* Basically, these "stealth" tactics include "voters' guides," which are mailed out containing misleading information about

Ralph Reed who opened the Road to Victory Conference presented the moderate, "healing" face of the Christian Coalition. That was frightening enough.

Celebrating the progress that had been made since the last conference, Reed boasted: "Howard Metzenbaum (BOOS FROM THE CROWD), one of our favorite members of the U.S. Senate, has been replaced by a pro-family, pro-life *Roman Catholic* (CHEERS), Mike Dewine." That's when the veins in my head started contracting.

Then he reminded the crowd that "we bear the name of He at which every knee shall bow and every tongue shall confess." By now my head had started throbbing.

Speaking of tongues, Reed urged participants in the conference to refrain from "violence of the tongue." Two minutes later, he engaged in a little tongue-violence himself, telling a bald-faced lie about Joycelyn Elders. Ralph claimed she had "called for the legalization of drugs," which is just plain false.

Reed also touched on the subject of my book. Noting that Mario Cuomo is now a talk-show host, Reed joked, "I know Rush Limbaugh. Rush Limbaugh is a friend of mine, and you, sir, are no Rush Limbaugh." The crowd loved that one, especially the towheaded 14-year-old Christian Coalition kid who, when he saw me on the edge of the crowd, rushed up to have his picture taken. I guess because I'm on TV. And I'm pretty sure he didn't know my politics. As he shook

---

opposition candidates; telephone smear campaigns; anonymous flyers which demonize opponents. That sort of thing.

How Big a Nut Is He?

"The feminist agenda . . . is not about equal rights for women. It is about a socialist, anti-family political movement that encourages women to leave their husbands, kill their children, practice witchcraft and become lesbians."

Pat Robertson,
fund-raising letter to Iowans

my hand, I got a very nervous feeling that his parents would burn the picture once this book comes out.

Reed, it turns out, is also a fan. Or at least he says so. Remember, he believes in "stealth" politics, so he might have just been "coming in under my radar screen." At one point, I tried to buttonhole Reed to see if we could talk. He saw me as he was coming offstage, smiled, and extended his hand. "Al," he said exuberantly, "I'm a big fan. What's the name of that character with the yellow sweater?"

"Stuart Smalley," I said, shaking his hand.

"I love him!"

I shouldn't have been surprised. As evangelical Christians go, Reed is very well versed in popular culture. In fact, a 1994 *People* magazine profile began with Reed extolling the virtues of John and Paul:

Sgt. Pepper was one of the most significant albums in the history of rock and roll. Lennon was a dark and troubled genius, and the Beatles elevated rock music to a kind of art form.

When I read that, my first thought was that Reed is just a real big Beatles fan. But then I remembered what Reed has said about his approach to politics:

It's like guerrilla welfare. . . . You've got two choices: You can wear cammies and shimmy along on your belly, or you can put on a red coat and stand up for everyone to see. It comes down to whether you want to be the British Army in the Revolutionary War or the Vietcong. History tells us which tactic was more effective.

This got me thinking that maybe Reed's hipster knowledge of popular culture had been a bit of camouflage, designed to lull the Baby-Boomer *People* reporter into letting his guard down.

How far can something like this go? Imagine Reed in a Florida condo complex trying to win over a crowd of elderly Jews. "Hackett was the master of the heartburn joke, whereas Rickles is still the consummate practitioner of the ethnic putdown. Yet at the end of the evening, Rickles makes it clear that he loves everyone and is just kidding."

Or suppose Reed wanted to sway a group of Harlem teenagers. "Public Enemy are more than just a fly posse. *Fear of a Black Planet* is a political manifesto, boyee. Chuck D is a prophet of rage, knowutImsayin'?"

But I digress.

Reed agreed to give me a five-minute interview and suggested I speak with his press secretary, Mike Russell. I found Russell, who also told me he was a big fan. He told me to call him in a few days to set up the interview. I called. Many times. He never called back. Frankly, I don't think that's very Christian. Then again, if I were him, *I* wouldn't call me.

I reentered the hall to hear Reed introduce Newt. "Newt Gingrich was pro-family before pro-family was cool." I tried to figure out if that meant being pro-family became cool *before* or *after* Newt got those blow jobs from the wife of a fellow college professor.

This was interesting. How would Newt address the oral revelations in the recently published *Vanity Fair* article in front of the Christian Coalition? As it turned out, he did it the usual way. By attacking liberals:

A number of liberals, particularly columnists and reporters, start with two standards, and these are their two standards: A number of Republican candidates for president . . . and I'm not one but I fit because I'm a national leader . . . who say they're pro-family are divorced. "Hah! We know what that means. So what right do they have?" Now, they have a second standard: People like Jesse Helms have been married too long to understand the problems of modern America. (BIG LAUGH) . . . So the only people you should listen to are social therapists who do not believe in God and who will tell you that you should simply relax and accept your decay and your depravity because it's the most you've got. (HUGE APPLAUSE)

Yes. That's us liberals, all right. When we're not attacking Jesse Helms for being married too long, we're paying our atheist therapists to tell us to accept our depravity.

I had a whole day of this stuff. I heard speakers from the podium refer to people like me as "lewd leftists," call liberals "corrupt and licentious," and say that "liberalism had made a pact with the devil." Also, it seems that the Prophet Isaiah had a real beef with the Great Society, saying all liberals were "vile. And they hate the poor."

I walked into a smaller "breakout session" on the 104th Congress, where one Christian referred to the President as "a scumbag," the First Lady as a "scumbagette," and their daughter as a "scumbagger."

Then there's abortion. Here's something I'll bet you didn't know. According to one speaker, "Of the four women listed in the genealogy of Jesus Christ . . . one [was] a product of rape and one a product of incest." Good thing for Western civilization that *Roe v. Wade* didn't take effect two thousand years earlier.

I heard a lot about prayer in school. Right now, the Coalition is pushing for the Religious Equality Amendment, which would allow "voluntary, student and citizen-initiated free speech in noncompulsory settings such as courthouse lawns, high school graduation ceremonies, and sports events." I think this means you could have a homecoming float with the nativity scene on it, but I'm not sure. I'm pretty certain, though, that if the Blessed Mother had pom-poms, it would spoil the whole thing for everybody.

By now you may be thinking that I'm showing an anti-Christian bias. Nonsense! Need I remind you that I *married* a Roman Catholic, whom I met in college, despoiled, and then convinced to renounce the Pope? So give me a break.

Convicted felons were invited to speak. Former Nixon aide Chuck "Let's firebomb the Brookings Institute" Colson, who found Christ in prison, not only spoke but, if I heard correctly, was the recipient of this year's Layman of the Year Award. I think that's fine. I'm all for redemption. But I'd be pissed if I had been Layman of the Year runner-up.

Ollie North spoke about the importance of electing local officials. And the Coalition has had tremendous success recently in taking over local school boards. All part of its attempt to rid curricula of "politically correct" liberal ideas like, say, evolution.

In fact, Creationism routinely won enthusiastic applause at the conference. I asked a nice 40-year-old woman named Pat from Florida about her views on the subject. She told me that God created man in his own image ten thousand years ago, not four billion, as those godless "experts" at universities believe. "Ten thousand?" I asked.

"Ten thousand." She nodded.

I asked her if she had seen *Jurassic Park*. She said that she had and that her entire family loved it. I tried to explain to her that she had to choose. Either *Jurassic Park* or Creationism. You can't have both.

Pat didn't seem to get my point. But she was very

Hey Gals, Check This Out!

"You know who's pushing [abortion]. You saw some of those women out there. I mean those women aren't ever going to have a baby by anybody. I mean, these are primarily lesbians, and lesbians don't have babies. And it's the one thing a mother has—that a lesbian can never have—is this femininity, and they can never achieve that. And so, in order to level the field, they say, 'Hey, let you abort your baby so you'll be like us, because we don't have them.'"

Pat Robertson, *700 Club*

nice, noticed I was ill, and wordlessly led me by the hand to her hotel room, where we spent an evening of unbridled passion.

Okay, that last part is just not true. What I actually did was go over to the American Enterprise Institute and take a nap on Norm Ornstein's couch.

So I missed Pat Robertson's speech. I learned later I would have been disappointed. He made no mention of any centuries-old satanic plots and, other than a passing reference to possibly repealing some of the sixties civil rights legislation, said nothing that could be construed as insane, apocalyptic, or even vaguely anti-Semitic.

I missed most of the presidential candidates, too.

But I understand that most of them gave their standard stump speeches, only with a lot more references to fetuses.

In fact, I missed so many of the speeches that I've decided to ask the Christian Coalition for a partial refund on the $40 registration fee. Which I'm going to do as soon as Ralph Reed calls me back. Of course, I figure the chances of that are about as good as the chances of an unrepentant Jew surviving the Apocalypse.

(Send anti-Semitic hate mail to Delacorte Press, attn: Jewish Media Conspirators.)

45
EPILOGUE:
A TIME FOR HEALING

By the next day my headache had disappeared. And yet, as I flew back to New York, I felt overwhelmed by a disquieting spiritual emptiness. In a way, I envied the absolute moral certainty of the people I met at the Road to Victory Conference. Sure, a lot of them were sanctimonious zealots. But some of them had seemed very nice. One or two had even offered to pray for me. And now it was my intention to make them objects of my ridicule.

I thought about what Ralph Reed had said about "violence of the tongue." Yes, Reed had been hypocritical about that himself, but it was Christ who said on the cross: "Forgive them, Father, for they know not what they do." Then I remembered that Reed knows exactly what he's doing and got mad all over again.

But I began to think about this book in terms of that phrase: Violence of the tongue. Is that what *Rush Limbaugh Is a Big Fat Idiot and Other Observations* had become? Is that what I was giving my readers? Don't I owe you more? Don't I owe America more?

I thought back to the Americans I had met at the Perot conference. Some of them were crackpots, sure. But I thought about Hank from Michigan, a retired autoworker who was worried about jobs moving overseas. I thought about Louise from Washington state, who was scared for her children because wages for non–college graduates have fallen 20 percent in the last twenty years. I thought about Gayle from Texas, who thought that members of the Bilderbergs, the Council on Foreign Relations, the Trilateral Commission, and the Skull and Bones Society were involved in a worldwide conspiracy.

I opened my briefcase and pulled out a stack of Frank Luntz's research. Most Americans think we're on the wrong track. Americans are working harder and longer for less. If there are two parents in a household (which is getting rarer and rarer), chances are they're both working. Sometimes at two jobs each. And they're spending less and less time with their kids.

We are all living in a wildly more complicated world than we were born into. And at the same time the trust in our institutions, in government, in family, in individuals, is eroding. And lack of trust creates fear, and fear creates anger.

I thought about how our political system appeals to the worst, not the best, in us. Not to the goodness of America. And again I thought about this book.

Maybe, I thought, maybe *I'm* on the wrong track. Yes, someone needs to take on demagogues like

Limbaugh and Gingrich and Robertson. But maybe I'm doing my country a disservice. Maybe I'm sowing the very seeds of distrust that I so decry.

Perhaps, I thought, I should throw away the 200-plus pages of cheap, tawdry, mean-spirited (yet accurate) bile, and start over on a book whose humor heals rather than wounds.

Then, as we flew over Manhattan, I happened to look down and catch a glimpse of the Delacorte building, and it occurred to me that my book was due in a week.

Then we flew over my daughter's private school. And then my son's orthodontist. Followed by the bank that holds the mortgage on my apartment.

And as the plane turned and banked its wings, a stream of light pierced the window, bathing my face in the orange glow of the sun setting over the American continent. And I thought to myself, "You know, Rush Limbaugh *is* a big fat idiot."

THE END

SPECIAL FOR THE PAPERBACK EDITION: NEW DIRT ON THE NUTCASE RIGHT

46
ADVENTURES IN MARKETING
JANUARY–APRIL 1996

I Go on a Book Tour, Bask in Glory, Taunt My Enemies, and Learn Terrible Things About Deepak Chopra

My book tour officially began on January 17, 1996, in Washington, D.C., our nation's capital. That morning, I hawked *Rush Limbaugh Is a Big Fat Idiot* on a D.C. TV show and a local public radio broadcast. By noon, when I was walking to another appointment, drivers in Washington were rolling down their car windows and yelling, "I love your book!" Of course, they didn't really love my book. They loved the *title* of my book.

Most of the callers who got on the air during my first national TV appearance did not love the title of my book. In fact, they were very angry about it. I probably should have anticipated this. A lot of dittoheads watch C-SPAN.

I was on *Washington Journal* with host Susan Swain. (Immediately before coming to C-SPAN, Susan did advance work for *Up with People*.) Her first question was "Why the title?" I gave her my prepared answer:

"Well, first of all, Rush is very fat. He's enormous. Just a huge, huge fat guy."

To my surprise, Susan did not laugh. After this happened a second time, Susan felt she owed me an explanation: "I'm not supposed to laugh." She said this on the air.

I asked, "Is this some kind of Brian Lamb rule?" Brian Lamb is the founder and CEO of C-SPAN.

"Yes," she said. Susan explained Brian's reasoning: Viewers might interpret a laugh as an indication of some philosophical bias on the part of the host, thereby eroding C-SPAN's standing as a paragon of neutrality. So, it's C-SPAN policy—no laughter.

At least from the host. I'm sure I can get the callers to join in the fun, I thought. I was so wrong. One angry caller accused me of snorting cocaine in the seventies.* Another tried some withering sarcasm. Did I think my book would sell one-tenth the copies that Rush's had?

"At least *I* wrote my book."

That's what I wish I had said. After the show I realized that I was going to get a lot of this, so I might as well be ready for it. In fact, probably the most fun I

---

* I assume he got this from Bob Woodward's exploitation book on John Belushi, *Wired*, which claimed, accurately, that there was widespread use of cocaine at *Saturday Night Live*. The only thing is, I was one of the few staffers not singled out for snorting the stuff. I think I escaped Woodward's focus because my one interview with him abruptly ended after about thirty seconds. He asked me if I had ever seen John do cocaine. I answered, "Only once, when he was snorting it with Carl Bernstein."

had on the rest of the tour came from taunting didiots.

"You wouldn't have a best seller if you hadn't put
Rush's name on it!" I got that one a lot on call-in
radio shows. My pat response: "That's a very good
point, caller. You're absolutely right. If Rush wasn't
such a vile and loathsome demagogue, hated by millions and millions of people, I wouldn't have a best
seller. Thank you for your call."

Then there was the guy in Boston. I was on *The
Jerry Williams Show*. Jerry is a conservative talk radio
host, and like most conservative talk radio hosts he
actually despises Rush. Which I was surprised to dis-
cover. As it turns out, about half of them think he's a
terrible demagogue, while the rest are just insanely
jealous. Anyway, Jerry and I were having a good time
for about a half hour. Then he opened up the phones.

"Yeah, Al. I've been listening, and nothing you have
said is even remotely funny."

"How about the joke I told earlier?" I asked. "Having Al D'Amato lead an ethics investigation is like
having Bob Dornan head up a mental health task
force?" (I'd been flogging that joke on the tour.)

There was a pause. Finally, "Okay. That was a little
funny."

"Well, then you've contradicted yourself."

"No, I didn't."

"Yes, you did. You said that nothing I said was even
remotely funny."

"No, I didn't."

"Yes, you did, caller," said Jerry.

"Cut him off, Jerry," I said. And Jerry cut him off.

My appearances on right wing talk shows didn't always infuriate dittoheads. Sometimes they were just confused. Like when I went on Ollie North's radio show and he really liked me.

The reason Ollie invited me on the show was that he'd read the "Operation Chickenhawk" chapter, in which he single-handedly kills almost an entire company of North Vietnamese. The chapter had just appeared in *Playboy*, and Ollie told me he'd read it when some kid handed him a Xeroxed copy while he was on an airplane.

I wondered what the chances were of a kid running into Ollie North on an airplane while carrying a Xeroxed copy of "Operation Chickenhawk" from the March issue of *Playboy*. Probably not quite as good as the chances that Ollie would tell a white lie to cover up the fact that he reads dirty magazines. I mean, he does lie now and again.

Mostly, though, the tour was one big coast-to-coast lovefest. In Seattle, 1700 people showed up for a book signing. In St. Louis, people lined up for hours to thank me for insulting so many Republicans. In Berkeley, a University of California professor introduced me by saying how important my book is and putting it into some kind of historical perspective that I didn't understand and probably wouldn't agree with if I did.

Terrible Things about Deepak Chopra

The day my book hit number one on the *New York Times* bestseller list, I flew into a large midwestern city. I was greeted by my "media escort." Let me explain what a media escort is. A media escort is almost always a woman, usually in her forties or fifties, who got into the media escorting business when her kids went off to college. Her job is to drive authors around to book signings and TV, radio, and newspaper interviews. She also tips the doorman at your hotel.

So this particular media escort picked me up at the airport and said, "I'm so glad your book has hit number one. You know, when it first hit the list, I was escorting an author who called it a fluke. He said it was going to fall off the list right away."

"Who was the author?" I wanted to know.

"Oh, I really shouldn't tell you," she said.

"Well, you can't say something like that and then not tell me who said it."

"I really shouldn't."

"Is it someone famous?"

"Yes, yes."

"At least give me a hint."

"Okay," she relented. "He has two books on the list."

"Deepak Chopra?!"

"Yes!"

She was surprised I figured it out so quickly. But when you're on the list, believe me, you study it obsessively. Evidently, no one knows this better than Deepak Chopra.

After that, I kind of made it a point to ask all my media escorts if they had any good Deepak Chopra stories. While no one came up with anything as juicy as *The Weekly Standard*'s Matt Labash (who managed to dig up credit card receipts for a hooker Deepak allegedly "visited" in 1991*), the general picture that emerged was of a hypercompetitive, condescending jerk.

My favorite Deepak story was this: Arriving at the airport in a state that had just passed a seat belt law, Deepak gets in the car with his media escort. She asks him to put on his seat belt. He refuses, saying that he has foreseen his own death and it will not be in a car accident. I just wish she had responded, "Have you foreseen whether I'm going to get a $200 fine?"

But enough about Deepak Chopra.

A SORT OF HOMECOMING

The highlight of the book tour was going to be my whirlwind trip to the Twin Cities. Hometown boy makes good, that sort of thing. Two solid days of print, radio, TV, book signings, with just enough time for dinner with my 78-year-old mom and some old friends. I was scheduled wall-to-wall. But that's the way it is when you're promoting a #1 best seller. You've got to travel light and strike fast.

* See *The Weekly Standard*, July 1, 1996, pages 22–24.

Unfortunately, the entire trip was colored by an unscheduled event. As I sipped Evian in the first class section of Northwest Flight 44 to Minneapolis, my mother's apartment was burning.

Mom was safe. But homeless. She had escaped the fire and was at the home of her friend Eleanor. I learned all this when I called my wife from the airport. Franni told me to call Eleanor.

"You're here!" That's what Eleanor said when I called.

I said, "Yes, Eleanor, I just landed."

"You're here!" Eleanor said again.

"Yes. Is Mom okay?"

"He's here!" Eleanor yelled to Mom.

It turned out that Mom couldn't stay with Eleanor, and this leg of my tour had just become infinitely more complicated. In addition to being homeless, Mom had no clothes or any personal belongings whatsoever. Also, she was slightly hysterical.

I got Mom a room at my hotel. We decided that it would probably be best for her to accompany me on my interviews. Spending the time together might help calm her down. The first stop was KSTP radio and *The Barbara Carlson Show*, which Mom listens to a lot. This could even turn out to be fun, I thought.

"Just one thing, Mom. You're not going to be on the radio."

Now, I make it a point to use the bathroom about five minutes before I do an on-air interview. I don't think I need to explain why. When I returned to the Green Room, Mom was gone. Frankly, I was a little concerned, so I searched the radio station but couldn't find her. Finally, it was time for the inter-

© 1996 Star Tribune/Minneapolis–St. Paul

My mother's apartment building burns to the ground.

view. As I was led into the studio, my heart sank. There was Mom, sitting in front of a mike, wearing headphones.

Mom did three radio interviews that day. I believe she was on two television shows. Minneapolis learned everything about my childhood that my mother felt it should know. Including my SAT scores.

The Twin Cities also heard all about the fire. Which turned out to be a good thing. Someone from the insurance company came to my next book signing and ended up helping Mom a lot. All in all, it was a pretty productive trip. My Minneapolis media escort, Isabel, volunteered to be Mom's personal shopper, and thank God for our friends the Watsons, who gave Mom a place to live while she looked for a place to live. Without them and my wife handling things from New York, I could never have abandoned my homeless mother to move onto yet another city to flog my book.

It Ain't Over Till the Fat Guy Sings

Probably the question I got asked the most on the tour was "Has Rush responded?" First off, we did send Rush the book a month before it came out, along with a note from my editor that said:

Dear Rush,
    Al feels it might help sales if you mentioned the book on your show.

Best wishes,
Leslie Schnur

Rush never did mention the book on his show. Nor did any of his prescreened callers.

So I took to the airwaves in an attempt to draw him out. I appeared on Comedy Central in a series of spots challenging Rush to a debate on the proposition: "Resolved: Rush Limbaugh is a big fat idiot." I even offered to let him take either side.

Still no word from Rush. Actually, I expected that. If I were Rush, I wouldn't have dignified my cheap, vulgar insults with a response.

But then, surprisingly, Rush *did* respond. While reading the Limbaugh-related newsgroups on the Internet, my research assistant, Geoff, found a message from Rush himself.

It was on the alt.fan.rush-limbaugh newsgroup. First, on April 8, 1996, Rush posted a message entitled "Message to My Fans." Referring to the large number of posts from Limbaugh haters, he wrote:

> It would seem that the liberals have to resort to name-calling instead of common sense. But common sense will prevail, so don't worry, you people.

A dittohead from Ohio State then replied to Rush's message with the following bit of "common sense":

> Greetings and Salutations!
>
> Here's some book ideas:
> • Al Franken is a desperate, washed-up loser.

- The least funniest wash-out comedian: Al Franken
- Gene Shallot's [sic] love for Barnyard Animals, aka, the birth of Al Franken
- Al Franken: The adventures of butt uglyman
- Me and my grotesque froglike appearance by Al Franken
- Al Franken: Abortion Posterchild
- Adventures in Beastiality: [sic] The Al Franken Story

I hope you get a kick out of this!
Thanks, Rush!
Keep up the good work!
Best regards,
xxxx xxxxx

The next day, April 9, Rush responded to the Ohio State kid's response under the title "Re: Message to My Fans":

Thank you for replying to my article. I like my fans praising me and my great wisdom. Anyway, about Al Franken, I did read his book and I did not think it was very funny, just stupid. You really came up with some excellent book ideas about Al Franken. Let me tell you something. The liberals are running scared. They are scared of the wisdom and common sense that I spew out in my radio and television programs. They are unable to challenge my wisdom, so they resort to names such as fatboy and old blubber ass. They are so scared that they embrace Al

Franken. But do not worry; common sense will
prevail.

Rush Limbaugh
Excellence in Broadcasting Network
http://www.rushties.com

Now, I could point out the logical inconsistency of
claiming that "liberals resort to name-calling instead
of common sense" and then turning around and com-
plimenting a fan for calling me "butt uglyman." Or
perhaps I could make light of Rush's own choice of
the word "spew" to describe what he does for a living.
And I suppose I could indignantly note that I have
never, ever, ever referred to Rush as "old blubber ass"
(blubber butt, yes; lard-ass, yes; but *never* "old blubber ass").

But I think I'll just let Rush's own words speak for
themselves.

One final note before I end this chapter. It is still
too early for historians to assess the ultimate impact
of my book on Western civilization. But I think it's
safe to say that it has fundamentally changed Rush's
life. For the better.

Because the guy has been shedding pounds like you
wouldn't believe. One night in the middle of June, I
stayed up late to watch Rush's television show (until it
got canceled, it was on at three in the morning, right
after a half-hour infomercial for Ab Roller Plus). Immediately, I was struck by how . . . normal-sized he
looked. Then, a few minutes later—as if to drive
home the point—Rush was flailing his arms wildly in

mid-rant, when his wedding ring flew off his finger and sailed off camera. Surprised, he said, "I've lost some weight."

Boy, has he! I mean, the guy really looks good! Sure, he's still fat. But not fat enough to write a whole book about it.

Of course, if the "Rush at a Glance" timeline in Chapter Two proves anything, it's that Rush has been seesawing back and forth for a couple of decades now, and every time he loses weight he eventually gains it all back and then some.

But for the time being, I'm going to give him the benefit of the doubt and accept the thanks that Rush owes me for providing the toughlove he needed to reverse his harrowing descent into food-assisted suicide.

You're welcome, Rush.

47

ADVENTURES IN POLITICS THE 1996 PRIMARY SEASON

I Cover the Primaries for *Newsweek* and Do a Very Bad Job

Part One: The Forbes Juggernaut Stalls in new Hampshire.

You'll remember that there was a brief period of time in early 1996 when it looked like a geeky, awkward rich guy who'd never held either elective office or a real job anywhere outside of his dad's publishing company might become the Republican presidential nominee.

In January, Steve Forbes was actually ahead of Bob Dole in the polls in New Hampshire. He managed to do this on the strength of two things. The first was a relentless barrage of negative ads accusing Dole of being a lifelong Washington insider who had raised our taxes a couple of hundred times.

The second was the flat tax. Which, since my book did so well, I now support. I feel that being taxed 17 percent instead of 39.6 percent on my royalties would really unleash my creative energies.

The week of the Iowa caucuses, *Newsweek* asked me to follow Forbes and interview him. It was my first foray into serious journalism. And I was delighted. See, I really didn't like Forbes. And neither, it would turn out, did Iowa Republicans, who ultimately resented the millions of dollars he spent soiling the caucus punch bowl with his sleazy attack ads.

Also, he had not been particularly forthright. When asked at the Des Moines debate how much he personally would save if his flat tax were adopted, Forbes answered in a very interesting way. He said, "There have been various estimates of that from $100,000 to $250,000." That may have been true. But whoever made those estimates would be off by several million dollars. According to *Fortune* magazine, Forbes is worth $439 million. Assuming, say, an eight percent return on investment, that's over $30 million a year in interest and capital gains. None of which would be taxed under his plan. I figure that means Forbes would save a good $10 million. Per year. Of course, there's no way to really know. The irony of the Forbes campaign was that his main issue was taxes —and he wouldn't release his taxes.

So my assignment was to interview the man. And the Forbes campaign promised me fifteen minutes of face time. The woman in his press office who made this promise asked me what I planned to ask him. I said I didn't know but mentioned that I was a humorist.

"You're not going to make fun of him, are you?"

"No," I lied.

The plan was this: I'd catch up to him in Iowa for the caucuses, then fly to New Hampshire, follow him again for a day, then use my fifteen minutes to ask the kind of tough, substantive questions that provide a window into the soul of a prospective president.

"Mr. Forbes, you grew up in a house called Timberfield. I was thinking of giving my apartment a name. Do you have any suggestions?"

In Iowa I noticed something very odd about Forbes. By then everybody had picked up on the fact that the man almost never blinks. But I noticed that when he laughs, the tip of his tongue goes up to the roof of his mouth. Very disturbing. It's like women who cover their mouths when they laugh. The purpose of the Forbes Tongue Shift seems to be to prevent you from seeing his uvula. My guess is that Forbes was taught at an early age that it's impolite to show your uvula. Which is very impressive. To this day, I am in awe of the social graces of the wellborn.

On caucus night I went to a school gymnasium in suburban Des Moines. There I talked with some Buchanan supporters. A man in his fifties told me he was against gays in the military. Then he added that he was against gays in the *workplace*. Looking back, I guess I should have pointed out to him that this would inevitably swell the welfare rolls.

Buchanan came in a close second to Dole in Iowa. Forbes, a distant third. All told, he spent over $400 per caucus vote. I estimated that at that rate, he could buy only about a million votes nationwide before he'd have to sell his island in the Pacific. So the Forbes campaign canceled the next day's events in New Hampshire to cut some new spots in the hope of getting it down to $385 a vote.

But the Forbes press office assured me I could have

my fifteen minutes at the Milford Rotary Club on Wednesday. So I used Tuesday night to check out the other campaigns. I went to a Dole spaghetti dinner at a VFW hall in Manchester. It was a terrific event. A real morale booster for Dole, because there were actually some people there who were older than him.

In a banquet hall across town, a giddy Pat Buchanan mounted the stage to the pounding strains of "We Will Rock You," sung by Queen's Freddie Mercury, who died of AIDS. Which I thought was very progressive for a Buchanan event.

There was a kaffeeklatsch for Lamar at the home of a utilities lawyer, where I chatted with Ben Wattenberg and David Gergen after the candidate blandly explained his ABCs: "Alexander Beats Clinton." And his ABCDEFGs: "Alexander Beats Clinton, Dole, and Even Forbes and Gramm." That actually got a laugh. Of course, presidential historians will probably remember Alexander's ABCs as simply "A Bad Campaign."

On Wednesday, it was very cold in Milford. All hundred or so of us in the press had to stand outside the Rotary Club freezing for two hours because, according to Forbes's press guy, we had scared the Rotarians. When Forbes arrived, there was this awful crush on the porch, and I got to know Mary McGrory of the *Washington Post* far better than I ever thought I would. Still, the press guy kept assuring me that I was at the top of his list for the interview.

While we were waiting for Forbes to leave, a Dutch TV crew decided to interview *me*. That's how little was happening. The Dutch correspondent asked me, "Who of the Republicans do you like the most?"

"Of the Republicans? I guess Dole," I answered.

"Ohhh, but he is so old!" the Dutch correspondent said, scrunching up his face.

"Well." I looked at him. "He wasn't too old to save your sorry Dutch ass." I wanted to make sure he understood what I was saying. So I asked, "How long did it take the Nazis to roll over Holland? Was that about an hour?"

That ruffled his Euro-feathers.

Then I decided to really cross the line. "Maybe I'd cut you a little more slack if you'd done a better job of hiding Anne Frank."

I just hope that got on Dutch TV.

After the event, Forbes gave a six-minute press conference outside the Rotary Club and then climbed on his campaign bus with Wattenberg and Gergen. I tried to get on, but was pushed off as I yelled, "Ben, help me out here!"

So I blew my first *Newsweek* assignment. But by then Forbes was sinking fast, and Buchanan was about to become the Big Story.

Still, Forbes's candidacy may start a new trend in American politics: vanity campaigns. By the next cycle, a presidential race might be a neat thing a rich guy can buy for his wife. "Happy birthday, honey. You're running for president!"

"Oh, honey, that is so sweet!"

"You've got media buys in Iowa and New Hampshire."

"Oh, that's great! What am I running on?"

"The flat tax."

I'm betting on Marla Maples in 2000.

PART TWO: I FOLLOW PAT BUCHANAN FOR THREE DAYS, AND HE STIFFS ME.

After I blew the Forbes assignment, *Newsweek* gave me one more shot. It was late February, and Pat Buchanan was on fire. His unique brand of vindictive populism had brought him victories in Alaska, Louisiana, and New Hampshire. Clearly fascinated, the media had dropped Forbes like a hot rock, and now Buchanan was the Story du Jour.*

I joined up with the Buchanan press corps in South Carolina and spent three days eating bad food, getting shoved on and off buses by the Secret Service, and being jerked around by the Buchanan press people.

I knew it was a long shot from the beginning. Buchanan's communications director, Greg Mueller, is a close friend of Rush Limbaugh's. At this point my book had been out for about six weeks, so there was a good chance Mueller had read the chapter entitled "Pat Buchanan: Nazi Lover."

Still, I was operating on the theory that of all the Republican candidates, Buchanan was best equipped to handle me and my snide questions. As he says, "I've been in the Crossfire." Heck, I thought he might *enjoy* talking to me.

---

* That's French. It means "Story of the Day."

Day One. The Greenville Marriott. The candidate was enjoying a few hours of "downtime." *My* "downtime" was spent waiting by the phone for Mueller, who was in Washington, to return my calls. Finally, I put on some shorts and headed for the gym. When you've written a book calling someone a big fat idiot, it's a good idea to stay trim.

I got in the elevator. And there was Buchanan with his entourage. Here was my chance! I thought I'd start by amusing him, so I went into a little something from my book. Reminding him that we had met in 1988 at the Atlanta Convention, I said, "When I got back to New York, I told my friends that Pat Buchanan was very charming. And they said, 'Yeah, well, Goebbels was charming.'" Buchanan laughed. This is working, I thought.

"I told my friends that was really unfair. Goebbels *wasn't* charming." That might have been a mistake. He stopped laughing.

Then he noticed my gym shorts. "Good treadmill here?" I found out later he uses a treadmill daily. Thank heavens the bum knee that kept him out of Vietnam isn't still bothering him.

"I use the bike—say, I'm on assignment for *Newsweek* and I need about ten minutes with you."

"Not now," said a young press aide as the door opened. The aide would say later with some admiration that I had "swung at the first pitch," but "it was low and inside."

"Good luck," said Buchanan as he patted me on the shoulder and headed into the lobby.

That night's event was at a nondenominational,

charismatic Mega-Church. There Buchanan sounded his theme: "Pat Buchanan means what he says and says what he means." He proudly defended his 1992 Convention speech. "I said, 'There was a cultural war going on in this country for the soul of America.' " Of course, that's *not* precisely what he said. Buchanan conveniently omits that he said, "There is a *religious* war . . ." It's a misrepresentation that Buchanan made at every stop. Buchanan means what he says and says what he means, but evidently he has trouble saying what he said.

Day Two. On the bus, the young press aide told me he'd call Mueller when we got to Columbia. I was skeptical. We were going to the debate: Buchanan, Dole, Forbes, and Alexander. At one point Forbes said he would outlaw abortions for the purpose of gender selection. Which confused me, because I didn't know that was a big problem in America. Then I remembered that Forbes has five daughters. Maybe it had crossed his mind.

Alan Keyes was excluded from the debate and announced that he would go on a hunger strike until he was allowed back in. He even said he would refuse *fluids*. Conceivably, he could have died if he hadn't been given a spot in the Georgia debate a week later.

Night Two was a big "God and country" rally hosted by Ralph Reed. I searched the place for Susan Smith's stepfather, who, you'll remember from Chapter 37, was a big mucky-muck in the South Carolina Christian Coalition. Or at least he was back when he was molesting his stepdaughter.

Reed got the evening off to a great start by, once

again, appropriating God for his side. "The pundits, the prognosticators, the self-appointed chatter-class, honestly believe that the most dangerous thing that could happen in America today is for people who believe in God, pray, and read the Bible to get involved in the political process." I guess that explains why the press was so scared of Jimmy Carter.

All the candidates spoke. Buchanan was the clear favorite. Strom Thurmond, who was only 93 at this time and running for reelection, appeared with Dole. A Buchanan supporter who told me she supported term limits also said she planned to vote for Thurmond. I asked her if she would vote for Thurmond if he ran for reelection in 2002. She said, "I'd have to see how senile he was." I asked her how senile is too senile? She said, "I'd have to make that judgment then."

Keyes spoke last. But I left because I was hungry.

Day Three. On the press bus from Columbia to Charleston, it was becoming pretty clear that I wasn't getting my interview. Buchanan's people kept telling me I was "on the list." That's bad. The Forbes people had told me I was at the *top* of the list.

We were headed to the Citadel, where Buchanan would stand up for the Southern tradition of excluding women from state-funded military academies. All across South Carolina, Buchanan had been standing up for other Southern traditions, like flying the Confederate flag and playing "Dixie" (wink, wink).

About two hundred cadets had turned out, wearing military-issue rain gear under the heavy drizzle. While we waited for Buchanan, the press stood under a tent that had been set up to keep us dry. But I grabbed an umbrella so I could berate a few cadets. See, all two hundred had skipped class to see Buchanan.

"Why am I paying taxes for you to go to school to skip classes?!"

"We're taking the consequences, sir," a cadet answered, standing at attention. The consequences, he informed me, were ten hours of solitary confinement. I pretended not to be impressed.

"What class are you missing now, son?" As long as he was calling me "sir," there was no reason not to call him "son."

"History of Western Civilization. Sir."

"Good thing to know about, son. Western civilization."

Now some of the cadets were getting angry. "Sir," asked one, "did you ever go to college?" I told him I went to Harvard. Perhaps he'd heard of it. "Didn't you ever miss class?" he wanted to know.

"I'm the journalist here!" I shouted indignantly. "I don't have to answer that!" Besides, I explained, the question was irrelevant, since Harvard is a private school.

The cadet was smarter than I thought. "Yes, sir. I understand about private schools. But you still get federal funding."

It sure didn't take much to stump me. I turned to Sidney Blumenthal of *The New Yorker*, who was under the press tent. "Sidney, help me out here. Does Harvard get federal funding?"

By now a few of the about fifty cadets who had been

pulled into the discussion were beginning to recognize me and realize that I was just having a bit of fun. "Hey, that's Al Franken," a cadet shouted.

"How do I get on *Saturday Night Live?*" another shouted.

"You want to know how you get on a show like that?" I asked. "You study. You think I missed a comedy class even once?"

On the flight from Charleston to Florence, I was getting desperate. I was up against my *Newsweek* filing deadline, and I still couldn't get my interview. I agreed to read my questions to yet another Buchanan aide, a humorless guy named John Condit.

• Mr. Buchanan, in your autobiography you write proudly about your penchant for brawling. Can you remember the name of the last guy you slugged?

• You have said that Holocaust survivors had "group fantasies of martyrdom and heroics." Is the same true of your supporters?

• Have you ever had a homoerotic dream?

Not a snicker. John cut me off, saying I was "on the list."

While I may still be on some kind of list within the Buchanan organization, I didn't get my interview. But after three days of following him around, I'm convinced of this: Pat Buchanan speaks in code.

Like any code, it's deliberately ambiguous. Which can lead to a lot of confusion. Case in point:

Back in 1992, when Buchanan was running for the first time, a screenwriter friend of mind went undercover to a Klan rally to research a movie. At one point a Klansman told him, "There's a lot I like about Pat Buchanan. But I worry that he's not really a racist."

48

ADVENTURES IN POLITICS
MAY 4, 1996

THE WASHINGTON HILTON. I DELIVER A SPEECH AT THE WHITE HOUSE CORRESPONDENTS DINNER AND RANKLE NEWT GINGRICH, WHO THREATENS TO SLUG ME.

Carl Lubsdorf, president of the White House Correspondents Association, called last September. Who could I recommend to speak at their dinner in May? I suggested myself.

Carl's immediate reaction was not positive. After all, I had just been the after-dinner speaker at their 1994 dinner. "How about David Letterman?" Carl asked.

"Great, if you can get him," I said bitterly.

Carl thanked me and said good-bye. A couple of days later he called back. Would I like to be the speaker? Surprised and flattered, I modestly accepted.

COCKTAIL BANTER WITH G. GORDON LIDDY

To get a feel for the Washington dinner gestalt, I decided to attend all the big D.C. fetes that precede the correspondents dinner on the Washington social calendar. First up was the "Salute to Congress" dinner in late January. Once again I was the guest of Josette Shiner of the *Washington Times* and this time was seated next to Maryland Lieutenant Governor Kathleen Kennedy Townsend, Bobby Kennedy's daughter. Seated to Kathleen's immediate left was Watergate felon and radio talk show host G. Gordon Liddy.

During dinner Kathleen excused herself for a few minutes, and I took the opportunity to ask Liddy about his 1995 comment suggesting that the best way to kill a federal agent was to shoot him in the head. "That was taken out of context, right?" I asked.

Not really. Liddy was very matter-of-fact: "All I said was that if law enforcement officials knock on your door, announce themselves, and state that they have a warrant, your obligation is to admit them, stand aside, and let them execute their warrant. If, on the other hand, they smash in your door and come in shooting, you have two choices: you can let them kill you, or you can defend yourself by firing back."

By now Kathleen had returned to the table. As she sat down, Liddy continued: "Now, if that's the situation, you have to remember that you're wearing a T-shirt while they're wearing a flak jacket. So if you shoot them in the center of mass, it won't do you any good. If you're a good shot, you can try the head, and if you're not, you try the groin area."

Kathleen, whose father and uncle had both been shot in the head, immediately stood up again. "We are stopping this conversation. We are not talking about this anymore."

But Liddy continued: "Now, I was an FBI special agent. I'm a trained handgunner. I can hit someone in the head."

"Stop it!" Kathleen was adamant. "We are not talking about this at dinner! We are going to talk about something else."

Liddy sort of shrugged. "Well," he asked, "what should we talk about?"

"About feeding the hungry and helping the poor," Kathleen suggested. As far as Liddy was concerned, this was a real conversation-stopper.

After dinner I was accosted at the coat check by the wife of an aide to Newt Gingrich. My book had just gone to number one on the *Times* best seller list, and I guess she was a little p.o.'d: "Why don'shoo getta real job?!"

"I'm sorry?" I said.

"Why don'shoo do somethin' useful?" Her eyes were a little glassy.

"Have you had a little too much to drink?" I asked gently.

"Why don'shoo getta job?" she sputtered.

"I *do* have a job," I said. "I'm a writer. In fact, I wrote a film about alcoholism that you might want to see."*

I thought that was a pretty good zinger. But she

---

* Actually, I *co*wrote (with Ron Bass) *When a Man Loves a Woman*, a film in which Meg Ryan plays an alcoholic married to Andy Garcia. I've added this mainly as a way of showing you that I have a serious, sensitive side, and that I make the kind of

came right back at me with a snappy comeback. It was: "Why don'shoo getta job?"

Don Imus: A Tough Act to Follow

Next came the Radio and TV Correspondents Dinner in March. This was the occasion of the infamous Don Imus speech, in which the shock jock offended pretty much everyone in the room. Which sat close to 3000 people. I was pretty impressed. That's hard to do.

By the time Imus finished his collection of jokes about, among other things, adulteries committed by both the President and Peter Jennings's wife (although not with each other), the audience was silent and Imus was soaked with flop sweat. As uncomfortable as the whole thing looked on C-SPAN, it was far worse if you were actually in the room experiencing the extraordinary displeasure of the President and First Lady as they sat fuming at the dais.

Carl Lubsdorf called me the next day. He was in a panic and wanted to update me on the "damage control." He had already called Mike McCurry, the President's press secretary, and assured him that I was "not going to be another Imus."

"Actually, Carl, my first joke is about Imus. 'Ladies and gentlemen, the last time I was in this room was for the Radio and TV Correspondents Dinner, and I

---

movies that best-selling compiler William Bennett would approve of.

came up with the title for my next book: Don Imus Is
a Big Dick.' "

"You're *not* going to say that at the White House
Correspondents Dinner!" Carl was in a lather. "*Tell
me* you're not going to say that!"

"Okay. Carl, what are you worried about?"

"I'm worried about the President not coming to
the dinner!"

"Carl, the President *always* comes to the dinner."

"There's always a first time. And it's not going to
happen on my watch!"

KNOCKOUT NEWT, THE MARIETTA MARAUDER

The President and First Lady did come to the dinner. So did the Speaker of the House. And I am very
happy to say that I did not offend the President or the
First Lady.

I opened with a cleaned-up version of the joke I
told Carl.

"The last time I was in this room was a little over a
month ago for the Radio and TV Correspondents
Dinner. And during the dinner I came up with the
title of my next book: Don Imus Is a Big Putz.

"Quick. My impression of Don Imus at the 1944
Radio Correspondents Dinner. Don Imus at the 1944
Radio Correspondents Dinner: 'For those of you lis-
tening on radio, the President is a cripple.'

"I guess Imus was trying to demonstrate his shock-
jock credentials. Let me tell you what my goal is. If at
the end of the evening Newt Gingrich leaves the ho-

tel thinking, 'Hey, that Al Franken is a pretty funny guy.' Then I'll know that I've failed miserably."

I was killing. Even Newt laughed at that.

"But the White House Correspondents' Association was afraid of a repeat of the whole Imus debacle. So the board of governors had a meeting and drew up some ground rules for tonight's talk. For example, there are a number of subjects I've been instructed to avoid:

- Whitewater

- specifically Web Hubbell

- Susan Thomases

- either of the McDougals

- I am not to do jokes about any aspect of the President's personal life. Except his eating habits. Evidently, sir, you eat quite a lot. And the Correspondents Association seems to think we could have quite a bit of harmless fun with that.

"Other subjects to avoid:

- Newt Gingrich's first wife

- Bob Dole's first wife

- Phil Gramm's first wife

- Dick Armey's first wife

- Rush Limbaugh's first wife

- Rush Limbaugh's second wife

- Rush Limbaugh's third wife."

There was some palpable discomfort on "Newt Gingrich's first wife," but the crowd was with the joke by "Phil Gramm's first wife" and applauding by "Rush Limbaugh's third wife."

"Now, here's an odd one—I can do jokes about abortion, but only first trimester abortions.

"So, Carl, you can rest assured. I'm not going to do any jokes that could make the President or the First Lady even remotely uncomfortable. And if you believe that, I've got some land in Arkansas I'd like to sell you."

Frankly, I was brilliant. And I thought it might be interesting for you, the reader, to see the transcript of my entire speech. It would give you some insight into the comedic process. In particular, you'd see how a truly great comedian recycles his old material, as I cannibalized jokes from both the first and second editions of this very book. But for brevity's sake, I've decided to go right to the stuff that pissed off Gingrich.

Now, the whole point of *Rush Limbaugh Is a Big Fat Idiot* was to satirize the breakdown of civility in our public discourse, which is having a tremendously corrosive effect on society in general. Case in point. Don Imus. And that's why tonight I'd like to do my part to move the national dialogue forward, not backward. And in all modesty I really hope that historians will look back on this speech as a watershed event that ushers in a New Age of Civility—which will begin immediately after I tell the following jokes about the Speaker.

Now, I did read Newt's book *To Renew America*, and there were an awful lot of futuristic, Third Wave ideas: the diagnostic health chair, honeymoons in space. You know, a lot of us smoked dope and read Toffler in the 70s. I think the Speaker's dirty little secret is that he smoked dope and watched *The Jetsons*.

But Newt is nothing if not a man of ideas. Some of which have been very controversial. For example, his gender theories. You'll remember that last year Newt said, and I quote: "If combat means living in a ditch, females have biological problems staying in a ditch for thirty days because they get infections."

Now, I read this and the image that immediately came to mind was that of Newt, about fifteen years ago, explaining to his thirteen-year-old daughter that she just got her first "infection."

You know the good news is that there are more ideas like that to come, because even though his poll numbers are at a historic low, the Speaker is writing another book. Once again he's taking a one-dollar advance. Not voluntarily, that's the most he could get.

You know, I kid the Speaker. But I knew he'd enjoy it. After all, it was his own press secretary,

Tony Blankley, who said, "Don Imus has demonstrated once again that Washington has little capacity to laugh at itself." And it's so great to see that the Speaker is not one of these Washington insiders who can't laugh at himself. Let's hear it for the Speaker.

And, of course, I'm going to take a few jabs at the Speaker. Anyone who's read my book knows I am basically in the President's pocket. And there's actually a lot of perks being the President's water carrier. For example, Harry Thomason books all my travel. And he's very good. That's what gets lost in that whole Travelgate thing. He does a heck of a job. He got me a supersaver, Denver to Seattle, fifty-nine bucks. 'Course, he had to backdate the ticket in order to do it, which, I guess, is kind of illegal. Anyway, Harry's great.

And, of course, when *Air Force One* is available, I get to use it. Let me tell you, *Air Force One* is great. Anybody here been on *Air Force One*? Table forty-one? Isn't it great? Especially the *front* of *Air Force One*. Now, not too many people know this, but there's a zoo up there. All kinds of animals. A Komodo dragon. Couple of koala bears. If you like that kind of thing, it's great. A full skeleton of triceratops. Right up there in the front. And the food. Man, you can just stuff your face! If you're the type of person who has absolutely no regard for his body, you can just eat and eat and eat!

After the speech I stepped down from the dais to meet my guests at their table, which, as it so happened, was right next to the *U.S. News and World Report* table, where the Speaker had been sitting. As I received hearty congratulations from my smiling friends, I noticed that Newt was standing about ten feet from me and that he was not smiling.

I thought that it might seem like a deliberate snub if I didn't say something, so I stepped over, extended my hand, and said, "Mr. Speaker, I hope you took everything I said with good humor."

He was angry. "I think you went over the line."

We were quickly encircled by our respective camps. Sort of a Sharks and Jets kind of thing. Not wanting a rumble while the C-SPAN cameras were still present, I tried to be conciliatory.

"Really?" I said. "What did you feel was over the line?"

"The thing about my *daughter*," he spat.

I honestly couldn't remember telling a joke about his daughter. "Your daughter? Help me out."

"The *infection*!" Smoke was coming out of his ears.

"Oh! That wasn't about your daughter. That was about you not understanding the difference between a period and an infection." I thought that cleared that up.

But *U.S. News* writer Michael Barone was indignant. "Any father of a daughter would have been offended by that joke," he fumed.

"My daughter is fifteen," I said.

That stopped Barone for an instant. But then he

one-upped me. "Well, my daughter is *seventeen*." Boy, he had me there.

Then he two-upped me. "And I'm a single parent!" I was smart enough not to ask why.* Then his coup de grâce: "And I've been through that!"

Now the Speaker was pointing to his chest. "You can take me on all you like. But stay away from my children."

"The children you abandoned?" I did not say that. Instead, I said, "It wasn't about your daughter. It was about your comments on women in the military. 'Women can't be in a ditch for thirty days because they get infections.' It sounded like you were confusing infections with the menstrual cycle."

I turned to Mort Zuckerman, the chairman and editor in chief of *U.S. News.* I had met him a number of times, and he seemed like an intelligent man. "Mort, help me out here."

Mort shrugged. "Al, you shouldn't have brought his daughter into it," he said with great regret. Intelligent, yes. But also an incredible toady.†

"Thanks for selling me out, Mort." I turned back

---

* His wife passed away when their daughter was very young. According to a couple of people I've talked to since, Michael is a terrific father. Which doesn't change the fact that he was kind of being an idiot here.

† The next day I spoke to Mort at a brunch at John McLaughlin's house. There Mort admitted that he hadn't heard the "thirty days" part of the joke. Evidently, he'd had his head too far up the Speaker's ass.

to the Speaker, who had something very macho to say:

"I just about walked up and punched you in the nose."

"Yeah, right. Believe me, you're not man enough. No real man would fail to pay his kids' child support." Actually, I didn't say that. What I said was "Yeah? Well, you better have hoped I went down on the first punch, because otherwise I would have wiped the floor with your fat ass."

Okay. I didn't say that either. I said: "Oh, c'mon! The joke wasn't about your daughter. The worst thing I said about your daughter was that she has a father who doesn't understand women's physiology. I don't know anything about your daughter. It was a *generic* daughter!"

I was looking for some glimmer of understanding from somewhere in his camp. My eye again caught single-parent Michael Barone, who was still in high dudgeon.

"Look," I continued to Newt. "Your friend Rush Limbaugh told this joke on his television show . . ." I recounted the incident where Rush put up a picture of Chelsea Clinton and called her "the White House dog." I asked the Speaker if he saw any distinction between Rush's joke and mine.

"I would have told him not to do that either," he said, refusing to concede my point because he's such a jerk.

As the Speaker walked away, Barone stepped in with an adamant "I think you owe the Speaker an apology."

"Oh, Jesus!" I said.

To this day I am not really sure why I bothered having this conversation. In retrospect, the "you can take me on, but stay away from my children" posture seems like it was a tactical move by the Speaker. Instead of just admitting that he's incredibly thin-skinned and can't take being ridiculed for his many glaring shortcomings, he took the "high road" and "defended" his daughter (whom, I regretfully must repeat, he abandoned).

Still, I have this hopelessly naive faith that as long as you're arguing a position that's logically correct, you can convince anyone of it. That's why, when I saw the Speaker in the hallway a few minutes later, I went over and tried again.

"Mr. Speaker, I am genuinely sorry if you were offended by my remarks."

He seemed much calmer this time. As we shook hands, he said, "I do think you went over the line." Back to square one.

I very gently put both my hands on his shoulders and looked straight into his eyes. "Mr. Speaker, *please* listen to me."

He seemed a little startled by the depth of feeling, and met my eyes with his. Maybe it was my imagination, but for just an instant I thought I saw the hurt little Newt of his childhood. But the vulnerable Newt was gone in a flash, and he straightened like a rod and said, "I'm listening," as if he had learned that in a management seminar.

I knew I was repeating myself, so I tried to be as succinct and precise as humanly possible: "Mr.

Speaker. You said, 'Females have biological problems staying in a ditch for thirty days because they get infections.' Thirty days is a month. Women get their periods once a month. It sounded like you were confusing periods with infections. *That's* what the joke was about."

And the Speaker said, "That's a very interesting concept."

The next day the Associated Press quoted Gingrich as saying that my remarks were "not as grotesquely obscene as Imus." Which, I guess, is a compliment.

Speaking of grotesquely obscene, a week later Gingrich spoke to what he thought was a closed session of Republicans. Without offering any evidence whatsoever, the Speaker told them that the Clinton administration had delayed the announcement of Ron Brown's death so that Commerce Department workers could shred incriminating documents in Brown's office.

Gingrich spokesman Tony Blankley later confirmed that the Speaker had made the accusation. Blankley did not apologize for Newt's charge that the Clinton Administration had committed a major felony. Instead, when asked if these were serious allegations, Blankley replied: "They are serious allegations if subsequent facts support them."

Oh, by the way. Tony Blankley is a cross-dresser. Which is a very serious allegation if subsequent facts support it.

49
MY RESEARCH ASSISTANT IS NOT DEAD

One of the occupational hazards of being a comedian is that people don't always get your jokes. For example, shortly after I published this book, I learned that if you kill off your research assistant and then don't specifically say you were kidding, you'll get a lot of mail.

Some of it will be confused: "Did your research assistant die or not?" Some of it will be angry: "How dare you criticize Republicans when you killed your research assistant? You horrible, horrible man!" Finally, some of it will be both confused and angry: "I see that Clinton increased aid to Israel. I have heard a great deal about the kindness of the Jewish people, but you, sir, are a disgrace to your race."

Let me try to explain where I was going in Chapters 40 through 42. I wanted to shed some light on three pretty serious issues—health care, tort reform, and the social security system—by using what I thought was a clever little satirical device: a completely untrue story about how my research assistant, Geoff, gets sick and, because I won't pay for his health care, ends up getting a whole lot sicker and eventually dying.

I want to be very clear about this: Geoff is not dead. He also didn't contract Lyme disease, pass out and hit his head, spend any time in the hospital with a shunt draining fluid from the lining of his brain, or sue my pants off when he got out.

In fact, Geoff continues to work for me—happily, I might add—as my research assistant. And although my company is too small to actually have a group insurance plan, I pay Geoff more than enough for him to afford private health insurance coverage, which he has. I even recommended a good primary care physician for him.

So please stop sending me letters telling me what a horrible man I am for what I did to Geoff. Because the honest truth is that none of it ever happened.

Actually, the honest truth in many ways is much, much worse.

I know this because I am Geoff. This may sound confusing. Let me explain: It is I, Geoff, who is writing this chapter, just as I have written approximately seventy-five percent of this book (the remaining twenty-five percent consists entirely of fat jokes. Mr. Franken did not write the fat jokes either. He hired someone who used to write for Don Rickles to do them).

You may wonder why I would continue to work for such a jackass. The unfortunate truth is that while Mr. Franken is indeed a jackass, he retains excellent legal counsel. When I first agreed to work for him, he presented me with what he called a "standard" seven-hundred-page contract. He assured me that it was perfectly safe to sign it without reading "all of that legal mumbo jumbo." When I suggested that perhaps I should have a lawyer look it over, he insinuated that the job would no longer be mine unless I signed on the spot.

As I later discovered, the bulk of the contract was devoted to the issue of "noncompetition." To make a long story short, I inadvertently signed away my right to publish any work of any kind in any form for the fifteen years subsequent to my leaving Mr. Franken's employment.

When I first attempted to quit my job, Mr. Franken gleefully pointed out the relevant sections of the contract. I immediately hired a lawyer, who confirmed my fear that I had unwittingly entered into the contractual equivalent of white slavery. If I stop working for Mr. Franken, I will be unable to publish anything I write until the year 2011. Since I have no other marketable skills, I am stuck with the thankless and frankly immoral job of making Mr. Franken appear competent.

I write this with some ambivalence, for I am sure that Mr. Franken will someday take credit for this chapter as just another one of his "brilliant comic conceits." Yet I urge—no, I *beg*—any investigative reporter who may read this (possibly but not necessarily someone from *The American Spectator*) to devote at least a small amount of time to an investigation of Mr. Franken's work habits. Not only does this man desperately need to be exposed and discredited, but I continue to hope beyond reason that a sufficient public outcry might convince him to free me from the chains of inhuman servitude in which I remain helplessly bound.

(Mr. Rodkey died of complications from Sick Building Syndrome in August 1996. He was 26.)

INDEX

Ailes, Roger, fat like
    Limbaugh, 123, 146
ass, Limbaugh's fat, 3, 12,
    17–19, 21, 23, 27–31,
    48, 53, 56–112, 113,
    114, 115, 123–134, 146,
    148, 151–175, 176

blimp, Limbaugh size of, 6,
    18, 76, 94
    (see also dirigible)
blubber, Limbaugh as pile
    of, 2, 77
butt, Limbaugh's fat, 7, 13,
    14–16, 20, 22, 24–26,
    32–47, 54, 116–122,
    133–145, 177
    balloon butt, Limbaugh's,
    72, 112–114
    lard butt, Limbaugh's, 18,
    75, 177

butterball, Limbaugh as, 3,
    17, 24, 112

chubby, young Limbaugh as,
    3, 6, 21
    as cause of early problems
    with women, 17, 32, 145

diets, Limbaugh's failed
    attempts at, 32, 57–89,
    77, 208
    Grapefruit 500 diet, 67–
    113
    denounced by
    Limbaugh, 114–120
    NutriSystem, 28–37
    called "a fraud" by
    Limbaugh, 37–66
    Slim-Fast, 176–193
    Limbaugh's lawsuit
    against, 194–208

dirigible, Limbaugh size of, 6, 18, 76, 94
   (see also *Hindenburg*)
doughnuts, Limbaugh's consumption of, 27–31, 112, 123, 127

eating, Limbaugh's inability to stop, 14–156, 158
exercise, Limbaugh's failure to, 23, 39, 97

fat, Limbaugh as, 1, 3–7, 9, 12, 14, 17–19, 21, 23, 26, 27–28, 31, 34, 35–54, 55, 56–76, 78–99, 100, 101, 102, 103, 104–143, 144, 145, 146, 147, 151, 152, 154, 159, 160–163, 165, 167, 171–182
   (see also ass and butt)
fatboy, Limbaugh referred to as, 12, 14–16, 96, 124, 132, 147

gas, hot, Limbaugh full of, 3, 27, 90, 108
Gingrich, Newt, gaining weight as fast as Limbaugh, 39–42
girth, Limbaugh's enormous, 7, 77, 117, 137, 177
gut, Limbaugh's huge, 6, 76, 116, 136, 176

health, obesity as risk to Limbaugh's, 16, 23, 43, 63, 127, 132–5
Hindenburg, Limbaugh size of, 6, 18, 76, 94
   (see also zeppelin)
hot weather, Limbaugh sweating in, 43, 158, 182
   (see also weather, hot)

immense, Limbaugh described as, 23, 56, 78, 98, 191

jelly, Limbaugh shaking like bowl of, 45

ketchup, Limbaugh smothering fries in, 36–38, 47, 78
   smothering hamburgers in, 38–45, 48, 79–80
   smothering hot dogs in, 46–47, 49, 51–77
   smothering pancakes in, 203

lawn, Limbaugh's inability to mow his own, 43
Limbaugh, Rush Hudson III and fat, 1, 3–7, 9, 12, 14, 17–19, 21, 23, 26, 27–28, 31, 34, 35–54, 55, 56–76, 78–99, 100, 101, 102, 103, 104–143, 144,

145, 146, 147, 151, 152, 154, 159, 160–163, 165, 167, 171–182
and lack of exercise, 23, 39, 97
and overeating, 13, 16, 28, 37, 45
and pathetic history with women, 18, 29, 136
body parts of, 13, 17, 40, 57, 123, 132, 167
ankles, swollen, 13, 17, 123
ass, big fat, 24, 56–78, 80–97
butt, lard as primary component of, 97, 120–130
feet, 117
as last seen by Limbaugh in 1978, 57
fingers, sausagelike, 1, 4, 79
gut, largest in Missouri, 13, 67, 89, 201
knee, mentioned as excuse for avoiding draft, 77
knees, tremendous pressure exerted on, 78, 90
waist, inability to measure without special instrumentation, 66

liposuction, Limbaugh's visits to Sweden to undergo, 123–189
Luntz, Frank, likelihood of his immediately turning to index and looking up his name, 48

metric measurements, Limbaugh's preference for expressing his weight in, 178
moderation, Limbaugh's failure to eat in, 117, 186–187
mountain, Limbaugh's size compared to, 2, 24, 109
muzzle, 43, 47
as briefly worn by Limbaugh in attempt to stop eating, 43

nuggets, chicken Mc-, 23, 56, 87, 89–97, 103, 105, 109, 123, 154, 167, 175, 197

outhouse, Limbaugh as big as, 65, 79, 83, 143

physician, Limbaugh's, 78–85
resigns in disgust, 83–85
porker, Limbaugh unfairly described as, 73, 98, 203–207

quantity, Limbaugh's
    preference for food in
    large, 83–85

record, world, Limbaugh
    sets for eating most hot
    dogs in an hour, 98–103
restaurants, Limbaugh's
    favorite
  Chinese, 13, 17, 74, 198,
    203
  Ethiopian, 165
  Diners, 3, 11, 14, 17, 22–
    27, 45, 62, 88, 119–123
  Fast food, 7, 9, 12, 28–31,
    34, 41, 49, 53, 61, 77,
    91, 112, 121, 151–156,
    199–203
  French, 12, 45, 47, 89,
    123–127, 156
  German, 21, 23, 39, 182,
    187
  Ice-cream parlors, 4, 14,
    29–32, 72, 91, 132, 149,
    178
  Indian, 83, 151, 189
  Indonesian, 173
  Italian, 3, 12, 19, 23, 26,
    28–31, 38–40, 45, 56,
    71, 101, 104, 106, 113,
    134, 142–147, 163, 201
  Japanese, 36, 77, 121
  Korean, 164
  Malaysian, 167
  Pie shops, 16, 21, 27, 32,
    37, 43, 59, 71, 87, 91–

    97, 119, 123, 132, 146–
    147
  Portuguese, 171
  Rib joints, 14, 19, 32, 46,
    73–77, 98, 153
  Steak houses, 15, 20, 33,
    47, 78–83, 99–101
  Trattorias, 28–31, 56
  Waffle houses, 7, 9, 47, 72
  Wurst stands, 12, 46
    (see also German)

sag, tendency of Limbaugh's
    jowls to, 18, 197, 201,
    203
self-loathing, Limbaugh's
    weight as cause of, 47
sex, 47
syrup, Limbaugh's purchase
    of in thirty-gallon
    drums, 17, 43, 67, 89,
    134, 189

talk radio host, Limbaugh as
    fattest, 15, 23, 94, 103
Titanic, Limbaugh's mass
    compared to iceberg
    that sank the, 1

underwear, Limbaugh's
    custom ordering of, 117

vehicles, automotive,
    Limbaugh's custom
    ordering of, 117

vests, Limbaugh's custom
ordering of, 117

weather, hot, Limbaugh
sweating in, 43, 158,
182
(see also hot weather)
whipped cream, 8, 13, 19,
21–26, 30–33, 39, 45,
50, 99–104

X ray, Limbaugh's distressed
skeleton revealed by,
152

yolk, egg, Limbaugh soaking
toast in, 71–72, 139,
200
yogurt, non-fat, Limbaugh's
supposed allergy to, 76

zeppelin, Limbaugh size of,
6, 18, 76, 94
(see also blimp)

ACKNOWLEDGMENTS

This is my second book. The first book, *I'm Good Enough, I'm Smart Enough, and Doggone It, People Like Me* (Dell, $9.95), was a work of fiction. Basically I just made things up. Which meant I didn't have all that many people to thank. The foundation of this book, however, is hard, factual information. And that means I had the help of a lot of people who know things.

My research assistant, Geoff Rodkey, was responsible for pulling together the information in a way that was useful to me and, hopefully, entertaining to you. This meant culling the newspapers, reading books by people like Rush Limbaugh and Pat Robertson, and nagging people at think tanks. As the process of writing the book progressed, Geoff became more and more indispensable, not just as a researcher, but as a source of humor, inspiration, and good sound judgment. And more than occasionally, he cleaned up my prose.

On that score, bad stuff that got past Geoff did not get past the keen eye of my editor, Leslie Schnur. Despite being pregnant with twins, Leslie worked tirelessly and gave me constant encouragement, mainly so I'd finish on time.

My agent, Jonathon Lazear, also gave me a tremendous amount of encouragement, and not just in the form of the sizable advance he negotiated.

Jonathon's wife, Wendy, was among the friends who read that manuscript as I was writing it. I apologize to Wendy and to David Mandel, Hazel Lichterman, and Melissa Mathis for my neediness, but thanks to all of you for spending so much time with me on the phone.

And special thanks to Norman Ornstein of the American Enterprise Institute, who spent the most time on the phone with me, fulfilling the triple function of friend, reader, and think-tank expert.

Which brings me back to the people who know things. They include Thomas Mann of the Brookings Institute, Brian Blackstone of the Competitiveness Policy Council, Jonathan Alter and Howard Fineman of *Newsweek*, John Camp of CNN, Steve Talbot of *Frontline*, Peter Boyer of *The New Yorker*, Ben Jones, Mandy Grunwald, Steve Jost, Dave Mizner of People for the American Way, Diane Colasanto of Princeton Survey Research, Brian Johnson from the Council on Environmental Quality, Kathleen Hall Jamieson of the Annenberg School for Communications, Mark Mellman of Mellman and Lazarus, and Kenan Block of the *MacNeil/Lehrer NewsHour*.

I had lunch with James Carville, who told me I could call his researcher Lowell Weiss for assistance. I did. A lot.

My friend Wendell Willkie II gave me the benefit of his expertise on tort reform. My pal Lawrence O'Donnell, likewise, on welfare. All my information on Lyme disease came from my friend-since-junior-high Dr. David Griffin.

James Retter gave me insight into Rush Limbaugh,

as did Warren Hudson. Dan Bateman helped conceptualize the bar graphs for the Reagan Years chapter. Dick Benson and John Drony, two Vietnam vets, consulted on "Operation Chickenhawk."

William Bramhall's illustrations are the perfect complement for that piece. I thank him for his artistry.

Kristin Kiser from Delacorte was terrific to work with on the mechanics of the book. For that matter, everyone at Delacorte has treated me with far more respect than I deserve.

Then there are the Conservatives whose kindnesses I took advantage of: Frank Luntz, Josette Shiner, Arianna Huffington, George Will, Richard Viguerie, John Kasich, Bob Dornan. None of them knew the title of the book when they agreed to cooperate with me. I think I did tell Ben Stein the title. Also, a hearty megadittoes to those Conservatives who didn't call me back.

And finally, I want to thank my family. My kids, Thomasin and Joe, whose dedication to social justice is ever inspiring. Well, that's not actually true. But they're good kids.

And mostly, to my wife, Franni. Who, believe me, has *tremendous* patience. Honey, thanks.